The Headhunters

The Headhunters

JOHN A. BYRNE

MACMILLAN PUBLISHING COMPANY
New York

Macmillan Publishing Company
866 Third Avenue, New York, N.Y. 10022
Collier Macmillan Canada, Inc.

Library of Congress Cataloging-in-Publication Data
Byrne, John A.
The headhunters.
Includes index.
1. Executives—United States—Recruiting.   I. Title.
HD38.25.U6B97 1986   338.7′61658407111′0973   86-129
ISBN 0-02-517950-0

10 9 8 7 6 5 4 3 2 1

Printed in the United States of America

Contents

Acknowledgments

To Sharon, Jonathan, Kathryn and Sarah, a sincere thanks for the patience and understanding they showed during the missed vacations, holidays, weeknights and weekends devoted to this project.

Introduction

"Headhunters collect visible young men."

THE PHONE RINGS—a headhunter is calling.

"Hello," the voice says plainly but pleasantly. "I'm Robert Smith with Runaway Recruiting, the executive search firm. We've been retained to find an executive vice-president for a midwestern company I can't yet name. Someone suggested I call you."

The call may be an intrusion, but the executive who receives it doesn't hang up. He rises from behind his desk, closes his office door and begins to talk.

Each year, the conversation is replayed hundreds of thousands of times. On the other end of the line are 10,000 executive predators stalking the best and brightest managerial prey in the nation. They run through the ritual questions in a game hunt for some 400,000 final candidates to deliver to corporations, all with the hopes of filling more than 100,000 executive jobs a year.

Some bristle at being called headhunters, preferring instead the more formal and less pejorative title of executive search consultant. Others acknowledge what they really are: "I've come to see the popular phrase as colorful, descriptive and accurate," says Lester B. Korn, who has built Korn/Ferry International into the largest outfit in the business. "We are hunters, skillful hunters in search of talented heads."

The average annual salary for the over 100,000 hunted heads annually delivered—although not mounted as tribal trophies—is not much more than $50,000, but some reach over the $1 million mark. And roughly one out of every five executive jobs paying more than

1

$100,000 a year at the nation's 1,000 largest corporations are now filled by headhunters. The remaining 80 percent are accounted for by promotion and internal recruiting efforts.

Executive search's healthy growth in recent years is both a symptom and a cause for the widespread mobility of American management. The business has loosed an army of hunters on the corporate elite. More than 1,500 executive search firms are working the phones daily, using their persuasive skills to lure the desired from their corporate homes. Over half of these headhunting outfits were nonexistent 20 years ago. Their calls have helped to create a class of mobile managers, willing to move from one job to the next for a few extra thousand. The Organization Man of the Fifties has given way to the Migrant Manager of the Eighties.

"You don't get brownie points for loyalty," contends William Battalia, chairman of Battalia & Associates, a New York search firm. "Being with a company thirty years is almost a black mark, and executives with that kind of record have it very tough if they find themselves out on the street." The underlying message to all: Entertain my offer while you've got it.

Executive hunting remains, despite the business's pervasiveness, a small cul-de-sac of the consulting world: Its total revenues of $2 billion a year make the entire profession much smaller than many of the corporations which engage them for the hunt. And the vast majority of the search firms, about 70 percent, bill less than half a million dollars a year. Even the Big Four—Korn/Ferry International; Russell Reynolds Associates, Inc.; Spencer Stuart & Associates and Heidrick & Struggles, Inc.—account for less than 10 percent of the total business.

Yet, these hired guns of the professional services world have helped to change the nature of executive mobility and the way managers switch jobs. Headhunters have become such an integral part of the corporate landscape that up-and-coming executives often measure their worth by the number of calls they receive from them annually. If the phone fails to ring often enough, it's a telltale sign that something is wrong. At General Electric Co. (GE), a favorite hunting ground, "If you don't get four calls a year you begin to worry," notes one former GE manager. At least one executive unabashedly lists on his resume the search firms responsible for putting him in his last two jobs. He considers it "an indication of my marketability and upward mobility." Gloats one headhunter, "Those men who've not been approached by executive searchers are getting worried about their market value."

So it is that executive search consultants, once corporate pariahs, now lecture M.B.A. classes and professional groups and have become sought-after guests at cocktail parties. "Nowadays, even chairmen carry their resumes in their inside pockets," says Russell Reynolds's David Joys half-jokingly. "They figure that with merger mania and other factors at play, they may just have to move on."

And the notion of headhunter as savior has seeped into the popular culture as well. In Wendy Wasserstein's comedic hit play, *Isn't It Romantic?* one of the lead characters, Harvard M.B.A. Harriet Cornwall, winds up marrying the headhunter who landed her a job at Colgate-Palmolive. When Apple Computer sought to plug the Macintosh for small businesses, it created the fictional Recruit-A-Suit headhunting firm in advertisements. One popular newspaper cartoonist recently drew three sweating, towel-wrapped executives chatting in a country club sauna. "I'm in public relations," says one. "We make heroes." "I'm in executive search," piped another. "We distribute them."

No wonder executives flood the mailboxes of search firms with resumes, hoping that one will land in their infamous databanks. They cultivate their favor, thinking that when the ideal job comes along their name will surface and they'll get a call. But headhunters work for and are paid by management to lure Mr. Right into the fold. They owe no allegiance to their candidates.

If anything, headhunters can often be accused of oversell. Today, acknowledges Allan Stern, of New York-based Haskell & Stern, "There are many more instances where recruiters are misrepresenting candidates' rights . . . not telling a candidate all we know about a given position or (not) letting him know in a timely or truthful manner where he might stand in relation to his candidacy. If we continue to oversell candidates, our credibility among them is going to decline."

Rarely a day goes by without a high-level search making headlines on the business pages of a newspaper: Korn/Ferry's recruitment of a corporate messiah for troubled Storage Technology, Russell Reynolds's luring of a savvy executive to run Convergent Technologies, Spencer Stuart's picking of an airline executive to rescue loss-plagued Pan Am or Heidrick & Struggles's landing of Peter Ueberroth as the new baseball commissioner. The musical chair game is chronicled daily in *The Wall Street Journal*'s "Who's News" column, which keeps tabs on top-level executive changes. Headhunters are behind half the corporate job hoppers who make the column every day. Newspaper classified ads today account for less than 2 percent of the job switches noted in *The Wall Street Journal*'s pages.

Turnover at many American corporations is endemic, a tragedy and a crisis aided and abetted by the rise of the executive hunter. It is shocking how many giant U.S. companies fail to groom qualified senior executives within their own ranks. Some of the strongest, most profitable concerns aren't immune from the problem. Executive churning at $8 billion (sales) PepsiCo, for example, became so severe that the company called in consultants to alter the corporation's fast-paced culture. The food and soft drink company had found that its top 470 executives stayed in their jobs an average of only 18 months. Most of the turnover resulted from the company's policy of rapid mobility. Still, only 16 of PepsiCo's 26 top officers listed in its 1982 annual report were around when the 1983 listing came out. In one short year, the company's executive ranks resembled a cotton field after a boll weevil attack. Headhunters did most of the picking.

Yet, that was nothing compared to the transformation that rocked the troubled Chrysler Corp. in the early 1980s. Within three years of Lee Iacocca's arrival there in late 1978, he had given the axe to 33 of Chrysler's 35 vice-presidents. Executive recruiters, of course, had little to do with that. But the unparalleled executive bloodletting confirmed again that there was little security in corporate America—another reason why headhunters have been given a welcome reception by the nation's managerial elite. You don't know when the axe could fall.

Trying to hold onto their best and brightest, corporations have been known to fight back. Some have employed the "Al Capone" theory of protection by hiring several search firms that could do the most harm. By throwing these headhunters a few bones, they keep their own employees off limits. Others, including AT&T, Hewlett-Packard and CBS, are attending seminars which teach defensive tactics to protect themselves from what a New York consulting group calls "the unscrupulous raiding and trading of key executives."

By stimulating executive job jumping, headhunters have been catalysts for huge increases in compensation, too, often responsible for negotiating some of the most controversial and lucrative pay packages ever granted. When headhunter extraordinaire Gerard Roche enticed PepsiCo President John Sculley to Apple, Sculley wrangled himself a whopping 400 percent jump in pay to make the switch. For finding Sculley a $1 million-a-year job with a $1 million sign-up bonus, Roche pocketed a cool third of a million dollars plus expenses. Yet a headhunting competitor, expressing disdain over the fee, boasted that he would have garnered twice as much. He would have billed Apple on the basis of both salary and bonus, not just the $1 million salary as Roche had done.

Headhunters, like Roche, are inherently deal makers. If they weren't hunting heads and closing deals, they would find a career in horse-trading just as challenging. With each transaction, of course, there is the money which comes with it. The sleepless nights thinking that if this deal is done, I'll have the thousands of dollars I need to buy the Porsche, the sauna, the accouterments of success. Beyond the money, beyond the greed, there is the thrill of making the deal. Bringing together two people who never met before and striking a connection. It is the challenge of moving someone perfectly happy from one job to another simply because you have the assignment and want to complete it. There is the sense of power that comes from having something, in this case a job, that other people want. And dangling the prospect of this position before the desiring eyes of talented, ambitious executives.

"We have an unconscious motivation to seek power out of the frustration of not having it before or never being able to achieve it," confides a headhunting millionaire. "The enormity of the power is awesome for some. They can't go back to college and restart their lives so they become search consultants and can cast value judgments every day of the week."

For people who are ostensibly gregarious, this is an almost cruel and ruthless power to wield. But deal makers are ruthless; they can be cool and uncaring. They are men with the streak of an actor, smoothly changing moods and manners as necessary to clinch the deal. And those who hunt heads are disarmingly gregarious in persuading another to overcome caution. When all is said and done, people are products. "They collect visible young men," says Arthur Taylor, himself once a young, visible man who had been collected and delivered to CBS as president at the age of 37, only to be ousted four years later.

"Headhunters?" a candidate once told the business's self-appointed watchdog, Jim Kennedy. "They think they control the whole situation and they wine and dine you and promise you the moon . . . and suddenly when you're out of the running, they treat you like they never met you. For so-called professionals they don't even have the faintest concept of common business courtesy. They're terribly rude to the very products they'll be wanting to peddle the next time an appropriate search comes in . . . not returning calls or answering letters . . . and yet, when they see the dollar signs dancing in their eyes, they'll call you again and expect you to jump through the hoop as if nothing had happened."

Headhunters thrive for that power. And sometimes, there is wonder, too. Wonder over what it would be like to slip a profile of yourself in the pile to the client. Because headhunters are largely people who have failed to achieve success at something else. Disenchanted with other professions, they drift or fall into this business. No one grows up wanting to spend his life hunting managers. No successful corporate executive climbs his company's hierarchy thinking about a headhunting detour. For the disillusioned corporate dropout with entrepreneurial pretensions, however, it is a safe haven. "When I was at IBM, I never enjoyed the politics," says John Sullivan, who became a headhunter after spending 13 years at IBM. "Now I look at them and have the luxury of not being a participant. It's fun to peek at the politics of a corporation from the outside and know that your turn to be it isn't going to come up. I won't get caught in the game."

Yet, there is this sense of power, of superiority, that comes with the job. It is a comforting and reassuring feeling for someone who wasn't able to taste success elsewhere. Still, it is not enough. They endure the grinding tedium, the endless telephoning, the weary traveling, the pure boredom of a repetitive job because of the occasional contact with the truly powerful. Headhunters are ambitious men who enjoy knowing, or at least feigning to know, interesting and powerful people. These are generally ephemeral associations, but the meetings might never have occurred if they had remained in the corporate world. There is the vicarious excitement of being part of the decision making, of rubbing shoulders with those who exercise the corporate power that had always been frustratingly out of reach.

The headhunter may help make some of these stars, too, by delivering a once-unseen opportunity to a person enveloped by his job. But they are not unlike the groupies who cluster near the backstage door after a rock concert, those star-struck adolescents who trail a favorite performer in the hopes of striking as close a relationship with him as possible. To have touched the anointed in some cursory way is to be granted a certain privilege or standing among one's own peers. The headhunter's stage door is the country club, the golf course, the city lunch club, even the airplane. Places that may grant him access—if only temporary—to the executive suite, time to gather enough of an anecdote to more than drop his name at an appropriate moment.

"Remember in high school," says Arthur Taylor, "there were always some guys who got their biggest thrill going along on the bus with the football team, even though they never played. There's some of that in the executive recruiter."

The danger, of course, is that after years of recruiting, after placing hundreds of executives, after thousands of hours chatting with them as an outside counselor, he wants to do more than tag along. He wants to advise the quarterback on the next play. Amid the name-dropping on the golf course, there is the sheer audacity of the Monday morning quarterback. The second-guessing by a nonplayer not capable of making the team.

"They think they know about management," continues Taylor, with a trace of bitterness in his voice. "They've never managed anything at anytime. They think they know how companies ought to be structured and how compensation ought to be devised. They don't. And yet it's a very scary thing because you've got a talented candidate who is talking to the chief executive officer and he's got this executive recruiter whispering in his ear. It's unbalanced. Fundamentally these fellows have virtually no management experience. They are selecting the managers of the future yet they couldn't manage themselves."

It is easy to pretend, to make believe you have been given true power because you get so close to it. And when that happens, it is easy to believe, comforting to the ego even, to think you play a critical role in the overall scheme of things. Why not? You put an executive in a company, he succeeds, affects his corporation in a way that increases its value, allows it to employ more people. That is the essence of success. And it easily entices the headhunter into elevating himself to a higher sphere. "They go through periods where they think executive recruiting is excessively important to society," agrees Taylor. "Then a lot of arrogance sets in and they lose business. It drags them back to a certain kind of reality that executive search is a useful adjunct to what a company wishes to do. But its demise is not going to shatter the stock market or the growth of the gross national product. Frankly, it could cease to exist tomorrow and the world wouldn't notice."

That may well be too severe. Their rising prominence and prestige parallels their growing acceptance by the corporate world. While it is true that only 15 percent of all executives jobs are filled through executive search, they tend to be the most critical and powerful jobs. Sometimes, they are jobs calling for a corporate savior, like Apple's John Sculley, Storage Technology's Ryal R. Poppa, Pan Am's Edward Acker or Allied's Edward Hennessy. For the average executive search consultant, these big jobs are once-in-a-career opportunities. But they are the chances to make a difference.

The business talent hunters can be forgiven the pretensions for the mundane job that it can often be. It is a business many have tried and abandoned. "The process is too repetitive, too passive," says Gerry Riso, a former management consultant with Booz, Allen & Hamilton who lasted all of 14 months in the business as a vice-president at Korn/Ferry. "I don't enjoy spending six to eight hours a day on the phone, going through a fairly routine list of questions, of what have you done, what schools did you attend, where have you worked, what were your major accomplishments, what were your major disappointments, how does your background match the job I've described. I might be able to do that two or three times a day, but 60 times over a week gets pretty boring."

Far from the glamorous picture often painted in the media, the lives of headhunters wouldn't interest a Hollywood scriptwriter. There are no geniuses in the business, only hard workers. Miracle-working executives are seldom extracted as effortlessly as a dentist might pull a loose tooth. "Search," says Karl Pierson, a director of personnel at ITT Corp. who employs them, "is not glamorous. It's a lot of hard work. Some of these characters drive around in limos and try to make it seem glamorous. They spend my money on fancy oil paintings and beautiful suites, but that doesn't get the search accomplished."

The business, too, is not yet a full-fledged profession commanding the respect of lawyering or doctoring. No license is granted, no test need be passed to hang out a headhunting shingle. It takes all of $9.95 to print 1,000 calling cards and go into the business. "Is this business a profession?" asks Alan Lafley, who turned headhunter after a successful career in human resources with Chase Manhattan Bank and General Electric. "Not with the kinds of people who use to walk in my office regularly a year ago who wanted to sell me search. I used to call them used car salesmen, and my secretary would not allow them through on the phone. It's a quick buck business for too many people."

Even some of the most prestigious search firms, the ones which strategically place English foxhunting prints on their walls and lush Oriental carpets on their floors, have embarrassingly fallen victim to ethical lapses. Some have had headhunters who claimed educational degrees they lacked, who pirated executives from angry client firms, who were happily employed by companies to skirt antidiscrimination rules.

Who are these executive merchants at the end of the telephone? What are they like? How do they evaluate the executives they screen? How do they entice executives to jump ship? What is this business all about? Where did it come from and where will it go? For anyone who has ever received a headhunting call and wondered, they'll soon find out.

Where the Jungle Is Wildest

"Every fifth person in New York is either an executive recruiter or a tax shelter salesman."

NEW YORK IS the headhunter's greatest jungle. More major corporations are headquartered here than in any other city in the world. And New York executives tend to be a wild, roaming bunch, comprising the most mobile population of executives anywhere. The sheer numbers of executive talent and their love for the musical chair game makes Manhattan the capital of headhunting, too.

Nine of the ten largest U.S. executive search firms make their headquarters in New York, where more than 260 firms have offices from which to recruit, nearly three times as many as Chicago, five times more than Los Angeles, Dallas or Boston. More than 25 headhunting shops in New York drum up a million or more in revenues annually. "Every fifth person in New York is either an executive recruiter or a tax shelter salesman," quips Peat Marwick's Dwight Foster.

The boulevard of hunting is Park Avenue, where the skyscraping office towers house most of the business's big-league recruiting strategists. More than 40 percent of the offices are clustered on three New York avenues, Park, Madison and Fifth, where the rents are as high as the buildings. Russell Reynolds Associates, Heidrick & Struggles and Handy Associates, three of the top ten firms in the business, all make their corporate homes in the imposing American Brands building at 245 Park Avenue.

These are offices made to awe, or at least impress, visitors by their cool elegance. Oftentimes, the elaborate reception areas feature private anterooms for the migrant managers who would rather not be seen in a headhunter's quarters. In offices hung with chandeliers and furnished with deep-grained chairs, pricey artwork and Oriental carpeting, they work the phones, spurring revolving-door turnover at corporations like ITT, Revlon, CBS, International Paper and more.

Executive search consultants find the hunting far less lucrative at such companies as Du Pont, Procter & Gamble, General Motors, Cummins Engine and Cargill—all firms where loyalty still means something, and all of them are located outside this massive executive jungle. "If you're going to create a company like that," says Robert Cox, president of PA International's U.S. search practice, "don't put it in New York. In Cargill-land, however, Cargill is the universe and it's a comfortable one."

The records for the musical chair game are played fastest on Wall Street where trading skills command large salaries and, therefore, huge fees for New York's headhunters. Some super-achievers in their early 30's boldly list as many as a half dozen affiliations with different companies on their resumes. "On Wall Street, they've stopped asking why you've left a certain company," says one headhunter.

It's little surprise, then, why headhunters from the very start of the business gravitated to New York, making it from the start the headhunting capital. One of the first was Thorndike Deland, a handsome, dapper man who combed his hair back from his face. He put starch in the collars of his white shirts and a crimp in his ties, and he wore wire-rimmed spectacles that lent him a professorial look. Deland not only helped to father a business, he brought two sons, Rawle and Thorndike, into it as well. The pair, who refer to their late father as TD, still hunt heads from the same New York building at 1440 Broadway where Deland opened his first office in 1926. Rawle, now 63, teamed up with his dad in 1947 after graduating from Harvard with an M.B.A. Thorny, as his 66-year-old brother is known, joined in 1945 after the war.

Little is known of Deland's early background. At best, he graduated from high school, but his sons aren't quite sure of that. He lost his job at an oil company due to one of the split-ups. Somehow, Deland talked himself into a job with the Chamber of Commerce, working with local chapters in Detroit, Chicago, Boston, New York and Denver. At night, he literally pulled rabbits out of a top hat as a professional magician. Deland finally got a job as labor manager with a Baltimore clothing maker, but soon quit that position in 1920 to head up an "executive placement bureau" for the Retail Research Association (RRA), a trade group of retailers.

When he hung his own shingle out six years later in New York, Deland boasted of having placed more than 1,000 managers and executives at average salaries of $5,000 during his RRA stint. "There is hardly a buyer in the country he has not heard of and whose progress he has not watched," noted *The Garment Weekly* in announcing that he would go off on his own to specialize in hunting down merchandise managers and retail buyers. What immediately made him different was his fee: Deland charged a client a $200 retainer to do a search. If he filled the job, Deland would pick up 5 percent of a manager's first year compensation minus the $200 retainer fee.

A peripatetic huckster of the first order, Thorndike Deland would scour the nation by rail spreading the gospel of executive search. He boasted the stamina of a traveling politician, the bravado of a carnival barker and the selling skills of an early-day vacuum cleaner salesman. Wherever he would go, local newspapers would write articles on his chats, and the datelines were far flung: Los Angeles, Vancouver, Portland, Minneapolis, Chicago, Milwaukee. He'd address groups on topics such as "What the Store Expects of Display Men" or pen trade magazine articles with titles such as "Do You Beg, Borrow or Steal Your Executives?" A marketing master, he never lost track of his need to establish himself as an authority. It was a carefully constructed image to insure that stores would come to him when they needed new talent. "Mr. Deland," one newspaper noted, "believes that more and more heads of big stores are ridding themselves of the idea that important posts should be delegated to individuals simply because of blood or marriage relationship."

Under one article entitled, "Let's Develop Executives Instead of Swiping Them," Deland claimed that 80 percent of the executive vacancies are filled by outsiders. "Occasionally it is a very good thing to bring in an outside person who has had experience with different methods and who can contribute new ideas and fresh enthusiasm to a store's personnel. It tends to put the organization on its toes, and has a healthy influence on some of the older executives in the institution who have fallen into a rut and think that there are no new ways of improving the business."

13

Deland met up with Edwin G. Booz at Montgomery Ward & Co. in the 1930s when chairman Sewell Avery was trying to improve profits at the mail-order company. Deland's role was to help recruit certain store managers around the country. "They got on the road and started to travel from town to town and the companies they were after began to spot them," says Rawle, who recalls his dad's storytelling at the dinner table. "They could tell where they were going. They were met in some towns by the management of companies who told them to please leave because they didn't want them fooling around with their people."

Among Deland's early placements was Raymond Fogler, who was put in as general operating manager and vice-president of Montgomery Ward and rose to become president. Charlie Kelstadt was placed as a Sears Roebuck store manager and later became president of the company. Deland also established close relationships with certain clients—Associated Dry Goods, Carter Hawley Hale, The May Co., Hartmarx and Edison Brothers—all of whom continue to work with the firm on a unique retainer basis under which Thorndike Deland Associates carries out consulting and headhunting work.

Like other headhunters through the years, he toyed and experimented with new ways of evaluating people. At one point Deland tried handwriting analysis. At another he took to sizing up an executive's frontal lobes as a measure of his intellectual capacity.

"My father was full of bananas and a lot of fun," says Rawle Deland. "He was a very outgoing and gregarious person. The reason we came into the business is that he was such a marvelous person that you liked to be around him." His father retired in 1966 and died four years later at the age of 83 in a nursing home. "Even in his declining years," says Rawle, "he loved the business. In the nursing home he was asking people if they'd like to make a change."

At the outset of World War II, Deland lent partner Edward Raisbeck to the U.S. War Department to help them identify and recruit business executives for the Army Service Forces. Raisbeck, who remains active in the firm today at the age of 81, became assistant to the Pentagon's director of personnel. But it wasn't until after the war in the late 1940s, when management consulting became respectable enough to be dubbed a profession, that headhunting began to take off. Consultants like Booz, Allen & Hamilton and McKinsey & Co. would come in, study a company and file a thick report of recommendations oftentimes urging changes or additions to management. They made executive search a logical extension of their consulting practices. And they would internally grow many of the entrepreneurial pioneers of the business who would splinter from them and start their own firms.

Jack Handy, who had dabbled in search for McKinsey as early as the 1930s, jumped the McKinsey ship in 1944 to open up shop as an executive search and management consultant. He pioneered the use of computers in search as early as 1955 to keep track of candidates and sources. Sidney Boyden, who had met Deland during a 17-year career in personnel with Montgomery Ward, quit Booz, Fry, Allen & Hamilton in 1946 to go out headhunting on his own.

Handy, the story goes, left McKinsey because he couldn't convince the firm to separately charge their clients for the service. At that time, McKinsey would recruit managers as part of their general consulting work. Handy's earlier background was a harbinger of his entrepreneurial leaning. A descendant of a prominent family which arrived on the Mayflower, he lived the charmed life of a blueblood. Handy was graduated from Milton Academy and Harvard University. He joined a rubber brokerage firm in Akron and enlisted in the Army as an officer in World War I. When he returned from the war in 1920, he co-founded his own brokerage outfit, French & Handy, Inc., in New York. Three years later, he put together his own brokerage firm, Handy & Co., eventually latching onto a role as managing partner of a stock brokerage company which preceded what was to become Paine, Webber, Jackson and Curtis. He started his own firm, Handy Associates, Inc., in 1944.

A colorful, engaging man with the personality of a shrewd salesman, Handy relished the elegant lifestyle and he enjoyed being the boss. "Uncle Jack knew the business, he knew people and he knew how to get business," says Lonsdale Stowell, who Handy hired after Stowell was fired from Compton Advertising in 1949. "But he had an ability to spend more than he could make."

Stowell, who can talk a good game himself, wasn't above openly criticizing Handy for his lack of personal financial control, which affected Handy's firm as well. "He couldn't take it after awhile," claims Stowell. "So one time he simply sealed up my office with masking tape after going through my personal effects one weekend to try to prove I was going competitive against him. I wasn't, but he hired a fucking detective and went in there at night to make sure I wouldn't burn the files and all that stuff."

After ten years with Handy, Stowell found himself out on the street again. He started his own shop, specializing in advertising agency assignments and has since placed nearly 80 people at BBD&O and nearly 50 at Ogilvy & Mather. Stowell, a heavyset man in his early 60s, now works out of a converted-apartment office in New York as L. F. Stowell & Associates, Inc. Handy sold his firm in the late 1960s, and it is now, as a subsidiary of Science Management Corp., the only publicly-owned headhunting firm.

Sidney Boyden, a tall, broad-shouldered man given to placing a handkerchief in the breast pocket of his suit jackets, had been manager of Booz, Fry, Allen & Hamilton's executive search department. A former lumber salesman who graduated from the University of Wisconsin with a business degree, he joined Montgomery Ward as a trainee in 1925. By 1941 he was personnel director of the giant Chicago mail-order house. When he stepped out on his own after World War II, Boyden ran his firm as a "beneficient monarchy." One headhunting friend called him a "dominant pedagogue" who had written volumes of text on every aspect of search. Boyden's timing was near perfect.

Top executives were hard to find in the war-thinned ranks of many corporations in the 1940s. Along with the havoc generated by the war were a slew of new products—from synthetic fibers to computers. Companies hoping to diversify into these promising areas lacked the managerial experience to do so. The shortcut, obviously, was to pirate knowledgeable executives from other corporations. The market for recruiters of talented managers seemed limitless, and it nearly was.

But Handy and Boyden, as had Deland before them, faced a similar problem: They had to persuade corporations to pay up for the service. Applicants paid fees to employment agencies. Why shouldn't job candidates pay Boyden or Handy? Because, Boyden would argue, "we're working for the corporation not the candidate. It was difficult in the beginning," says Boyden, now a trim, silver-haired man of 86 years who has retired to Fort Lauderdale, Florida. "I really had to educate industry with the idea that there was a way to get executives without going to an employment agency. When I called it took a little doing. It was a brand-new profession."

Boyden initially started in his Bronxville, New York, apartment, switching to the mezzanine of New York's Roosevelt Hotel for his private interviews of executives interested in jumping ship. He plied a clubby network of old acquaintances from his years at Montgomery Ward and Booz. Boyden especially cultivated what he termed "business feeders"—bankers, lawyers and trade association executives who would be in a position to recommend him to others for additional assignments. There was little to it. "I'd sit down with an executive I knew, say a personnel guy somewhere, and ask him, 'Okay, well do you know who would be able to work in the chemical business in the Philippines?' "

Boyden was, like all of the most successful headhunters, a savvy salesman, too. "When I employed an associate I was interested in a man who could be a business getter and a merchandiser," he says with refreshing candor. "I was looking for widely acquainted top sales executives. Because the ability to go out and promote business and get business is more important than finding the men. I was least interested in somebody who would know how to track down a man and find him."

Unlike Deland, who charged a nonrefundable retainer, however, Boyden would only earn his fee of 10 percent of an executive's first year compensation if he delivered a body who was hired by his client. His fee was contingent on his success. Indeed, if Boyden would have continued to bill clients on that basis he eventually would have been excluded from the professional association he helped to found in 1959. That group, the Association of Executive Recruiting Consultants, specifically required its members to charge fees on a "retainer" basis regardless of whether the headhunter could locate and move a successful candidate. They consider themselves professionals, who like attorneys and physicians are paid even when they fail to win a case or fail to nurse a patient back to health.

This distinction remains important today. Headhunting firms essentially fall into two categories: contingency firms and retainer firms. The retainer firms sniff that their contingency colleagues are mere employment agencies which shuffle papers. In many cases, that is true. Contingency recruiters often will send to their clients candidates who they have not met nor interviewed in person. Conventional executive recruiters consider that practice unethical. Corporate human resources chiefs tend to use the contingency firms for searches on jobs paying $60,000 or less, while they turn to retainer firms for the more senior level assignments.

The friction between the two groups was enough to cause the retainer firms to change the name of their trade association in 1982 to the Association of Executive Search Consultants. As Boyden puts it, "I always say you recruit truck drivers. You search for executives." Maybe so. But Boyden gladly collected his contingency fees for years until he and the other firms which sprouted in later years could convince their clients to pay them as professionals.

It was a vastly different business then—most of the executive trading was done on a network basis and competition was not severe. Some corporations would even help headhunters recruit their restless executives. "In the old days you could call General Electric and say I need a financial executive," recalls Rawle Deland. "And they'd say well we have this guy and that. Once I called and said I need a chief financial officer for a wine distributor and they said we've got a great guy. We can't use him. We're going to promote him, but it won't be for another year and he's getting restless. At their expense, they flew him to New York 20 years ago and our client hired him."

Most of the work Deland and others did in those early days were for lower and middle management jobs. "We were still about ten years behind Booz and McKinsey in respectability," says George Haley, another of the early pioneers in the business. "If we got a $30,000 salary for an assistant vice-president or a divisional officer it was an occasion." Haley latched onto a headhunting job with fellow Yalie Henry Wardwell Howell, the son of an Episcopalian minister in Pennsylvania. Howell had left McKinsey to assemble his own firm in November of 1951 after McKinsey believed its recruiting practice posed a conflict-of-interest problem and dropped it. The 29-year-old Haley had been fired as executive assistant to the president of Vanadium Corporation of America and was hanging out at New York's Yale Club when Howell invited him to come aboard in early 1952. "We basically did middle managers. There were no senior positions at all. Then, gradually people became conscious of what we could do and we moved up the ladder."

One of the first breakthrough searches occurred in 1959 when ITT, a sizable but lethargic maker of telephone equipment, called on Boyden to find a chief executive to succeed the retiring General Edmund Leavey. A ramrod stiff West Point graduate steeped in military protocol, the General took over ITT when the company's legendary founder Colonel Sosthenes Behn died in June 1957. Leavey was to find and develop an executive to take his place in two years when he would turn 65 years of age. When his time was up, however, Leavey recommended himself. ITT's board would have none of that. Instead, it named a search committee that immediately turned to Boyden, who had known a couple of the company's directors, to find ITT a new leader. This was a rare assignment in a time when virtually all major corporations took pride in growing their own loyal men.

"They wanted somebody who could come in there and really crack down and know how to coordinate all their branches," recalls Boyden, who worked on the search with his colleague G. Lawton-Johnson. Boyden delivered Harold Geneen, an executive vice-president at Raytheon Manufacturing Co. who had earned a reputation as a no-nonsense manager who could impose financial controls on a company. "I had known Geneen for a number of years when he was with other companies. I had never moved him before, but I knew about him and he had the kind of experience I was interested in."

Geneen did not require much convincing. Amid rumors that he would never be named president—the position he coveted—he already was fishing for an opportunity to run his own show. Lawton-Johnson arranged a meeting with ITT's search committee and Geneen took over as ITT's $125,000-a-year president and chief executive in June 19, 1959, the very day Leavey turned 65. This was when search fees were 20 percent of an executive's first-year compensation—a rate which would have allowed Boyden a $25,000 fee for coming up with Geneen.

Sidney Boyden hit the big time. So did Geneen, who garnered the further reputation as being "the General Patton of industry." He used search firms extensively to staff the sprawling conglomerate that ITT became under him. When Geneen stepped down as chief executive in 1977, ITT's annual sales had approached $17 billion with earnings of $562 million.

Boyden, who, says one colleague, used to secretly photograph candidates as they walked through the doors of his New York office with a hidden camera, got one big assignment after another. His firm plucked presidents for Chrysler (Virgil Boyd), Philco-Ford (Robert O. Fickes), General Foods (Arthur Larkin, Jr.), Anchor Hocking Glass (John L. Gushman), Investors Diversified Services (Stuart Silloway), Warner-Lambert Pharmaceutical (Stuart Hensley and Bruce Giblin), Midland-Ross Corp. (Harry J. Bolwell).

Meantime, as Boyden's hair thinned and grayed, a new big-league headhunting guru also emerged. His name was Bob Gette, a distinguished, gentlemanly man who up until only 1984 still did searches

19

in semi-retirement from Florida. By 1964, Haley left Ward Howell in a huff when Howell altered his deal with him. Within six months, Haley picked off Gette, one of Howell's most promising headhunters. Together they laid the groundwork for some of the most important chief executive searches of the 1970s.

The first big one was U.S. Plywood-Champion Papers, Inc., the forerunner of Champion International Corp. Haley already had placed at Champion a couple of senior executives, including a vice-president of finance. So when Chairman Karl R. Bendetsen needed a president in 1972 he turned to, who else, but Haley. There was, of course, a rather obvious reason why Bendetsen, soon to turn 65, lacked a successor in house. A tough curmudgeon who supervised the internment of Japanese-Americans during World War II, he had scared away many of the company's top executives.

Haley found for the demanding taskmaster an equally tough manager in Ian MacGregor, an executive at AMAX, Inc., a metals and mining concern. But Bendetsen wanted to meet the candidate's wife before completing the deal. It was just a last-minute formality before the contracts were signed. The dinner meeting was set at 6:45 P.M. at the Pierre Hotel in New York. "I went home," says Haley, "took my shoes off and said this is going to be a real breeze. The terms were set; the papers were being drawn. And then all of a sudden the phone rings at my house."

The caller was Bendetsen, and he was steaming. "Smoke was coming out of his ears," says Haley. "It was 7:30 and this fellow still hadn't shown up and he hadn't even called. What MacGregor did was take that offer, go back to his company and used it to become president and CEO of AMAX. I phoned next morning and called him everything I could think of. It took me half an hour, and I used every possible vile word."

Despite that handicap, Haley eventually put in Thomas F. Willers, a man who had quit as vice-chairman of Occidental Petroleum Corp. after clashing with its autocratic chairman Dr. Armand Hammer. It was a less than successful match. Willers was fired in two years by Champion's board reportedly because of his commitment to a failing strategy. Caught up in the jargon of the 1960s, he wanted to transform Champion into a company that would "serve the total home environment." Champion succeeded him with a loyal insider who started with the company over 17 years earlier as a sales trainee. Before it was evident that Willers would be unsuccessful, however, that search led to another big assignment to find a new chief executive for the St. Louis-based Monsanto Co. Haley got to make his pitch for the job because a member of Champion's board, familiar with his work there, also was a Monsanto director. And when The Singer Co. required a new president in 1975, the chairman of the search committee, Ian MacGregor, invited Haley to compete for the assignment with a few other search firms. Haley won the job and Gette extracted from Xerox Joseph B. Flavin to become chairman, chief executive and president of Singer.

Haley and Gette were on a roll. The year after the Champion and Monsanto assignments, one of Haley's bedrock clients, International Paper, called up asking him to hunt for a chief executive. There were many others, too: presidents of Rockwell International, Mobil Chemical Co., Crocker National Bank, Admiral Corp., Dr Pepper Co. and more.

Gette, a quiet professional who refused to allow the high-level work to dazzle him, was the first of the big-game hunters to rack up annual headhunting fees in excess of $1 million. So well known did Haley and Gette become for their high-level search work that corporations would enlist the firm to evaluate its internal candidates over outsiders before promoting them from within. Before Howard Clark stepped down as chairman and chief executive of American Express in 1977, Haley was called in. "The board wanted to be sure there wasn't somebody better outside than President Jim Robinson," recalls Haley. "We did a full assignment. And, of course, Clark went with Robinson. He was his boy and he was going to be head of American Express." Similarly, Olin Corp., Armco, Inc. and Lockheed Corp. called on Haley for such consulting work before picking insiders for the top jobs.

The greatest growth of the business occurred in the 1970s as more search firms proliferated and the major firms emerged. By the mid-1970s, more than 900 recruiting firms had sprouted in the U.S. alone. The total climbed to more than 1,500 by 1985. Corporate appetite for outside management talent rose as the traditional promotion-from-within notion of advancement grew fusty and executives viewed ship-jumping mobility as a career strategy. Before World War II, largely homegrown executives had a near-familial loyalty to their corporations. Managers equated their career interests with the success of their employer. The outsider was unacceptable to most company value systems.

The phenomenal growth of search coincided with a growing belief that managers were interchangeable—not only from company to company but from one industry to another. Demand for managerial savvy rose, too, as the supply dwindled, a result of the low birth rates during the Depression. The jobs of human resource executives grew more complex, permitting them less time to recruit senior-level managers. So corporations began turning to headhunters for help as routinely as they would call accountants, lawyers and management consultants.

William A. Spartin, his red hair flecked with gray, has watched the phenomenon grow as a bystander and a participant over the past 30 years. Now president of Washington, D.C.-based MSL International Ltd., the U.S. recruiting arm of compensation consultants the Hay Group, he had been recruited and had employed search firms himself. An engineer by background, he was at Du Pont Corp. when Gardner Heidrick, founder of Heidrick & Struggles, lured him from Wilmington, Delaware, to Chicago to work in human resources for International Harvester. At IH, he employed dozens of search firms himself. Years later, a Ward Howell recruiter got him to jump ship to *The Washington Post*.

Why did he often turn to headhunters? "My networks were predictable and traditional when I recruited in the corporate world," he says. "There's a tendency to keep going back to the same networks. You find yourself starting to cut corners in the search process because your time is limited." As a corporate human resource executive, Spartin would have as many as 35 executive openings to fill at any one time. It was impossible for him or his staff to search for the best talent.

Beyond time, he also steadfastly adhered to another rule. He would never hire someone at or above his level on the organization chart. "There are just too many pressures on an individual to put someone there for the wrong reasons," he contends. "It's a very dicey situation. A lot of them go on ego trips and say I'm going to hire the executive vice president myself. Once you start doing things above you, watch out. It may be difficult to maintain your integrity."

The flood of government regulation protecting an individual's right to privacy during the seventies also caused more companies to turn to executive search. Headhunters, after all, are hired partly to find out what many corporations cannot legally discover themselves, to discreetly ask delicate questions about divorce or alcoholic abuse, and to obtain references colleagues would normally refrain from giving.

What can a headhunter ask a candidate that a client legally cannot? "Almost everything," replies Brenda Ruello, of Heidrick & Struggles. "My attitude is that I can ask a candidate any question I want to ask. I work for my client and the more I know about a candidate is better for my client. And I don't like surprises. I don't think a client can ask all those good questions like 'Who's going to take care of your children. Tell me about your divorce' or any of those things. I can set up an interview in an environment that encourages you to talk. By the fun of it, the warmth of it and the non-threatening way of asking a question."

Extracting nitty-gritty detail on candidates is seldom easy. And the less than ethical recruiters have been known to employ everything from intimidating interviews to ruse calling—when a headhunter assumes a false identity to weasel private information on people and companies. In one rare instance, an alleged ruse drew a lawsuit from McGraw-Hill Inc., publisher of *BusinessWeek,* that charged that a headhunter with the San Francisco-based search firm of F. R. Bacci & Co. posed as a *BusinessWeek* reporter to more easily gather information from several companies.

But most often, headhunters cleverly ply their subjects. Typically, they will work from reference check lists that remind them to bring up areas that corporate personnel staffs would be chary to explore. "We don't want to put him in over his head or underrate his potential," is a common opening line to a reference source. A series of softball queries leads up to the hardball questions. Examples: "Is his personal life clear? Sincere and honest character? Drinking habits? Community relations-good?"

Besides, corporate chieftains prefer not to directly raid their competitors for talent. "Corporations do not want to pirate directly from one another so there is a need for the search business," affirms Karl Pierson, ITT's outspoken director of staffing. Executive vanity plays a role as well. "No chief executive wants to be turned down," maintains Robert Cox, who started recruiting for John F. Kennedy's administration in 1961, later bringing in recruits for cabinet and sub-cabinet positions during Lyndon B. Johnson's reign in the White House. "L.B.J. would refuse to have people tell him no. My objective was to insure that the President of the United States was never told no. Chief executives could live with that, of course, but why should they have to? So we're a lot like Japanese marriage brokers."

When Katharine Graham, chairman and publisher of the Washington Post Co., was seeking a president for her firm in the 1980s, she had read that Richard Simmons was passed over for the presidency of Dun & Bradstreet. Simmons seemed an ideal choice. But Graham didn't call him direct. She telephoned Gette, who had left Haley to work on his own in Florida, to inquire whether "we" should be calling this guy up. Gette made the approach, and Simmons was subsequently hired in 1981 as president.

All these trends combined to fuel staggering growth for executive search as the pirating of executives became pervasive. Two of the most powerful forces in the business today did not exist in early 1969: Korn/Ferry International, with revenues of nearly $60 million, and Russell Reynolds Associates, Inc., with revenues of $50 million.

Both firms' origins stretched back to a couple of the Big Eight accounting firms, again proving how incestuous a business headhunting continued to be. Price Waterhouse delivered William H. Clark which led to Russell Reynolds; Peat, Marwick & Mitchell brought into the world Korn/Ferry International, which can lay claim to dozens of offspring. Booz, Allen & Hamilton alone has spawned four of the top ten U.S. search firms from Boyden Associates in 1946, Heidrick & Struggles in 1953, Spencer Stuart & Associates in 1956 to Lamalie Associates in 1967. Spencer Stuart, in turn, begot European-based Egon Zehnder in 1964, while Boyden brought forth Paul R. Ray in 1965. McKinsey bred Handy in 1944, Ward Howell in 1951 and Canny, Bowen, Inc. in 1954. Ward Howell, in turn, led to Haley Associates in 1964.

While Haley was carving a niche for himself in the U.S. as a hunter of the biggest executive game, another early pioneer was actively exporting the new American product abroad. Spencer R. Stuart, yet another Booz, Allen alumnus, began paving this ground as soon as he opened the doors of his firm in Chicago in 1956. His first assignment: to hunt down a managing director to run an American pharmaceutical company's operations in Caracas, Venezuela. "They said, 'Spence, we want you to find an executive who not only knows the pharmaceutical business, but who also speaks Spanish, understands the business climate in Venezuela and whose wife and family will be happy living in Caracas,' " recalls the now retired Stuart. "Once I heard those specifications, I knew the only place I was going to find the right candidate was in Caracas, and either his wife was happy living there or not."

That job successfully completed, Stuart discovered that well over half his time was spent outside the U.S., where he endured 36 "propeller trips" to Europe and Latin America during his first two years. He had astutely set up an international operation in Zurich and Mexico City by 1958, becoming the first American executive search firm to establish a thriving international practice. By the end of 1960, his firm hunted heads in 28 countries outside the U.S. Offices followed in London, Frankfurt, Paris, Dusseldorf, Brussels and Sydney. Most of Stuart's work was for the myriad American companies that moved into Europe in the postwar years. By the time he sold out and resigned in 1973, his strategy had served him well. Stuart had amassed a fortune to live a life of early-retirement luxury with residential addresses in Sugarbush Mountain, Vermont; the Eldorado Country Club in Palm Springs; Lake Tahoe, Nevada and Dallas, Texas.

His partners continued the firm's international bent, increasing their business with foreign corporations. Headhunting abroad has often been less lucrative because employees there tend to be far more loyal to their employers than in the U.S. and foreign companies do not use headhunters as extensively as U.S. concerns. Egon Zehnder International, Europe's largest headhunting firm with billings of $25 million a year, still does 40 percent of its business with U.S. companies which it estimates recruits outsiders to senior management positions by a four-to-one margin over European concerns.

Zehnder, a charming Harvard M.B.A. lured into the business by Spencer Stuart in 1959, claims to be the first professional consultant in Europe who specialized exclusively in search. He broke from Stuart in 1964 to open his own shop, finding, like the U.S. pioneers before him, the going rough at first. "I got nasty letters from company presidents," says Zehnder, whose baldness is hardly disguised by the few strands of hair curled atop his head. "They even notified my bank, trying to exert pressure. It was very difficult. Today the banks call me and ask if they should do business with certain companies."

Headhunters, like Zehnder, have successfully chipped away at the loyalty factor abroad, most dramatically in Europe. "Ten years ago, some people would say 'How dare you call me!' " affirms the Amsterdam-based Arnold Tempel, chairman of Spencer Stuart. "Today most people in Europe consider it an honor to be called. They're flattered to be considered for a better job." Tempel, whose firm is one of the largest in the U.S. and now garners half its revenues from searches outside the U.S., is well equipped to lure them away. The Dutch-born recruiter, who boasts graduate degrees in law and social economics, speaks Dutch, Engligh and German and is conversant in both French and Portuguese.

The key to many of these foreign searches is having access to the social networks that count, whether it's some link to the male-dominated public school cloisters and Oxbridge common room that lead to London's corridors of power or the rather closed, aristo-cratic circles of wealthy Latin American executives. "In Brazil, for instance, you wouldn't think of making a cold call to a senior ex-ecutive even today," Tempel says. "You're talking about the most important thing a man has—his career. Therefore, you can only communicate with someone if you have the proper introduction or entree."

In certain areas of Europe, headhunting has become as prevalent as in the U.S. and as despised by entrepreneurs who fear that their best executives might become prey. "Headhunters are a destructive, pernicious breed who feed on a small circle of executives," the chairman of a major retailing combine in London was telling an En-glish journalist in 1985. "I loathe them. Headhunters go around prodding people—making them discontent. The more people they can move, the better for business. Three years later, they come back and try to do it again."

In many parts of Asia, however, corporations feel betrayed if an employee jumps ship for someone else. Defections aren't taken lightly, either. When Chemical Bank hired away a young ambitious execu-tive from a South Korean company in 1984 it provoked headlines and a major flap. Samsung Group, the huge South Korean industrial producer, was so irked that it asked Chemical Bank to pull out of a $100 million syndicated loan the New York bank was helping to arrange for the Korean company.

Back in the U.S., Haley Associates' reputation as a recruiter of major corporation heads came to a rather abrupt end when Gette went into semi-retirement in Florida in 1978. "Bob and I," Haley says, "were like brothers. I would get the business and he would do the work. And when he left things fell apart."

Haley figured he could maintain the high level work by luring over one of the rising stars at Heidrick & Struggles, Gerard Roche. But the swaggering Roche remained with Heidrick and would later emerge as the grand acquisitor of top executive savvy, the man who would pull more chief executive rabbits out of corporate hats than any other headhunter. "Roche allowed Heidrick to replace us and took an awful lot of business away," says the 69-year-old Haley.

Notwithstanding the firm's loss, many of the pure headhunting firms found a welcome, if unexpected, boost when Booz, Allen closed down its highly profitable executive recruiting arm in 1980. The management consultant's retreat occurred shortly after a series of disastrous recruitments: Archie McCardell to International Harvester in 1978 and Jonathan Scott to A&P in 1975. Both presided over the near demise of two once great American corporate institutions. Then, Booz apparently made a mess in trying to recruit a new chief executive and heir apparent to Greyhound Corp. chairman Gerald Trautman. "We almost ended up suing Booz Allen because of the way they conducted the search," Trautman later complained to a *Fortune* journalist. "They kept pushing five or six different candidates."

"A lot of the placements came apart and consequently didn't work," says James A. Newman, vice-chairman of Booz, who once headed up Booz's search practice. "Of course, you could do a bad consulting study, too. But the chief executive could put it in a drawer to collect dust. If you placed a bad person in a company it had a different effect. Everytime he comes into the CEO's office, he looks at him and reminds him of Booz, Allen. That happened a few times." Newman guesses that roughly half of Booz's placements lasted no more than five years in their new jobs. Hardly a record worth preserving.

The official word from Booz was that it withdrew from the search business for the same reason that caused McKinsey to ditch its involvement years earlier: a potential conflict of interest with consulting clients. Management consultants, the reasoning went, could simply recommend changes in personnel and then collect from a corporation twice: once for producing the study and again for producing a candidate. There were other obvious problems as well. Booz's headhunters ethically could not raid any of the consulting practice's 3,000 clients for candidates. That made it doubly hard to find the best available executives on the market.

Similar limitations among the Big Eight accountants—who initially got into the business by sending to clients their own employees who likely wouldn't make partner—hindered their efforts to make an impact. "I remember that two or three times I had searches where a Warner-Lambert executive I knew would have been perfect, but I couldn't take him out because the company was an auditing client," says Mathew J. Beecher, formerly head of Price Waterhouse's search group. "My partners were always afraid we would put someone in a job who would be in a position to fire us as auditors."

Then, in 1978, the big certified-public-accounting firms voluntarily agreed to curtail a good chunk of their search activities. Under pressure from the Securities & Exchange Commission (SEC), they decided not to recruit for their SEC-registered audit clients due to the same potential for conflicts. Already blocked from recruiting candidates from their accounting, auditing and management consulting clients, this new barrier severely limited their future growth in executive hunting. Some, such as Price Waterhouse, totally quit search. Only one Big Eight firm is in the headhunting top ten, Peat, Marwick, Mitchell & Co., and only 5 percent of its clients are Fortune 500 companies.

Meantime, many of the old traditional firms that pioneered the business and labored hard for credibility with the corporate world to handle those big jobs began to fall by the wayside. Some failed to realize that their views and approaches to the business were dated and stereotyped. Others lost their driven and dynamic leaders and floundered. Thorndike Deland Associates, the first and oldest executive search firm, still boasts only one office in New York. Under Thorndike's less ambitious sons, the firm failed to venture from its retail specialty until the late 1960s when it moved into the consumer goods field. It remains a small, highly respected, specialty outfit—one that Russell Reynolds has unsuccessfully tried to acquire. But its annual $2 million billings are but a fraction of the revenues that any major search firm generates in New York today. William H. Clark Associates, Inc., in the sixties one of the major, elite headhunting firms, now boasts only a single office in Chicago. It, too, had trouble surviving the trauma of succession when founder Clark retired. Handy Associates, also, is a one office firm—although it has managed under different ownership to be among the top ten largest search firms.

During most of the 1960s, Boyden could comfortably claim his firm was king. But when he retired in 1971 and sold the $3.9 million (revenues) firm to Los Angeles-based Shareholders Capital Corp., things rapidly unraveled. The West Coast company wanted to use Boyden's headhunters to connect with well-heeled clients to sell investment counsel. It was a disaster. Profits turned to losses, and Boyden's associates bought the firm back for themselves in 1977. Momentum, along with several heavy-hitters, had been lost. Boyden Associates still remains one of the largest firms in the business, but five other U.S. firms which didn't exist when Boyden opened his doors have since eclipsed it in size.

A sad, but true irony, became well-known: The headhunters charged with finding corporate America's most savvy, urbane and talented managers couldn't manage themselves. Few of their companies were run like legitimate businesses, but rather like loose collections of overbearing egos. Turnover among their own staffs, in some cases, became critical problems as did the management of overseas offices. These were not large companies, either. If any of the major headhunting firms had to enlist a chief executive for a similarly sized business it would be considered a small assignment.

How could the searchers of managerial talent lack so much of that talent themselves? Was it possible for a poor manager to successfully and consistently recruit good ones? "This business is unique," claims Carl Menk, who nursed Boyden back to health after the headhunting pioneer foolishly sold out. "It attracts strong personalities with an entrepreneurial flair who are not always good managers. If they were good, strong managers, they would have stayed on the client side."

The Management Succession Game

"If you are planning for centuries, grow men."

THE CHINESE PROVERB was beautifully framed on the wall of the executive's well-appointed office at General Electric's corporate headquarters. "If you are planning for one year, grow rice; if you are planning for twenty years, grow trees; if you are planning for centuries, grow men."

It was a gift to J. Stanford Smith from his GE associates, and it hung prominently in his office at a company known for its succession planning, a corporate institution which has written the book on it. Now Smith was leaving GE for International Paper (IP) and hoping to take a leaf or two on the subject with him from the manual. At IP, management development was weak and corporate morale was low.

Smith's departure in 1974 for IP, the world's largest producer of paperboard, paper and pulp and North America's largest private owner of forest lands, was a lucky break. George Haley, a well-known headhunter, had been called in by IP to find a chief executive who could succeed Paul Gorman, a former Western Electric executive. After an exhaustive search, Haley had worked up a list of five candidates, including Lee Iacocca, who had been named president of Ford Motor Corp. three years earlier.

Smith was not on the list, not until Haley's client insisted upon having a sixth candidate from which to choose. Haley threw in Smith, a 37-year veteran of General Electric, who had been passed over for the top spot at GE.

"He decided he wanted to leave GE and the first place many top executives would come to was me," boasts Haley. "We figured we would just slip him in and that they would quickly discard him. Goddamn it. Against our recommendation they hired him."

One of Smith's duties was to improve the depth of management at the company, to grow its own managers instead of importing them. Smith failed miserably at this task. Five years later, when it was time for him to retire, he had no inside successor in place. Instead, he turned to Heidrick & Struggles's Gerard Roche and David Peasback to find yet another outsider to take over IP. They found Edwin A. Gee, a senior vice-president and member of Du Pont's ruling executive committee, who had a Ph.D. in chemical engineering. When Peasback first met him at a secretly arranged meeting in a room of the Key Bridge Marriott in Delaware, he was shocked to see him dressed in a dark suit wearing white athletic socks. Smith was a fastidious dresser, the ultimate New York executive, sophisticated and urbane. What would he possibly think?

"My question was what do we do?" Peasback wondered. "Tell him to change his socks during the first interview? Or do we alert Stan and tell him, 'Hey, if this guy comes in and crosses his legs don't get turned off?' It didn't matter whether he wore a brown, blue or gray suit, he'd still wear white socks." Peasback, hoping that Smith either wouldn't notice or wouldn't care, ultimately decided to cross his fingers and stay mum. It was the right strategy.

After landing the job, Gee dashed off a letter to Heidrick & Struggles thanking them for arranging the linkup. Under a P.S., he wrote: "And I kept wearing the same socks." Gee signed off by drawing a funny face and an exclamation point.

When his appointment was announced by International Paper in early 1978, it drew jeers from Wall Street analysts who followed the company. They were immediately critical of IP's failure to groom top management from within the company. "They've had to go outside the company for nearly every recent top management change," one analyst told *The Wall Street Journal*. "The Gee election is the wrong decision for a company which has visibly underperformed in the paper market. They needed a competent guy like Gee but one who had experience in the forest products industry as well."

Chalk another one up for the headhunting fraternity. That seemed like nothing new. As one former company executive told a reporter even before Gee came aboard, "IP hasn't had a chief executive in years who knew one end of a paper machine from the other." Added another: "Some of IP's top managers don't have the business in their blood, and that's never a good thing." Heidrick & Struggles, meantime, considers IP one of its bedrock clients since it has performed some 60 searches for the company.

The turmoil began in the early 1970s after poor performance led to the firing of then IP head Edward Hinman. Paul Gorman, former president of Western Electric Co. and chief executive of Penn Central Co. was the first outsider named chairman, CEO and president of IP in 1971. Then came outsider Smith three years later. And Gee five years after that. Soon after Gee's arrival, he was introduced by Smith to nearly 200 of IP's top managers at a special meeting. When Smith asked all the executives who had been with the company before he joined it to stand, only about a dozen men did.

When Gee picked John A. Georges as his successor as chief executive officer in 1984, International Paper essentially went with another executive who was not a product of the company's culture. This time, however, the outsider had come to IP five years earlier. Georges was recruited as an executive vice-president from Gee's old stomping grounds, Du Pont, where he had spent 28 years; the last position he held there was as general manager of Du Pont's textile fibers department. Georges succeeded Gee as chairman in 1985 when Gee finally retired. For over a dozen years, the company was run by outsiders who at least initially knew little, if anything, about the paper industry. Yet Gee still failed to groom a true insider for the top job. What kind of signal did that send to IP's demotivated troops?

Gorman, Smith, Gee and Georges all were brought into IP on the theory that an astute executive can perform well in any business—it is an underlining notion that has propelled the use of search. But realistically what did a telephone man know about the paper industry? An automobile executive? A chemicals manager? A textile fiber man?

Sometimes, it's necessary to reach outside for a senior executive because the managers being groomed for the chief executive officer's suite left for other opportunities. Those behind them may require further seasoning and development before taking on the top job. In other cases, the board may want an outsider to spur a dramatic change in strategy, to lead the corporation in new directions. But four outsiders in a row?

Most honest headhunters will tell you the odds for success for the outside chief executive officer are less than 50–50. Sometimes it works. More often it does not. One study, by two business professors at Utah State University in 1976, found that top-level executives do not readily transfer between firms. Of 270 major corporations in the study, only 29 had recruited a chief executive from outside. Of the 29 outsiders, only 14 could boast the dubious distinction of arriving from outside the industry, like all of IP's three previous chief executive officers. The same professors also concluded that insiders in the top job increase a corporation's chance to attain greater profitability.

"Executives promoted from within are aided by knowing the company, its traditions, personalities and unique ways of functioning," says Dr. Y. K. Shetty, a co-author of the study. "In other words, knowing the organizational culture is a crucial factor in defining the effectiveness of a chief executive. When a company hires an outside man, he generally brings with him his own people to fill top management positions. The result is an executive exodus."

A former International Paper executive confirms the trend, noting that the recruitment of each outsider brought with him scores of other outsiders, each trained in his former employer's style and culture. "Gorman spoke AT&T management language," the executive told *BusinessWeek*. "Then Gorman brought in a lot of senior people from Mobil Corp., and they had their own language. We had some more of that with Smith's GE language. And now we've got Du Pont. You have to keep learning a new vocabulary."

The greatest single barrier to a successful transfer is the institutional acumen an executive is likely to lack in a new environment. Success is not dependent solely on the technical or managerial skills of an executive. Instead, a successful manager must rely on the people who work for and above him. Personal contacts, in turn, are closely tied with his knowledge of the company's traditions and culture and his understanding of how things get done in his new work place.

The best executive headhunters can help ease the transition by feeding their recruit some of the skinny they've picked up on the company and its executives during their search. "We sit down and talk him through our assessment of the people he'll work with," says Robert Slater, managing director of Spencer Stuart & Associates' U.S. operations. "When you conduct a senior-level search, you talk to a lot of people who assess the corporation and its people. So we're able to present a profile of the organization and how it's perceived by competitors and insiders. And we can typically identify those people who would be embittered or disappointed at having been passed over for the job."

The odds are almost always against the outsider. After all, when the headhunter brings in an unfamiliar face it means several internal candidates were perceived to be less than qualified for a promotion. Passed-over executives might resent their new outside boss; they're likely to be less committed to his success. "Corporations have a higher tolerance for people they have grown and much less tolerance for those who come in from the outside," believes William Gould, founder of Gould & McCoy, a small New York headhunting firm. "They want outsiders to prove themselves because they really don't want to go outside. It's still a bit of a trauma to reach outside for a senior executive."

No less crucial, the sense of camaraderie critical to good performance is often lacking. "As corporate executives increasingly accept job hopping as the way to succeed, the trust essential to teamwork almost certainly suffers," writes McKinsey & Co.'s Arch Patton. "As more companies come to rely on executives trained by others, often with different work standards and internal corporate cultures, the common will to attain company objectives must lose something."

Consider an assignment undertaken by George Haley, chairman of New York's Haley Associates, Inc., to find a president for AMF Corp., a conglomerate whose products ranged from Harley-Davidson motorcycles and Head skis to industrial equipment. Haley believes the search resulted in the most egregious mistake of his headhunting career. The assignment was handed to Haley by AMF's soon-to-retire chairman and chief executive Rodney C. Gott. Haley delivered to AMF Corp. as president and vice-chairman R. William McNealy, Jr. in March of 1978. An irreverent 50-year-old Irishman, McNealy had been fired as vice-chairman of American Motors Corp. six months earlier.

Simultaneously, however, Gott elevated his 44-year-old president W. Thomas York as his successor just as McNealy assumed his roles as an outsider. A classic numbers' cruncher, York spent ten years in accounting and finance at Philco-Ford before joining AMF in 1968. He rose rapidly through the ranks as a controller and vice-president of finance. But he clearly lacked the broad-based management experience necessary for the top job. "He had no training whatsoever," says Haley. "He had about a year in general management. I told Gott that was not the way to do it. He should have brought in an older man as chairman and chief executive who could train York and let him succeed the interim president. Well, he wouldn't buy it."

Rejecting Haley's suggestion that an elder caretaker chief executive officer be put in place, Gott moved up York to chairman and chief executive as McNealy moved in to work under him as president and vice-chairman. "York didn't want this guy, and he just castrated him," says Haley. "He was not wanted by the inner circle of the company. York never gave this guy any duties. He just sat by the window for a year. What disturbed me was that Gott had arranged this thing yet wouldn't protect him. I knew the thing wouldn't work and a guy's career was really damaged. I knew it and I never should have done it. We should have refused to take the assignment."

McNealy lasted less than 18 months in the job before he suddenly resigned in September 1979, walking away from the mess with $190,000 in severance pay. Five years later enough time had passed to fairly assess York's performance in the job. He was simply pitiful. AMF's profitability sank to among the lowest levels in its industries. *Forbes* magazine ranked AMF 42 out of 48 industrial machinery companies and dead last of four recreation companies in return-on-equity, a standard measure of corporate profitability. Shareholders investing in AMF during this period would have been better off putting their money into the local savings and loan. They would have realized a puny gain of 6 percent on their investment over five years.

"It was a real tragedy," says Haley, shaking his head from side-to-side, "and in the meantime AMF went to pot. It's been downhill all the way." Justice was somehow done, however. York resigned in July 1985 after corporate raider Irwin L. Jacobs successfully captured the company in a takeover bid. In York's last full year as chief executive, AMF eked out a 1.5 percent return, a measly $14.9 million in net income on $1.1 billion of revenues in 1984.

The method Haley advocated is one frequently used today by corporations caught without inside successors. Headhunters are asked to find a caretaker chief executive officer in his early 60s so his appointment would not turn off the corporation's younger managers and cause them to flee.

Nonetheless, these are stopgap measures which simply are a consequence of poor succession planning. The fact remains that many corporations pay relatively scant attention to grooming top-level personnel. And that's what keeps headhunters in the money. "I live off the carnage of failed management development programs," says Gerry Roche, Heidrick & Struggles's chairman and chief executive hunter. "About 88 percent of the senior executives mentioned in "Who's News" in *The Wall Street Journal* are promoted from within and that's the way it should be. We live off the remaining 12 percent or so. If American management were paying more attention to developing people at the top, we would be doing less business."

Management development often is relegated to the human resources or personnel department, which spends most of its time working on development from middle management down. Careful cultivation at top levels tends to be overlooked at many companies. "Management development is woefully inadequate in American management today," adds Roche. "It is done from the hip, spottily, without much thought or formality. The key is that executives are afraid to tell people what they find lacking in them and what is improvable. Somebody once said that imperfect people are improvable. That's a great line. I love it. We don't work enough at improving them and this is how I make my money. They come to me and they say, 'Roche, replace my imperfect person.' And I say, 'Have you worked with them? Have you tried to improve them? Have you had a program?' 'No, just go get us a new one.' The president of a company should help to develop his executive vice-presidents, and he should be measured by his board on how good a battery of successors he has ready to go in."

The board of directors must oversee the career progression of these likely prospects to insure they have a meaningful slate of successors from which to choose when the chief executive leaves. "Several of the country's largest corporations, despite their reputation for following a promotion-from-within policy, have on their slates the names of one or two outside candidates," notes Roger M. Kenny, formerly a senior partner with Spencer Stuart & Associates. "If an emergency occurs and the position of president must be filled quickly, these companies' boards know of several 'outside' individuals who might be likely successors."

General Electric, IBM, Procter & Gamble, Exxon, General Motors and Du Pont have long been major exceptions. Outsiders have never risen to the top of these American institutions. Known as academies because they train and develop so many good managers, they are more often favorite hunting grounds of headhunters in search of executive excellence. Predictably, they employ headhunters sparingly, if at all, because they can simply dip into their own pools of executive talent to fill most of the jobs that come open.

"I still feel very strongly that companies ought to be primarily devoted to growing their own," says human resources executive-turned-headhunter Alan Lafley. "It's the poorer companies which give search firms most of the business because they just constantly keep turning people over and bringing outside people in."

Before they became human resources professionals, Lafley and others like him were called personnel directors. They were the "happiness boys" of the business world: They tried to keep smiles imprinted on everyone's face and to keep the unions far from the plant doors. But they typically were excluded from the senior management team, seldom reported directly to the chief executive and often were thrust in offices off the floor where executive power was exercised. They were implementors; never decision makers.

That is changing and Lafley has ridden the crest of this wave. Acknowledged by many as a pioneer in the human resources field, he was one of the first to function as a key member of senior management. Lafley spent 22 years with General Electric, in roles ranging from head of human relations at the company's monmouth Schenectady, New York, plant to manager of executive manpower and compensation. In 1968, he joined GE corporate to determine how general managers should be identified, selected and developed. General Electric makes succession planning a corporate way of life. The company maintains a management development school at a 50-acre estate in Crotonville, New York, which rivals most of the nation's finest graduate business programs. More than 50,000 GE managers attend classes at this center annually.

Yet, while at General Electric, Lafley was one of the early pioneers to encourage the company to use search. Not to willy-nilly recruit outsiders for jobs, but to employ headhunters to drum up outside candidates to compare against its internal people for key jobs. "I asked if we were sure our people were as good as we thought they were. We had done a reasonably good job of assessing our people within the company and sorting them out. But how did they compare with the outside?"

To find out, GE employed several headhunting firms to bring them talented and experienced outsiders who would be matched up against GE's own crop of managers. "Generally, we never hired the outside candidates," adds Lafley. "We did not, in my opinion, bring in as many people as we should have. But we started to change the views of key managers and we recruited a number of outsiders in the 1970s in strategic planning."

More recently, as a headhunter with Korn/Ferry International, Lafley was engaged to help GE decide whether it should, for the first time, reach outside for a human resources executive for GE Credit, an important money-making subsidiary. With GE, Lafley identified the two best internal candidates and then found two external executives to compare them against. The GE executives were grilled as extensively as the outsiders in interviews which lasted as long as three hours each. Even at General Electric that type of scrutiny for a single promotion is not common. An insider eventually got the nod.

While headhunters increasingly hope to play these true consulting roles in corporate America, such assignments remain elusive. "In most cases," notes Lafley, "corporations won't allow a search firm to assess their internal candidates because they don't trust the firms that much. And many of the firms think their job is just finding people."

That might well be one reason why so many mismatches occur. Search consultants fail to spend enough time deciphering the operating styles and personalities of associates with which the outsider must work. Haley's experience at AMF is no anomaly. Headhunting mismatches have been plentiful, resulting in the dismissal of many executives and contributing, in some cases, to the decline of several once-great American business institutions. It was Booz, Allen & Hamilton headhunting, for example, that led to the recruitment of Archie McCardell from Xerox to president of International Harvester in 1977 and Jonathan Scott to A&P in 1975. Both outsiders presided over the dismantling of two of the nation's most known and respected corporations. McCardell finally got the ax in 1982, as did Scott in 1980.

Booz's "skillful" headhunting work, along with McCardell's legacy, was eventually preserved in a book appropriately titled *A Corporate Tragedy: The Agony of International Harvester Company* and written by Barbara Marsh. It was Booz President Charles P. Bowen, Jr., no less, who insisted that International Harvester break its long-standing tradition of grooming leaders from within and search outside the company for a new chief executive. The recommendation from Bowen came after a major Booz, Allen management consulting study of the company for Brooks McCormick, then Harvester's chairman. But when Bowen suggested that IH turn to an outsider, McCormick was initially skeptical. He "demanded to know how other companies had fared after recruiting leaders from outside," writes Marsh. To satisfy his concerns, the consulting firm put together a study of thirty-one recent leadership changes at major corporations. Although largely inconclusive, it did show that none of the truly poor performers were homegrown.

McCormick might have taken the hint. The "spec" called for an executive between 45 and 55 years old with an undergraduate degree in engineering and an M.B.A. It required ten years of experience as the top executive in a capital equipment, automotive or industrial goods company or division with more than $500 million in annual sales.

"I clearly remember," a former Harvester executive told Marsh, "that Mr. McCormick said he was looking for someone who could come into Harvester's family environment without disrupting it. He was looking for a winner who would in fact fit into the culture." The list of candidates gathered by Booz's headhunters grew to some 34 names including, Rockwell International chief executive Robert Anderson, TRW Inc. assistant president Stanley C. Pace and Xerox President McCardell. Anderson dropped out of the race. Pace remained at TRW and in 1985 was recruited by Paul R. Ray, Sr. to General Dynamics as chairman.

Booz, Allen eventually delivered McCardell, an executive who could hardly be counted upon to maintain the old family culture. It did not take long before the inevitable mass exodus of veteran executives began in full. "It was horrible working there in the last three or four years," a former executive told Marsh. "There was so much change with top management being replaced from the outside that we lost all executive knowledge of products and markets." After several managerial miscues, including the taking of a prolonged and damaging strike by Harvester employees, McCardell left five years after he came. He left a company teetering on the edge of bankruptcy.

Corporations, of course, can often survive mistakes. Executives more often can not. Inevitably, too, any single assignment has a far greater impact on the individual. Executives, however, may watch helplessly as their careers disintegrate because of a mismatch. Dwight

Foster, the ebullient and witty head of Peat Marwick's search practice, quickly turns serious when he tells how he sold a reputable executive on a bum job. The search, he says, was for an automobile manufacturer in New York, presumably DeLorean Motor Corp. "The client did not tell me everything," he says. "He was very charismatic. I brought in a high quality executive to work with him as executive vice-president of finance. That executive came back to me three or four months later and said you've got to get me out of here. And I recognized what I had done because sometimes you fall in love with these charismatic figures. Sometimes people who engage you don't tell you the truth and you pass that scenario onto others and affect their career development. The end of the story was that my executive negotiated a settlement with the company, and a man with an excellent career record is now in early retirement with his last major executive responsibility tainted by an unfortunate relationship. So the guy spends 25 or 30 years building an excellent reputation and then this happens. I feel guilty, but you remember we're all consenting adults."

There are many success stories as well, however. If AMF and International Paper are case studies on how not to handle management succession, perhaps Haley's involvement in the recruitment of the first outsider to head up St. Louis-based Monsanto Corp. is an excellent example of how a search firm was employed to deal with the succession issue and how the move worked beautifully for the job jumper. In February 1972 Monsanto's president and chief executive officer, Edward J. Bock, a former all-American football player, had resigned under pressure. No one within the company was named to succeed him. The board believed it lacked an internal candidate to lead the diversified chemical company into the future. The following month, a search committee was organized by Monsanto chairman Charles H. Sommer to find a successor. The group met with Haley, among other headhunters, in a shootout.

"I met all these guys with vests on and stiff collars at Monsanto and told them I wouldn't consider taking the assignment unless I could talk to the top 25 people in the company," recalls Haley. "I couldn't believe there wasn't somebody inside who could be chief executive. All of these guys were looking at me saying 'Who the hell does this guy think he is?' I thought we would get thrown out, but I felt we were right. We're just not body snatchers; we're consultants. I wanted to find out what was inside that company."

Haley and Gette spent a week in St. Louis, interviewing senior management at Monsanto. The duo returned to the search committee and recommended a Monsanto executive for the job. "He was persona non grata with the board for a very unfair reason in my opinion. They blamed him for the decline of their fiber business, although I didn't think he was responsible. So they would not appoint him."

The only candidate inside the industry which Monsanto would have considered was C. Benson Branch who had been named chief executive and president of Dow Chemical only weeks earlier. "Dow was bigger and Branch was not likely to accept the post," says Haley. Monsanto, however, was thinking of diversifying into consumer products. So the search also focused on executives with experience in the consumer product field. Sommer's marching orders to Gette, who conducted the search, were: "Find the best man for the job."

The best man turned out to be John W. Hanley, an executive vice-president at Procter & Gamble (P&G) who had racked up more than 20 years of service at the consumer packaging giant. It was an opportune time for Gette to call him. A year earlier, in 1971, Edward G. Harness, also a P&G executive vice-president like Hanley, had been named president. The two had competed for the post and Hanley obviously was the loser.

Gette knew that Hanley had been passed over. He arranged through a mutual friend to meet him in New York in May. By the end of June, Hanley's name was atop a list of 20 prospects that Gette reportedly had compiled for Monsanto's search committee. There were some worries about pirating Hanley from P&G, which purchased about $50 million worth of Monsanto products annually. Sommer even made a courtesy call to P&G's aloof chairman Howard Morgens.

Morgens was enraged. "We had worked closely with Monsanto for years," he told a reporter later. "They could walk into our offices and talk to anybody. When a company does that, there is an unwritten code not to offer a job to one of your customer's people. It's an unfortunate thing for a good supplier to do to one of its best customers."

Monsanto went with Hanley, anyway. It helped that a study found that P&G had no alternative source of supply for the phosphates and other chemicals that P&G bought from Monsanto. Hanley quit P&G to join Monsanto on November 1, 1972 for an eye-opening compensation package of more than $400,000 a year—a deal which included the purchase of Hanley's Cincinnati house for $247,500 by Monsanto and a $125,000 guaranteed minimum annual year-end bonus in his first three years with the company.

Monsanto's decision to reach outside was a shock. For the company's 71-year history, it had been ruled by familiar faces. "They had worked their way up from lower echelons, step by step, to the accompaniment of cheers from the internal troops," noted the company's official biographer Dan J. Forrestal. "But when Jack Hanley became the tenth president he was a stranger to 98 or 99 percent of the company's 59,000 employees."

To his credit, Hanley wanted to insure that few other strangers would ever walk in and over other Monsanto executives like he did. After his first board meeting in New York, Hanley paid a quick visit to Haley to deliver a message that earned him Haley's immediate respect despite the implication that it meant Monsanto would be doing little business with him in the future. "The first thing he said was, 'We're not going to let you guys near the door. We're going to build this from within,' " recalls Haley.

Hanley kept his promise. When he retired as chairman and chief executive in 1984 at the age of 62, Hanley had behind him two loyal lieutenants who had climbed Monsanto's corporate ladder and who both intimately knew the company and its culture. Richard Mahoney, Monsanto's 49-year-old president, succeeded Hanley as chief executive officer, while 59-year-old vice-chairman Louis Fernandez moved into the chairman's suite. A company which had often pridefully declared that it specialized in promoting from within had restored its valued ethic.

Hanley's performance wasn't stellar. But it was no disaster, either. In the five years leading to his retirement in 1984, Monsanto ranked 14th in profitability among 19 diversified chemical companies on *Forbes*'s annual report on American industry. Its net profit margins of 5.9 percent, though, were the third highest in the group.

Headhunters trot out many of these success stories. Carl Menk, 64, a smooth blue-eyed man in a seersucker suit with wing-tipped shoes, is no exception. Menk, chairman of Canny, Bowen, Inc. and former chief executive of Boyden Associates, has tallied up more than 15 years in the search business. When Menk was enlisted to find a new chief operating officer for NL Industries, Inc. in 1972, he had but three years of executive search experience behind him.

NL, which had just changed its name from National Lead, was

mainly a lead recycling company with a record of uncontrolled diversification that resulted in 79 major divisions and subsidiaries making everything from Dutch Boy paint to castor oil. The company had as its president a man who came up through the legal route and who was perceived to lack an overall understanding of the company. "There was no one in the company who understood the whole company and all its diverse products," recalls Menk. "They needed a very aggressive, tough-minded manager who could pull all the different parts of the company together and call some shots without any emotion."

Menk discovered Ray C. Adam, a 26-year veteran of Mobil Corp. who rose to president of Mobil Chemical Co. "A lot of things Mobil was doing then was similar to National Lead, so he seemed a good fit," says Menk. So Adam was installed as chief operating officer—not chief executive. "If a company has to go outside, it's better to bring someone aboard as an executive vice-president or something and in two years move him up," believes Menk. "The client then has a chance to observe a person and find out if he's capable. The only way to learn whether a person has what is necessary to become chief executive is to observe him in a moment of stress. Have him make decisions in several stressful situations." Adam must have passed the test. Within two years, he was elected chief executive officer and chairman of NL.

A decade after Menk snatched Adam from Mobil and deposited him into the company, NL Industries had 26 fewer divisions, 5,000 fewer employees and was more than seven times as profitable. Adam also helped to increase NL's market value for shareholders by roughly $2 billion in the process. Widely credited with transforming the company into a major petroleum services corporation, he retired as chairman in 1983—a full 11 years after joining NL. "He built," boasts Menk with a sense of pride, "a strong organization that was good for the stockholders, for employment and for Uncle Sam because NL paid a lot more taxes than they did before. So they had a positive effect on the economy. That's what I consider doing the job in this kind of business. When I look back at the number of people I have found for clients in top-level positions, I think in my humble way that I have made a contribution to strengthen the economy."

One of the most delicate and tricky succession assignments for headhunters occurs when a corporate infant of a company has outgrown its founder's ability to successfully manage it. Occasionally, the entrepreneur realizes his limitations, swallows his pride and brings in an outsider to run the show. More often, the venture capitalists become venture vultures and employ a search firm to find a successor as they give the entrepreneur his walking papers. Peat Marwick's Dwight Foster refers to such searches as "lethal." "Those are the ones that will chew you up," he says. "No one can ever do things quite well enough for the entrepreneur who founded a company, builds it and has a personal touch with the business. That kind of search is just lethal."

It was just such a job which fell into the lap of Russell Reynolds Associates, and it rapidly became one of the most critical and intriguing assignments ever approached by an executive search firm.

Wanted: A Corporate Savior

*"Silicon Valley's shock troops meet Park Avenue's
Brooks Brothers-clad headhunters."*

FOR FIVE YEARS, Allen Michels, a scrappy, cigar-chomping physicist, had worked day and night to construct a counterculture computer company that meant as much to him as one of his own children. In Silicon Valley, the high-tech mecca of the world, his story and the story of Convergent Technologies, Inc. was well-known. Starting with little more than a business plan sketched on a paper napkin in 1979, Michels built his corporation into a $400 million player in the intensely competitive and volatile computer market. Convergent blossomed into the fastest growing public corporation in the U.S. Its swift success made Michels and dozens of others multimillionaires.

But his company's promising childhood threatened to give way to a stunted adolescence. Profits turned to losses. Michels and his top executives slashed their salaries in half. The irreverent, rotund wizard half-seriously joked he would match the company's percentage savings in expenses with an equal loss in his personal weight. Silicon Valley gossips prematurely wondered whether Convergent would turn into another dream gone bankrupt like so many others in the valley. Wall Street reacted in a panic. Convergent stock, once a $40.75 per share darling at its peak in 1983, plummeted to under $5 in 1984. The company, valued at $1.5 billion in 1983, was in 1984 worth a mere $36 million. Michels, downcast and defeated, watched as his own paper fortune dwindled to less than $40 million from over $300 million.

And now, at 1:00 P.M. on November 6, 1984, he was about to play host to four men he had never met before, strangers who he hoped could help him turn his company around. They were there to capture and begin what would be the big-game hunt for Michels's successor. The contingent was led by Russell Reynolds, a slim and handsome 52-year-old man who in his own right was an entrepreneur, too. In 1969, he had founded Russell Reynolds Associates, Inc., and made it one of the most elite and largest executive headhunting firms in the world. He was accompanied by P. Anthony Price, who was about to take charge of the firm's San Francisco office, Richard S. Gostyla, who headed his newly opened Menlo Park quarters and Reynolds's personal assistant and sidekick of two years, Steven Potter.

Reynolds and Potter flew in from New York that morning and Gostyla and Price picked them up at the airport in San Francisco and drove straight to Convergent in Santa Clara. During the 35-minute drive on Highway 101 South the four began choreographing the upcoming meeting. Reynolds would tell Michels the background of his firm. Price and Gostyla, both Harvard M.B.A.s, would do the actual search work if Michels awarded them the assignment. To get the more lucrative business for Michels's successor, Price would talk up his experience in doing high-tech searches for such multinational corporations as TRW and Eaton Corp. in Cleveland, where he had headed the firm's local office. Gostyla would explain why he could deliver a financial executive to Convergent—the second search they were expected to discuss. Potter, in training to become a full-fledged headhunter, would simply sit and listen.

As the car sped past rows and rows of monotonous industrial buildings that sprouted where orchards and fields once lay, Reynolds noted that he had chatted with Michels for the first time only a few days earlier. The telephone conversation was initiated by Reynolds's personal friend Michael Blumenthal, chief executive of Burroughs Corp. Blumenthal had used Reynolds's search firm to replace scores of Burroughs's old-line company executives with outsiders. Less than two years after joining Burroughs in 1980, Blumenthal was said to have installed outsiders in 20 of the company's top 25 executive positions. Reynolds's firm played a key role in this management overhaul. Among Reynolds's recruits was the company's current president, Paul Stern, who the firm had lured from Rockwell International Corp.

Their relationship started out awkwardly enough. One of Reynolds's earliest search assignments had been to find a vice-president of finance for Bendix in 1970. The firm helped to put W. R. Clerihue, the vice-president and treasurer of Celanese Corp., into the $100,000-a-year job at Bendix. But Clerihue broke no records for longevity. He left little more than a year later. Perusing Bendix's contract with the headhunter, Blumenthal, at the time chairman and chief executive, gave Reynolds a call.

"Mr. Blumenthal got out the file and read that I had promised that if the successful candidate left within a certain period, we would do another search to replace him for a dramatically reduced fee," says Reynolds. "He is a man with an eye for detail, which is in my opinion the mark of any good executive. And he's no fool when it comes to spending money.

"He called up and said, 'My name is W. Michael Blumenthal and we expect you to do this search.'

"Look," Reynolds said, "it's almost been nine months."

"Yes," replied Blumenthal, "but it hasn't been nine months."

"We negotiated an arrangement that we were both satisfied with and recruited someone else for him," says Reynolds. "And we've been good friends ever since." Blumenthal, in fact, has made an appearance at one of the firm's annual management planning conferences.

Reynolds's new replacement for Blumenthal was a young fast-track executive from Boise Cascade, a Harvard M.B.A. and comer called William Agee. It was easy for Reynolds to lure Agee to Bendix. Agee had risen quickly up the ranks at Boise, becoming treasurer at 29 and a senior vice-president at 33. But another "young tiger" at Boise, John Fery, was clearly the heir apparent. Agee was eager to bail out for a shot at the Bendix presidency. His hunch was right. Five years later, in 1976, Agee was named president; and when Blumenthal left to become Secretary of the Treasury in the Carter Administration the sandy-haired son of a farmer was named, at the age of 39, one of the youngest chief executives of a major corporation. Agee did not forget his friends at Reynolds who allowed him to connect. He gave them lots of business, including a high-level search that led to the recruitment in 1981 of Alonzo MacDonald, Jr., a McKinsey & Co. former managing director, to the job as Bendix president.

Blumenthal, now long distanced from his Bendix days, had reason to be interested in the meeting's outcome between Reynolds and Michels. He was Convergent's largest and most important customer. A year earlier, in 1983, Burroughs had accounted for 46 percent of Convergent's total sales. In late October, when the green of Central Park was turning to autumn brown, Michels had flown the 3,000 miles cross country to New York for a private dinner meeting with Blumenthal at the Helmsley Palace, one of the city's most elegant hotels. It was there, over what Michels calls a dinner "of mediocrity and abominable service," that he both shocked and disappointed Blumenthal with the news that he would seek a top executive who could do what he acknowledged he could not. "He wasn't happy that I made the decision," says Michels, "but once he too understood that it was firm and I wasn't going to change my mind, his help was invaluable." Blumenthal told Michels he knew Reynolds personally and would have him call to help. Two days later, Reynolds was on the phone to Michels arranging this trip.

In a memo preparing his troops for the meeting, Reynolds said that Blumenthal had described Michels as a "an effervescent fat man who eats too much and is full of energy and has really built a helluva operation. But it's a mess. Please get somebody in there quickly because we buy a lot of our stuff from them."

Still, the four had less than a week to prepare for the session and much of the information they had accumulated was flimsy and second hand. The firm's research department delivered a package of press clips on the company that told of its rollercoaster ride. And some customers were called for their views. "The picture was pretty consistent that Convergent had grown very rapidly, but had not been able to develop the operating systems to keep up with the growth in sales," said Price.

They pulled into the parking lot outside the Convergent building in an industrial park on 2500 Augustine Drive. It was a nondescript two-story, tilt-up structure, one of the hurriedly erected industrial barns built to house yet another quickly assembled business. This was the heart of Silicon Valley, where many of America's new industries are now taking shape. In this technological wonderland, the signs outside every other concrete box seemed to bear names like Advanced-this and Digital-that or Micro-this and Tech-that. Digital Equipment Corp. was across the street. Avantek was around the corner. Intel Corp., Michels's former employer and the first company to make a computer on a chip, had a facility a couple of blocks away. And closer than that was the building in which IBM had pulled its well-publicized "sting operation" on the Japanese. This was, in short, as far away as one could get from Reynolds's elegant suite of offices on the 35th floor of the American Brands Building at 245 Park Avenue in New York.

Inside, the building was no more impressive. "It looked like the entrance to a bakery," recalls Potter. "It was not corporate at all. There was a linoleum floor and there were posters all over the place announcing a 3:30 P.M. aerobics class. Russ looked around in his Brooks Brothers suit and said, 'Oh, okay, I can see why they're in trouble.' " Not long ago, Reynolds had visited one of his California offices during lunch time only to see a couple of his associates, dressed in gym shorts, breeze past him. "Where the hell are you going?" he demanded. "We've got our aerobics class," they answered. "After that," recalls Potter, "there was a flurry of memos about aerobics classes during business hours."

The visitors sat in the sparse reception area until Michels's secretary came a few steps down a stairway which led to the executive offices. "Come on you guys," she said with a wave of her hand, "up here." No one except Potter noticed her. "Russ," he said, "I think that lady at the top of the stairs wants us and she's too lazy to come all the way down to get us." The group filed up the stairs behind her and was led to Michels.

The four bluebloods found the 43-year-old idiosyncratic Jew sitting behind a small cluttered desk in a Spartan office. It was a drab and cramped 10-foot-by-10-foot room, not much larger than the sitting room outside Reynolds's personal office in New York. It was an office as austere and messy as Reynolds's was sumptuous and tidy. Over two walls were large white boards covered with scribbled numbers and organization charts. Hanging on another were faded advertisements for Convergent products. Books, leaflets and brochures were spilled about the room. Atop his desk, amid a pile of paper, was a Convergent work station and a box of Dominican cigars.

Michels is the antithesis of Reynolds's cultivated urbanity. He is short, balding, informal and overweight, not interested in acquiring polish. His style is direct and blunt. His conversation is laced with obscenity. He is the type of guy Reynolds would have tried to throw out of his country club or blackball at the college fraternity. His jacket off, collar loosened and tie askew, Michels was wolfing down a juicy hamburger when the four Brooks Brothers clad headhunters arrived.

"Come on in," Michels shouted. "We're a little informal around here."

There were only two chairs in the office, so Michels's visitors dragged in two more and sat crammed next to each other in horseshoe formation. A plant kept brushing one side of Reynolds's face, but it didn't distract him. He and his entourage became captivated with the little fat man. For the next hour, Michels delivered a near-monologue on the company's troubles. It was a brutally frank and self-effacing assessment in which Michels accepted much of the blame for Convergent's dive. At times, he would leap from his chair and pace what little space was left in the room to tell them of his joys and sorrows in running what he continually called his "baby."

"You may ask why I'm doing this," he said, "why I've asked you here. Let me tell you how it is. It's because I fucked up. I made a lot of mistakes running this company."

Not the least of which, he told them, was his decision to develop a portable, notebook-sized computer called WorkSlate. The project, carried out under the code name "Ultra" after an Allied method of deciphering Nazi communiqués during World War II, garnered Michels much publicity. He was featured in a long front-page story in *The Wall Street Journal,* and management guru Tom Peters, who had co-authored the best-selling book *In Search of Excellence,* praised Michels numerous times in speeches and a sequel book, *A Passion for Excellence.*

But WorkSlate turned out to be the company's biggest disaster. Michels strayed from what the company did best—producing innovative products for other computer companies like Burroughs, NCR, Datapoint and Prime Computer, which would then market the computers under their names. WorkSlate was both the first Convergent product to bear its own label and the first to be sold direct to retail computer stores.

Michels didn't know the market, never sold to it and was forced to drop the computer after selling it for slightly over six months because of disappointing sales only five months earlier. It was a costly diversion from Convergent's main business as well as a costly error, resulting in a $15 million charge against earnings. The once-profitable company was now heading toward a $13.8 million loss for the full year. "The market for portable business computers just wasn't there, at any price," Michels feebly explained.

Never mind. Michels wanted their help to repair the damage. "I have four children and this company is my fifth," he said. "It's my late-life baby. I love this company. And all I want is the best for it.

"I'll step back and be the cheerleader. I'll rally the troops, I'll do whatever this guy wants me to do. I'll be the marketing guy. I could sell this company better than anybody. I'm a sprinter and what the business needs now is a long-distance runner."

Employees occasionally wandered into Michels's office, interrupting the meeting for a quick word with the boss. Michels didn't mind. His company was without the bureaucracy and hierarchy of conventional corporations and he was proud of it. But to the visitors that day, it also reflected the lack of structure and formality needed in a company as large as Convergent had grown.

Michels picked a used cigar off his desk and began chewing on its end. "I'm looking for someone who understands the computer business," he continued, "although that isn't absolutely necessary. Somebody who is bright, aggressive and can command the respect of people here."

The strangers meeting Michels for the first time only an hour earlier were astonished with his candor and his emotionally-stirring enthusiasm for Convergent. Frequently enough, headhunters were called to find successors for entrepreneurs whose skills were outgrown by a company's success. But it was rare for a founder to admit his mistakes and give up control of his firm. "At times, he was almost in tears describing the damage he felt he had done to the company," says Gostyla. "It was quite a shock to see someone as open, honest and sincere as Allen." And Reynolds, despite their differing backgrounds and style, was taken with him. "He comes out of a Dick Tracy comic strip," says Reynolds. "He's a work of art, a bundle of energy."

Michels was far from finished assessing his own lapses in judgment when he launched into a personal critique, detailing what he perceived to be the strengths and weaknesses of several senior executives whom the headhunters would soon meet. "It was perfectly obvious that there were people in jobs who were totally unqualified in what they were doing," said Potter.

Michels named his co-founder Eliot "Ben" Wegbreit president of Convergent only two months ago, but he already was conceding it was less than a good idea. Wegbreit had been manager of software development at Xerox before joining Michels in 1979 to help him put together Convergent. A brilliant engineer and a former Harvard

University professor with a Ph.D. from the ivy-covered school, he had helped to develop some of the company's main products. Lacking the managerial skills necessary to run a $400 million company, however, he was over his head as a manager. Michels showered him with praise, called him a genius, but admitted, despite awarding him a recent promotion, that he probably wasn't yet ready for a major operating responsibility.

"I thought I would be able to fill the position from within the company," Michels said. "But as it turned out, that wasn't the case." He insisted that the recruiters treat the matter with great sensitivity, however, because he did not want to either hurt or lose Wegbreit. So he instructed them to get his perspective on the company and what it needed.

The other executive was Joe Willits, a 57-year-old numbers cruncher who had replaced chief financial officer Merrill E. Newman who retired in September. In addition to finding someone who could succeed him as chief executive, Michels wanted Reynolds to conduct a search for a controller who might later succeed Willits. Gostyla, it was agreed, would handle this search.

All told, the meeting with Michels lasted two full hours after which Michels escorted the headhunting group down the hall to meet other members of his executive team. On the way, Michels would stick his head into an office, move in quickly and pat a colleague on the back for a job well done, while his guests awkwardly waited in the hall. Michels sent them to see Willits, then board members Bill Rollnick and Merrill Newman, and finally Wegbreit before meeting again with the unusual entrepreneur.

When Michels left that night, squeezing his portly frame between the steering wheel of his Jaguar and its bucket seat, he was elated. "I left the building buoyant because I had found people who really would be able to help us and I was excited about it," recalls Michels. "I liked them, I trusted them, I felt they knew what to do and that I could rely on them for the kinds of support and intelligence I would need to get the right man. Contrary to my expectations, they were open and straight. There was no bullshit. Having worked with a number of lesser houses over the years, I had come to expect from these people a certain pompous arrogance and a lot of behavioral bullshit. I thought they were the genuine article."

Without question, they were a different breed from the high-tech West Coast body snatcher who would show up at Convergent with an open shirt and beads strung around his neck. A flashy, tenacious deal maker, he had the capacity to bait a candidate like a doomed gladiator in a Roman circus. For five years, he delivered to Convergent many of the valley's brightest young engineers. His walking orders, one computer publication noted, were to seek out highly talented people willing to work 60-hour weeks. Those less committed were automatically disqualified. Among this wooed crop of workaholic geniuses were some of Convergent's most important officials. So critical was he in the company's success that Michels rewarded him with a five-year company pin on Convergent's fifth anniversary. "They had encouraged me to use him to recruit finance people," says Willits, "but I wasn't enthusiastic about him. He didn't know one end of finance from another."

It wasn't until 7:30 P.M. that the four left to battle the massive traffic jam that daily snarls the highways of Silicon Valley. They inched their way back to the Amfac Hotel in Burlingame, five minutes south of San Francisco's airport, and later assembled in the hotel's Calcutta Cricket Club for dinner at 9:00 P.M. Reynolds and Potter, who didn't have time for lunch, were famished.

But they also were just as excited as Michels about the assignment they had won. Michels had indicated he would pay whatever was necessary, within reason, to entice the right man to Convergent. Because Reynolds's fee is based on a percentage of an executive's first-year compensation, precisely one-third, that meant the potential to collect one of the largest fees ever charged in the business.

"Everybody recognized that this was going to be one of the bigger and better searches we would do that year," said Potter. "Everyone concluded this was a great search, that it was going to make or break us in Silicon Valley because we had just opened up our Menlo Park office six months before. Here's a chance for some real visibility in the high-tech community by a relative newcomer in the area. The attitude was pull out all the stops on this one and don't screw around."

Luckily, the group was seated in an alcove of the restaurant, an area affording them the privacy for a brainstorming session on what had just occurred. The four began throwing out names as possibilities, including several nationally-known executives with backgrounds as far afield as banking and financial services. "Someone would come out with a name and someone else would say, 'Are you kidding? He's awful.' And then someone would come out with another idea and the response would be 'No, well actually maybe.' It got free form. We all had a couple of drinks and it was a very pleasant, relaxing dinner," recalls Potter.

Most of all, Reynolds thought, Convergent sorely needed a leader not unlike John Sculley, a PepsiCo marketing executive who had been lured to Apple Computer as chief executive by headhunter Gerry Roche of rival firm Heidrick & Struggles two years earlier. Sculley didn't know a thing about computers, but he was regarded as a marketing whiz. Reynolds, invoking the Sculley example, suggested that computer experience wasn't absolutely critical.

That was no surprise. In hiring his own people, Reynolds always zeroed in on leadership abilities. "Russ tends to believe in the qualities of the individual as being paramount," said Potter. "So he always goes for leadership ability."

Price, who had done a number of high-tech searches for Cleveland-based multinationals such as TRW and Eaton Corp., disagreed. "We really need to stick close to their industry to find someone who knows the customers and won't have a serious learning curve," said Price. "Convergent has serious problems that need solving right away. There just isn't time for a brilliant leader who doesn't know the industry to come in and get up to speed. We need somebody who could come in, be able to identify the problems immediately and set the tone."

"Doing a Sculley number—from soft drinks to computers—wasn't going to fly," said Potter.

Reynolds finally was won over. He volunteered that this new, as yet unknown, executive would have to restore the confidence of Convergent's uneasy customers. A man lacking computer know-how was not apt to inspire such confidence. "One of the key byproducts of this search will be the sigh of relief on the part of their big clients," he said. "A Blumenthal or an AT&T might feel uneasy if we put an ice-cream man in there. The best way to tell Mike Blumenthal he can relax is to put in a high-tech computer guy."

Still, they all agreed, Michels was so flamboyant and domineering a personality within his company that it would be difficult for anyone other than an exceptional candidate to fill his shoes. Here was an irrepressible man who once slipped into an assembly plant and began wildly spraying the walls with four letters, reportedly a code to workers which loosely translated as "Build the Machines Fast." And when production of one of the company's most important new products had been slowed by the shortage of a new 16-bit computer chip by Intel Corp., Michels showed up on the doorstep of Intel President Andrew Grove with a Cookie Monster Doll. On bended knee, it was reported, Michels handed him the blue furry toy with a sign taped to its tummy that bore the plea: "Give Me Chips!"

Convergent employees were highly motivated and obsessed workaholics who had earned a reputation as "Silicon Valley's shock troops." The parking lot was full on Saturdays and Sundays, and some of them were known to have worked 36 hours straight without time off. Michels was their spiritual leader and guru.

"It was clear he was not only respected as the founder, but as somebody that many would work 80 hours a week for," says Price. "So his successor had a tough act to follow and had to have a track record that would speak for itself."

The group drained a bottle of California's finest wine and lingered till the wee hours, laying out a strategy of how to do the search, debating whether Michels really needed a chief executive or a chief operating officer, and developing a list of 15 sources and potential candidates for the job. Among them was a Hewlett-Packard executive named Paul Ely, Jr., whom they had briefly mentioned to Michels in the last hour of their visit.

The task of delivering this savior fell to Price, a low-key and reserved man of 43 years who would soon be taking over Reynolds's San Francisco office because of a major scandal there just two months earlier. *Executive Recruiter News,* a monthly newsletter which serves up the good and the bad news of the business, reported that two Reynolds's professionals in San Francisco had been credited with advanced degrees neither really had in the firm's elaborate promotional brochure. One of the two was Joseph Griesedieck, Jr., a five-year Reynolds veteran who managed the San Francisco office. He had been listed as having a "Master in Business and Finance" from Washington University. Griesedieck, in fact, had only attended the university. He never earned a degree from it. This was a major embarrassment for a search firm which employed people to make character judgments on executives it would recommend to major corporations.

Griesedieck, the former chief executive of Falstaff Brewing Corp., said he had informed the Reynolds firm about the mistake, but a correction never found its way into print. Indeed, the bios of other Reynolds headhunters with advanced degrees consistently had recorded them with an M.B.A. or a J.D., never a "Master," giving validity to Griesedieck's claim that it was a mistake. Nonetheless, Reynolds announced that Price would immediately assume responsibility for the San Francisco office, and later Griesedieck resigned to join Spencer Stuart & Associates, another top firm in the business. Griesedieck would later admit to a Spencer Stuart colleague that he was less than persistent in getting the error corrected and that Ferdinand Nadherny, Reynolds's president, wanted him out of the firm because of it.

A sleepy-eyed and cautious man, Price has the appearance of a typical conservative midwestern businessman. He was, however, born in New York, raised in California, and graduated from the University of California at Berkeley with a B.S. in mechanical engineering. Son of a financial executive, Price was groomed a corporate capitalist at Harvard, where he received his M.B.A. He then went off to spend more than a dozen years with two old-line nuts-and-bolts companies in the American heartland. He joined FMC, a diversified multibillion dollar corporation in Chicago, climbing to the position of manager of planning. After nine years, Price quit to become chief operating officer of small privately-owned MacLean-Fogg Co., a maker of industrial fasteners and products for the railroad industry.

Like many who drift into the business of collecting people, Price got into recruiting by accident. He had left MacLean-Fogg in 1978 after three and one-half years because he wanted to run his own show—something that didn't appear likely at MacLean-Fogg. He made the rounds of business brokers, bankers and accountants, shopping for the perfect small business, but nothing seemed to fit. Answering a blind "Business for Sale" ad in *The Wall Street Journal* three months later, Price found himself being contacted by a small, three-man executive recruiting firm in Chicago's Loop. The founders were retiring and wanted to sell out.

"They kindly opened their books to me," say Price, "and I suddenly saw the kind of gross profit margins that we could only dream about in the manufacturing business. That was really the turning point for me. I thought maybe I should be looking at service-type opportunities. Still, I wasn't intrigued in buying out some retiring executives in a business I knew nothing about."

A mere two weeks after that session, though, Price received a call from Ferdinand Nadherny, the president of Russell Reynolds based in Chicago, a huge headhunting market that Nadherny had locked up for his firm. Price was lured into the office for "an unnamed job opportunity" and soon discovered Nadherny wanted him to join Reynolds. He talked to four of Reynolds competitors, including Korn/Ferry and Heidrick & Struggles, before concluding that Reynolds was the ideal match.

Price wondered if the business of plucking men from their jobs was beneath him. A man who seldom makes a move without thought or counsel, he spoke to several human resources executives about his move. They advised him that he could spend no longer than two years headhunting without losing his credibility as a general manager. His friends had mixed reactions. "I was sensitive to what my self-image would be after I got into the business," he says. Some friends, who viewed headhunting as something less than respectable, surmised that he turned headhunter only to get an inside peek at other jobs. "You'll be in an ideal position to see all types of opportunities, and then you can pick the general management slot you want to get back to what you really enjoy and are good at," his friends told him. They had Price convinced that it was the perfect escape hatch should things not work out. "Who sees more job opportunities than a good search consultant?"

He started out slow. It took him four months to complete his first search, for a vice-president of Gould's battery division in Minneapolis, but he took to the business. Nadherny, who in common with Price boasted a Harvard M.B.A., became something of a mentor to him. He would listen in on his first prospect telephone calls, later offering critiques on them. Reynolds liked Price and the country-club strokes of his tennis game immediately. "He's an extremely good manager, very precise, an excellent administrator and one of the four best tennis players in the firm," is the way Reynolds describes him. "He's got an extremely attractive wife and one child, about six or seven." Price worked out of Chicago for a year and one-half before moving to Reynolds's Cleveland office in May of 1980.

He learned how to use everything from social connections to old school ties to make it in the business. When Price, for example, moved to Cleveland, Nadherny flew in from Chicago to throw a luncheon for a dozen top executives at the Union League Club to introduce him to his Cleveland friends. "Some 15 minutes into that lunch, during stand-up cocktails," laughs Price, "four of these guys including Nadherny were down in a three-point stance reliving the Yale-Columbia game when Nadherny made the saving tackle. More than half the group there were CEOs of the major corporations in Cleveland, and most of them were Yalies who had played football."

Price is not your typical, overly gregarious headhunter. Neither witty nor outwardly sharp, he dresses like a mannequin in a Madison Avenue men's store window, and he speaks in a dull, weary monotone. "I find Tony hard to make out," says a business acquaintance. "He's very reserved. He's on the phone day and night, but he never makes any fuss about it. He's a 'Cool Hand Luke.' "

Above all, Price is the consummate professional who never lets his hair down. He is a man who has made the transition to headhunter without forsaking his traditional values and morality. Focused and committed, Price routinely puts in 12-to-14-hour work days. And he hauls home a briefcase full of work every weekend, typically spending another four hours on Saturday and Sunday doing paperwork and making phone calls to candidates and contacts. "Tony is the kind of guy who dots every i and crosses every t," says Griesedieck, who Price succeeded in San Francisco. "He's very thorough."

That has always been true with, perhaps, only one exception early on in his Cleveland days. Price had placed a division general manager in a company who turned out to be an alcoholic and was dismissed from his job in six months. "He fell into a drunken stupor after work one day and got into an accident," explains Price. "It was a great embarrassment to the company and to his employer. Of course, he was fired and the client was very unhappy with me and our firm for not having detected this beforehand."

Now back in California, Price would have to exchange his ability for cocktail party chitchat in Chicago and Cleveland about golf and tennis and master Valley talk about floppy disks, integrated software and spreadsheets. Reynolds and Potter caught a 7:00 A.M. flight back to New York so they could return to the office by late afternoon, while Price began plotting the strategy and placing the initial calls on the search.

Within a week, he touched base with more than 50 sources and potential candidates, venture capitalists, former IBM and Digital Equipment executives who had already made the transition to small companies and a slew of others. They were recommended by colleagues and Reynolds's researchers. Price rejected out of hand managers with small company backgrounds who could not boast a proven track record in growing a business to one of great size, stature and success. And he was hesitant in taking an executive from a large company who hadn't yet made the transition to a smaller concern.

The vast majority of those he contacted never heard the name Convergent Technologies slither off his lips; Price would only provide a rather oblique description to protect the confidentiality of his client. Convergent would be referred to as a "medium-sized company in the computer and electronics industry in the West." Hardly a tantalizing lure. Only when a telephone call uncovered an executive who would likely be a candidate for the job would Price reveal he was working for Convergent. Few of the 15 executives on his "hit list"—all of whom were interviewed by Price by phone in the first week—would know the company was Convergent.

Of the names swirling in his head, Price had thought that one candidate could be ideal. He was Paul Ely, Jr., a 52-year-old executive vice-president and director of Hewlett-Packard, a huge company in Palo Alto only ten minutes away from Convergent. H-P, as the company is familiarly known, was the product of a dream shared by two young electrical engineers named William R. Hewlett and David Packard some 45 years ago. The pair began their business in a narrow one-car garage at 367 Addison Street in Palo Alto, and they vigorously pursued a strategy of carving out lucrative niches in the instrument and electronics business. H-P had established itself as a model of American capitalism, a highly successful $6 billion institution known all over the world for quality and innovation.

Ely played an important role in the company's growth. For close to a decade, he ran Hewlett-Packard's computer business, guiding it from sales of $100 million in 1973 to more than $3 billion with over 35,000 employees. That record made the company the largest producer of electronic test and measurement instruments and the second largest maker of minicomputers in the world. Ely, who gained a reputation as a tough, aggressive manager, was highly regarded within H-P. A 22-year company veteran, he was one of the company's highest ranking officers and one of its five most generously paid executives.

Price met Ely for the first time in mid-1983 when he was searching for two top-level executives with high-tech backgrounds for Cleveland-based Parker Hannifin. The company was a $1.3 billion corporation, a part of smokestack America, which now was investing in electronics and sorely required a couple of outsiders with some experience in high technology on its board of directors. Price assembled a lengthy list of "target" companies—firms in which he would identify possible candidates for his client. Hewlett-Packard, naturally was one of them, and Ely, given his visible position there, was a logical prospect. Price approached him because he had often read of Ely's H-P exploits in *Electronic News,* a weekly bible of sorts for those in the computer industry. Ely had been getting lots of outside attention at the time because he was overseeing H-P's belated effort to get into the personal computer market in competition with IBM.

Price figured him to be a long shot. After all, why would a California executive want to trudge across the country to Cleveland a few times a year to attend the meetings of a ho-hum industrial equipment company? Much to Price's surprise, however, Ely had spent many of his formative years in Cleveland and still had a sister in the area. A directorship with Parker Hannifin would, at the very least, give him an excuse to go back. "It was just blind luck," says Price, who eventually delivered the heads of Ely and Allan Rayfield, president of GTE Corp.'s diversified products group, to Parker Hannifin. If that board assignment conferred any additional prestige on Ely within H-P, you wouldn't know it. In one of H-P's annual 10K reports filed with the Securities & Exchange Commission in Washington the company incorrectly spells the name of Parker Hannifin as "Parker Hanifen Co." in a brief bio of Ely.

Getting an H-P executive to consider joining the board of directors of another company was one thing. Prying loose an H-P veteran and enticing him to jump ship was entirely another. In a world in which loyalties are exasperatingly ephemeral, H-P is an anomaly because it had long been impenetrable to headhunters. The company's president, John A. Young, once boasted to a journalist that by maintaining Hewlett-Packard's people-oriented management style and by keeping managers engaged on exciting products "they won't have time to return that phone call from the headhunter." That was generally true. Although H-P alumni have begot an astounding array of high-tech start ups, from Tandem Computers to Apple Computer, few of their top executives leave simply to join other existing companies. Price had tried to nudge numerous H-P men out to no avail. "I've called many prospects and tried to interest them and in the vast majority of times it was without much success," he says.

Price, however, had at least some reason to surmise that Ely might finally want to leave Hewlett-Packard. Four months earlier, in July 1984, Hewlett-Packard had announced a major reorganization and had named Dean O. Morton, an executive vice-president on the same step of the corporate ladder as Ely, chief operating officer, the number two job. Ely lost his computer group in the shuffle and was reassigned to run the medical and analytical operations of the company. The corporate revamping was widely regarded as a major setback for him.

Price had read of the change in Ely's duties in *BusinessWeek*. Under a picture of a grim and tense Ely, the magazine reported that the executive had become increasingly difficult to work with during the ten years he built computers into H-P's largest business. "He has been a disruptive force in the company—lecturing, browbeating and intimidating people," one former executive told the magazine. A Hewlett-Packard director called him "able but cocky. Within the parameters of H-P's culture, he was just in bounds." In contrast, Morton, who clearly won out over Ely in the managerial overhaul, was viewed as a statesmanlike manager, a style more akin to President Young and founders Hewlett and Packard.

Once news of this broke out, the calls from headhunters began rolling in. "That put a lot of executive recruiters on my tail," says Ely. " 'Ah ha,' they figured, something has happened. There has been a change and finally he'll be available to recruit out of the company.' I was getting a lot of calls. I had some very startling propositions made to me on the telephone."

Ely would turn down the overtures out of hand, however, refusing to pursue them. But he found his new role at H-P less than exciting and the company's policy of mandatory retirement for officers at the age of 60 worried him. "The likelihood of my retiring at that age was close to zero," he says. "It made me nervous. I could see myself at fifty-nine-and-a-half saying, 'Gee, what am I going to do next year?' I said to myself, 'Look, don't be a dumb shit. Listen to these guys.' "

In the five months before Price rang him, Ely said, "I had given a polite no to at least 40 other inquiries. Only two of these got beyond the first phone call. Had it not been for the earlier experience (with Parker Hannifin) I almost assuredly would have responded with my usual polite no."

So Price was able to chat with Ely on the phone 12 days after his meeting with Michels on November 6. It wasn't a promising beginning. "I came right out and told him I wasn't interested," recalls Ely. "I'd be happy to hear about it, but it's more out of curiosity than interest," he told Price. Ely was about to leave to go sailing with his family, but the two arranged to meet at Hewlett-Packard on November 26, the Monday before Thanksgiving. Meantime, Price would scour the minds of his colleagues and other sources to unearth still more possibilities. But Ely was high up on the list.

Price, obviously, was apprehensive. "I figured that if he was willing to listen to me there undoubtedly were many others who called up. There might be even better offers floating around. His name had been rumored in connection with a wide variety of other searches." Price had read in *Electronic News,* in fact, that only a month after H-P's reorganization, Tektronix, another computer company, was considering Ely for a top job. Silicon Valley gossips suggested that Ely had interviewed with several venture capital firms as well as Apollo Computer, Inc., a Convergent competitor, in Chelmsford, Massachusetts.

On November 26, Price and Ely huddled secretly for one hour in a private conference room at H-P's corporate headquarters in Palo Alto, an unusual venue considering that Price was attempting to extract Ely from the company. Most executives would freeze in terror at the thought of entertaining a headhunter on company premises. Ely apparently did not, but he stressed that the meeting be highly confidential. For half the session, Price talked about his client without naming Convergent, while the remainder of the time was spent trying to better understand Ely's operating style and whether it would fit within the smaller company.

Ely was interested enough to allow Price to reveal his client was Allen Michels. The name didn't immediately register with the H-P executive. He had heard of him, but didn't know Michels or Convergent well, in part because there was little overlap between the two companies' products. That was an advantage for Price. If Ely had read all the bad press Convergent had received over the previous year he might have dismissed the possibility out of hand. "He was essentially starting with a clean slate," says Price.

"Paul's immediate reaction was: 'Gee, the business and the product line fits my background. The size is about right, I don't want something too small and probably a much bigger company wouldn't be much fun because it would be too hard to turn around. The location is clearly a plus because I wouldn't have to move. And the nature of the turnaround job was the kind of thing that could be done. The problems of getting product out the door played right to my greatest strengths.' "

Price was delighted. At least Ely was keeping an open mind. He asked how much Ely was making and quickly realized it would be a costly exercise to get him out. In the previous year, 1983, as one of five of the highest-paid executives at H-P, Ely collected $378,166 in salary and bonus as well as an additional $228,441 in cash from the exercise of special stock options. That was $606,607 in cash alone, not counting another $50,353 in deferred profit-sharing retirement benefits. At the end of 1983, Ely held nearly 20,000 shares of H-P stock worth over $1 million, and he had lucrative options to buy another 62,000 shares.

The two concluded that he should meet Michels as soon as possible. That night, when Price returned to his office, he wrote a five-page memo on Ely. It described his work experience: from his first nine years with Sperry Gyroscope to his 22 years with Hewlett-Packard; his B.S. degree in engineering physics from Lehigh University, and his M.S. degree in electrical engineering from H-P's Honors Cooperative Program. Most crucial, however, was Price's discussion of why he thought Ely, an energetic workaholic, would make the perfect fit inside Convergent's work-obsessed culture.

He wrote of H-P's "concern for the fellow man," of its strong commitment to customers, of its dedication to being in the forefront of technology and of its people-oriented work ethic. "As I looked at those characteristics and thought about what Convergent needed, it seemed to be a good fit," says Price. "Some people characterize Convergent as being like a Marine boot camp. And there was no way they could have achieved what they did in five years without it. But it was burning a lot of people out. So Allen wanted an individual who was sensitive to those interests.

"Where they differed was that Convergent had not put an emphasis on operating systems. This was why I felt Ely's background was so right. One of the hallmarks of his success was building the business in a controlled and orderly manner so that when they introduced a product they could produce it on schedule within the targeted cost range without quality problems."

The next day, Price hand-delivered to Michels two candidate profiles: one on Ely and another on a similar candidate he had interviewed the previous week. Like Ely, this other candidate, who had been recommended by another Reynolds consultant in New York, came from a large corporate background in high tech. Price dispatched to both candidates financial statements and analyst reports on the company to help them prepare for their meetings with the boss. Michels arranged to meet with the first candidate in his office for four hours on Friday afternoon. He would meet Ely on Saturday morning, December 1, at his rambling two-story brick home in San Francisco's opulent Pacific Heights district.

The meeting was held over sweet rolls and coffee in Michels's study, a handsomely furnished room that reflected many of his interests—from Japanese ivory carvings to pre-Raphaelite art that hangs on the walls of his home. A voracious reader, Michels takes great delight in having acquired a 30-volume collection of George Bernard Shaw's work and a complete set of *Foreign Affairs* dating back to 1921, both of which he proudly considers to be among the treasures of his collection.

A born storyteller, Michels launched into the tale of himself and his company all over again. Ely told him about himself and what happened at H-P. Both were candid and reserved, and Michels tried hard to repress the immediate enthusiasm he felt for Ely. "I fell in love with him," he says. "It wasn't ten minutes. I had never met him before. He came with a reputation for being a tough guy and I simply fell in love with him. I thought he was completely honest, open, a man of high principles, a man who is capable of developing a very deep affection for a company and its people."

That was crucial to Michels. Although highly driven, he displayed an unusual concern and sensitivity for his employees. Michels took pride in noting that divorce was not endemic to Convergent as it was in many of the other enterprises in Santa Clara County, which annually posts one of the highest divorce rates in the nation. When his salesmen racked up huge orders for products the company was unable to ship due to its internal disorders, Michels still would pay his sales people their commissions. As the pair spoke in the quiet of Michels's study, the light bulb in the entrepreneur's mind grew brighter and brighter. "It went from dark to dimly lit to bright in the space of around three or four hours and it never dimmed," Michels says.

Five long hours had elapsed when Michels closed the front door after Ely left. And he broke out in a wide grin, shouting out loud to himself:

"Son of a bitch! This guy would have the time of his life at Convergent. I hope he's able to see that."

Ely, for his part, found he could not dismiss the opportunity out of hand. "The last thing I wanted was to be involved in an unfriendly change of management," he says. "That meeting confirmed what Tony had convinced me of. This man was in pain for what he thought he did to his friends and stockholders and he was committed to change."

Michels felt Ely was so clearly the right choice that it was difficult for him to take any other candidates seriously. "The moment I met him I felt it wrong to pursue any of the others," says Michels. Price would only interview three candidates in person on the assignment and present only two. Still, the following day, Sunday, the first candidate met by Michels was to visit with Convergent directors Rollnick and Newman for three hours of additional interviewing.

Michels also put together a second session with Ely for Thursday evening on December 6. It would be the first meeting on Convergent's premises, and Ely worried that he would be recognized there. A number of H-P alumni were working for Michels, and Ely's picture had been published on several occasions in local newspapers and magazines. So Michels arranged to have a late dinner meeting at Convergent on Thursday, after work hours. The two spent another four hours together, with Michels showing him the facilities and getting better acquainted. Price also met again with Ely, in part, to prepare him for the next step and to act as the intermediary, collecting more information on Ely's stock options and his overall compensation. The latter information was conveyed to Michels so the board of directors would have a ballpark idea of what it would take to get him.

On Saturday, December 8, Michels assembled a majority of the board at his home to meet both candidates. One came in during the morning, the other in the afternoon. Michels would introduce each candidate, sit in on a portion of the meeting and then excuse himself so the board could grill each candidate privately. At Ely's session, however, the H-P executive wound up asking most of the questions—about the company's financial health, its past, its future and its founder.

On Sunday, December 9, at 7:00 A.M. California time, Michels spoke to Price, who had returned to Cleveland the previous Friday evening. Michels, who almost sounded like a hero worshipper for Ely, told Price that he and the board now wanted to put together a deal with the H-P executive. Price had been on the phone with Ely the evening before, just after his session with the Convergent board, so he already knew that things went well.

"Let's put it together," Michels told Price over the telephone. "What do we do next?"

"Do you have a lawyer?" asked Price. "We're going to be getting into some fairly sophisticated and complicated tax considerations on options and bonus payments."

Michels asked Price for a recommendation. Reynolds often used a Park Avenue lawyer, Joseph E. Bachelder, who behind-the-scenes has put together the compensation packages for many of the head-hunting firms. Bachelder had astutely crafted the multimillion dollar deals which helped convince many big-time executives to leave their companies for literally greener pastures. But this time, his New York location, Price thought, would hinder a speedy resolution of the search.

Working from his home in Cleveland, Price dialed Gostyla and another Reynolds associate in California to enlist them in the search for a local law firm that could swiftly put together a big-ticket compensation package. Telephone to his ear, Price interviewed three law firms that Sunday, in San Francisco. He wasn't convinced they could do the work as rapidly as he would like.

He also reached Wilson, Sonsini, Goodrich and Rosati, the leading Silicon Valley law firm in Palo Alto. Price was advised that he should try to get partner Larry Sonsini, a well-known securities lawyer on the West Coast, to personally work on the deal. Sonsini had gained a reputation as a savvy lawyering superstar, one of the nation's foremost venture capital practitioners and the driving force behind Wilson, Sonsini's success. He linked the firm to the Silicon Valley boom, carving out a niche in the care and feeding of young companies. When Sonsini joined the firm in 1966 straight out of the University of California's Boalt Hall, it boasted all of five lawyers. Now, with some 400 high-tech clients including Apple Computer, Rolm Corp. and Monolithic Memories, the firm numbered nearly 75 attorneys.

A firm partner told Price that 43-year-old Sonsini was unreachable Sunday, but that he would accept his call early Monday morning. Price called him then in the hopes that Sonsini would be able to handle what could be the most serious impediment yet to the negotiations with Ely.

"These are major parties on both fronts," Price told Sonsini. "Would you personally be able to assist?"

"Sure," the lawyer answered, "provided we don't have any conflicts with either individual. Have Ely give me a call this afternoon and we'll get together tonight."

Later that day, Ely met Sonsini at his office in Palo Alto and began the long process of going through a number of contract variations, balancing both stock and cash, to limit the tax consequences to the H-P executive. It was agreed that Sonsini would represent Ely, even though he eventually would send his bill to Convergent, and another attorney, Paul E. Kreutz with Ware, Fletcher and Freidenrich, would look out for Convergent's interests.

Price flew back to California and in a flurry of meetings with Michels, Ely and Sonsini, helped to hammer out a package acceptable to all. They had little time to do this. Ely was to leave for a two-week vacation only five days later, and Price wanted him to have the outlines of an agreement with him when he left.

One of the major obstacles was a mountain of H-P stock options held by Ely. By the year's end, he had accumulated a massive 98,484 shares of stock at H-P, a treasure-trove with a value of $3.2 million. But some 78,738 of these shares hadn't yet been realized through the exercise of options. "Because of a very generous option program, I was assured of a substantial estate by remaining at H-P," Ely told Price. "I don't feel I should have to re-earn this. " To offset the loss, he wanted a sizable bonus.

"I lost a fair amount of sleep that week just because there were a lot of places where the contract could potentially go wrong," recalls Price. "Some of the directors did balk a little bit during these discussions so it wasn't clear it was going to happen."

Neither could he be certain that Ely was ready to leave H-P for Convergent. Although Ely was proceeding with the negotiations, he still lacked a firm offer in hand to either accept or deny. Michels, who was lobbying his board of directors to get them to agree to Ely's various conditions, worried, too. "I thought that somebody would get him out of H-P," says Michels. "I thought that here was this guy, about fifty-two years old with a vibrant, activist personality, and I couldn't see him spending the next 12 years or so at H-P in the role he was in. Nonetheless," he adds, "I was afraid that he might not see, as I saw, the enormous compatibility between he and Convergent and its culture. Paul was 22 years at H-P, and it was very tough to sever that emotional relationship. And his attitude toward David Packard and Bill Hewlett was one of reverence, deep affection and respect. That made me love him all the more. I respect feelings like that. It was very important to me that he had them."

Ely wasn't so sure he had to leave H-P, and if he did whether Convergent was the right opportunity. "I had an attractive top-level job in one of America's most-admired companies," he said. "Why should I leave? In fact, I pretended as if a competing executive recruiter, like a Tony Price, was selling me on my job at Hewlett-Packard—nothing much sounded comparable. It was pretty tough to beat."

Price was doing his best to deliver the candidate Michels wanted. He wasn't trying to "sell" Ely on the job. Instead, Price had to play the "disinterested" career counselor, the confidant, who would bring Ely to his senses. He couldn't afford to be too disinterested, though. A lot was riding on Price's ability to deliver the head Michels desired.

Even if Ely decided to leave H-P, he wasn't sure he should go to Convergent. Another of his options, he ruminated, was to hook up with California's venture capital community, to become a venture capitalist himself and give birth to corporate infants like Convergent. Price assured Ely he wasn't suited for that.

"You could be highly frustrated in a venture capital situation," Price told him, "because your success at H-P has been as a builder of organizations and products. While venture capitalists have a critical role as builders it still is from the point of view of an outsider. When they have advice to give they can't always impose it on a business. That would be frustrating to you, Paul."

Convergent, on the other hand, could be the opportunity of a lifetime, assured Price. "It could be a much more satisfying capstone to your career to come into a Convergent, get it back on track and build it to the size and success that you and Allen Michels think would be possible."

In the extremely competitive sport of corporate headhunting, this is the essence of the business. The larger search firms, and Reynolds is among the top three, endlessly boast how their extensive databases full of executives help them locate and deliver the booty. But in big-game hunting like the Convergent job, finding the candidate is relatively easy and often dependent on having the right contacts and breaks. Persuading him to leave, though, is something else. It is here that the clever headhunter must slip into the roles of both amateur psychologist and private detective to "close" the deal. To ease a desired candidate through the traumatic decision to leave a comfortable environment where he knows he can succeed. To convince the client he needn't look ad infinitum for the nonexistent perfect being. And to get enough money on the table to pull it off.

In the offices of Wilson, Sonsini, Goodrich and Rosati, the latter requirement began taking shape. It became clear that Convergent would have to offer Ely a $1 million sign-on bonus just to offset his H-P stock options along with a $300,000 salary and generous stock options. Surely, this was a contract that would be difficult for the Convergent board to swallow. In his first year, Ely would be making in cash alone more than six times what Michels brought home in 1984. Michels was paying himself only $200,000 a year, while president Wegbreit was collecting $160,000. The highest-paid executive at the company was Richard Meise, an ex-Honeywell Corp. executive who was vice-president of field operations. He pulled in $650,000 in salary, bonus and commissions in 1984.

Even Price, whose firm would directly profit from the size of the contract, was nearly incredulous. "The economics surrounding some of these moves are just mind-boggling to someone who has spent a good part of his business career in the more conservative Midwest," he says. "The kinds of numbers thrown around both in cash and in stock are staggering. Some of the directors might have swallowed hard a couple of times, but it was clear that this was what was necessary to attract someone of Ely's character." The board agreed. "It was pricey," confirms Bill Rollnick, a Convergent director and a long-time friend of Michels. "My eyebrows were raised, and there were a couple of gulps. This wasn't a Macy's bargain sale. But it was the right thing to do. It was pretty pricey, but we were going after a superstar."

Even more difficult for some board members were Ely's nonfinancial demands. Over the myriad daily conversations Price had with Ely he had developed several key issues relating to Ely's role as chief executive as well as his relationship to Michels and the board of directors. In his contract, he wanted it made clear that he, not Michels, who would remain as chairman, would report directly to the board. Ely also wanted in writing the power to appoint new members to the board through a nominating committee of which he would be a member. And he asked that Michels's role be succinctly defined and that he be given primary responsibility for coordinating Michels's duties.

71

In Ely's mind, these points were critical. "A negative from my point of view was that Convergent wanted a chief executive officer, but the founder is still there, he's young, he's done an awful lot," Ely would later say. "He's gotten the company to $400 million. That doesn't sound like he's ready to take off." Ely wanted to ensure that Michels wouldn't change his mind after he came aboard.

It was a familiar, even predictable, scenario. The founder-chief executive of a company decides he needs to hire a professional manager, but is unable to tear himself away from the company to allow the executive the freedom to run the business. Silicon Valley was abuzz with the latest "I've-changed-my-mind" episode as Ely was considering his options. David Hanna, who had spent 15 years as an executive at IBM, ended up accepting a job at Altos Computer Systems, a Convergent competitor, earlier in the year to succeed founder David Jackson as president and chief executive. Roughly four months later he resigned, primarily because Jackson grew tired of fishing and had second thoughts about his decision to relinquish control. The H-P executive didn't want the same thing happening to him.

"Ely was clearly in a good position," says Price. "He didn't have to take the opportunity. And it only made sense to do it on his terms. Looking after his own interests and protecting his ability to operate unencumbered, he demanded some very hard terms that a lot of corporations and boards would have great difficulty swallowing."

So did Convergent, for that matter. Some directors believed such authority undermined and diminished the contribution Michels had made over the previous five years. Witness to a rare self-sacrifice, they weren't convinced Michels had to give up so much to get Ely. "They were worried about Allen's self-esteem," Price says.

It was, of course, one of the most painful decisions Michels ever made. "No one will ever know, not even me, how difficult it was for him to do this," says Rollnick, one of Michels's closest friends. "We barely spoke of it. It's like having a friend's wife run out on him. How do you discuss that with a guy? You know he's hurting like hell, and somehow you let him know you feel sorry for him and if there was anything you can do you'd do it. But there's really nothing other than emotional support to give."

That week Sonsini was putting the finishing touches to Convergent's formal offer of employment to Ely. Michels wanted to insure that it would be completed before Ely left for Vail, Colorado, where he and his family had traditionally spend the Christmas holidays without fail for the past ten years.

When Ely embarked for Vail on December 15, for a two-week skiing vacation with his family, it was ready. In his briefcase was a letter of agreement, approved by Michels and an informal search committee just days before and fashioned from Price's labors over the previous five-and-one-half weeks. Dated December 12, 1984, it read:

"Dear Paul:

"We are pleased to offer you the position of Chief Executive Officer and President of Convergent Technologies, Inc. The terms of your employment shall be as follows:"

What followed were eight single-spaced, typewritten pages of legalese that represented one of the most lucrative compensation packages ever made to a businessman. The ultimate high-tech carrot.

The letter, addressed to Ely's home in Portola Valley and signed with a flourish by Michels, offered him a starting base salary of $300,000 and $2.6 million of guaranteed bonuses. He would receive the first $1 million bonus as soon as he signed the contract, $900,000 in January of 1986 and another $700,000 in January of 1987.

The most extraordinary part of this package, however, had little to do with cash. Rather, it was the option to buy Convergent stock at a mere $5.50 per share, its market value on December 12, 1984, the date the offer was placed in writing. If Ely could restore Convergent to its previous glory point in the market, a peak it reached only 18 months ago, his stock options would be worth an eye-popping $3.2 billion. He would have to ante up less than $5 million to realize that $3.2 billion profit. If he didn't have the money, no worry. The company also would agree to hand Ely a five-year loan to help him cash in on this extraordinary potential bonanza.

If Ely was axed for any reason during the first five years, the contract assured that he would walk away a wealthier man. It guaranteed him his $2.6 million bonus, a minimum of $600,000 representing two full years of salary and at least 50 percent of his Convergent stock options.

Without the distraction of his duties at H-P, Ely was now expected to decide in the comfort of the relaxed mountain setting in Vail whether to accept what must have appeared to all except him

the proverbial offer one could not refuse. Ely felt he had to overcome any suspicions and doubts he had over the company's future.
"Over the past year," Ely later told a reporter, "partly around
WorkSlate but around some other things, there have been a lot of
questions about the viability of Convergent. "I wasn't interested in
walking into an Osborne," said Ely in a reference to one of the early
casualties of the computer slump. "So I spent some of my energy in
looking up the financial situation, trying to understand what was
going on."

Before he left for his spacious condominium in Vail, Ely already
had arranged a private meeting with the Coopers & Lybrand partner in charge of auditing Convergent's books. That session neither
allayed his worries over the company's financial situation nor caused
him additional concern. Now, while on his Christmas skiing vacation, came an unpredictable development for Price. Ely brought with
him a H-P personal computer, and with Lotus 1-2-3, a popular
business software program, he constructed several financial models
of Convergent and began crunching the company's numbers to convince himself that the company was no worse than Michels and others thought.

Ely brought with him all of Convergent's publicly available financial information, but soon found that wasn't enough. After skiing
the slopes with his family in the morning, breaking for lunch and
doing a couple of runs in the early afternoon, Ely would disappear
to his condo. There he would consume himself in the financial min-
utiae of Convergent, as he stared into the glowing screen of his
computer atop the dining room table. He would almost daily speak
with Price and Michels late in the day for what seemed like an hour-
and-a-half from his bedroom phone. His friends must have wondered about his unusual disappearances every afternoon.

Day after day, he would ask for more financial data on the company: esoteric digits and ratios hidden in the company's ledgers on
Convergent's order backlog, inventory, and cost and pricing strategies of new products being introduced. Among other things, Ely was
searching for a better understanding of Convergent's dwindling profit
margins. Were costs falling out of line or was the company pricing
its products incorrectly, he wondered.

Some of the analysis wasn't even readily available. If it were,
Convergent probably would not have had to recruit him. The absence of certain figures, particularly detail on production costs, un-

derscored the lack of financial controls necessary to efficiently run the company.

Chief Financial Officer Willits and his staff, already occupied with year-end financial closings, would have to frenetically work through the night to generate the statistics. "We were scrambling pretty hard to get it to him," says Willits. "It was a bit of a crisis because the demands were added on top of everything else going on in the last week of the fiscal year."

Price, drawing on an early background in finance, played the role of a senior finance analyst in helping Willits and his team get the information to Ely via Federal Express. "Tony," Ely says, "was helpful in stirring people up when I couldn't get the facts."

"He was looking at this much as he would as if he was acquiring Convergent," says Price. "Where are the skeletons? Are the inventories overvalued? Is the order backlog misleading? Where do we stand on margins on some of our new products? He didn't want the patient to die on the operating room table. He wanted to make sure he'd have enough time to establish the controls and make the firm successful."

At one point, Convergent prepared to send Willits to Vail with several pounds of sophisticated financial data. Ely, however, had been at Vail with other H-P friends including Dean Morton, who won the chief operating job. Some of them apparently knew Willits. So instead, Convergent hired a courier to deliver the information which Willits and his staff had frantically gathered. The messenger was dispatched in a blinding snowstorm so serious that the courier service thought it had lost their messenger.

"My God," Michels told Willits, "I'd never be able to feel good about this if somebody died in the process."

The messenger finally turned up, six hours late, at the executive's Vail condo at 11:00 P.M. with, laughs Ely, "ice dripping off his ears."

As the demands for more and more data dragged on, Price wondered whether Ely would ever make the jump. In seven years of recruiting, never before had he seen a candidate as demanding as Ely. Although Michels had difficulty understanding why Ely was asking for certain types of data, he fortunately didn't grow impatient with his constant requests. "Tony was there all the time making sure I did understand, getting clarity and definition and most of all keeping my nose to the grindstone because the work done for Paul was extensive."

Yet, the more questions he asked, the more interested Michels became. "I was not only surprised by it, I was pleased by it," says Michels. "It merely fortified me. It heightened my anxieties about his joining us because the more I saw of his analysis the more I was convinced he was the right man."

Price, meantime, had to keep the second candidate "warm" in the event that Ely turned Michels down. Price would call the other executive to explain that things were likely to drag out over the holidays and that it would take until early January before Convergent made a move. Price obviously didn't tell him that Convergent was actively courting another candidate for fear of losing him to someone else.

Price would speak with Ely by phone daily an average 45 minutes for two straight weeks with the exception of Christmas day. An avid skier himself, he would chat about the condition of the slope that day and then get back to business. Finally, on December 28, he told Price it looked like a go. But he still wanted to withhold an official yes until he spent a few more days talking the move over with his wife of 32 years, Barbara, and his two sons, both of whom worked at Convergent and could give their father a different perspective on the company. Three days later, on New Year's Eve, Ely finally said he would join Convergent.

In fact, Ely had been in Vail only two days when, unbeknownst to Price and Michels, he had made the emotional commitment to leave H-P. He would think about what it would be like to quit the company for this new and different challenge while sitting on the ski lifts in the quiet of the mountains. Before taking off on his vacation, he had informed both John Young and David Packard that he had been listening to a few offers on the outside but had not yet made a decision to leave. During his trip, Ely brought into his confidence as a personal friend, rather than a fellow H-P executive, Dean Morton.

The endless hours Ely spent processing Convergent's financial figures gave him a head start on his new job. "The net effect of it was that when I arrived here on January 7, I spent no time on paper for two months," says Ely. "I spent it with people."

When he returned to H-P on Thursday, January 3, 1985, he again met with Packard and told him about the opportunity he accepted with Convergent. "It was very, very emotional," recalls Ely. "I realized now there was no going back, and I realized how much I had valued my position at Hewlett-Packard. I had the most mixed set of emotions I could ever have."

Michels arranged a special meeting of the board of directors the following day, January 4, to elect Ely chief executive officer and ratify his contract. But Price's work was far from done. Ely wanted more time to talk to his key people at H-P and to manage the news of his job switch to the press. They figured all this would push the date of the announcement to the middle of the following week, perhaps January 9.

Michels, who not long ago had been hailed a genius by the media during Convergent's better days, had more recently taken on the costume of the goat. Rightly or wrongly, he felt he had been burnt by the media a number of times, but a story that appeared in *The New York Times* on November 5, 1984, the day after Reynolds and his entourage first visited, enraged him. The story, under the headline "Computer Struggle at Convergent," reported that analysts believed the company was running out of cash and that its new products could plunge it into bankruptcy. "According to my calculations, they can only hang on until late December," the story quoted an E.F. Hutton & Co. analyst.

Michels went into a rage, but the statement he immediately issued contained none of the obscenities which spilled from his mouth that day. "*The New York Times* story exaggerates our present difficulties and is largely based on Wall Street perceptions," Michels said. "It is not correct that we have serious cash problems. Reports to that effect are irresponsible."

"To hell with the media," Michels told Price.

"We'll just send out a press release out of our own office and if they pick it up fine. If not, that's fine too."

But Ely and Price thought otherwise.

"This is a material development in the history of Convergent and if properly managed it could be viewed as a very significant positive development," said Price. "If we don't handle the press well, they could find all sorts of negatives."

Michels agreed to use a professional public relations firm, and Price had the job of finding one that could do it less than a week before the announcement was to be made. After several frantic phone calls to colleagues and friends, Price identified three firms he would interview that afternoon on January 3. On top of the list was Regis McKenna, an image maker who orchestrated the highly successful publicity campaigns for Apple Computer and Intel. McKenna, much like Sonsini, owed his success to the Silicon Valley boom. And the firm which bore his name had become, like Wilson, Sonsini, Goodrich and Rosati in law, the leading PR machine in the Valley.

Price ruled McKenna out, however, because a member of the firm said McKenna couldn't personally handle the business. He also decided against the San Jose office of Burson-Marsteller because he believed they couldn't act quickly enough. The job was given to the San Francisco office of Hill & Knowlton, Inc., one of the largest public relations agencies in the nation. Price called Donald Winks, the 57-year-old manager of the office, on January 3 and arranged to visit with him that night.

Winks and his crew had the job by 9:00 the next morning, along with the instructions to hustle into his car to make the 48-mile drive on 101 South to meet Michels in Santa Clara by 10:00 A.M. When Winks and Diana Stark, a Hill & Knowlton vice-president, got there, Michels was waiting.

They met with Michels, Price and Wegbreit in the latter's office, a room just as modest as Michels's. And Michels gave them a quick fix on where they stood.

"This is not an overthrow," Michels told them. "I convinced the board to allow me to bring Ely here. We want you to convince everyone that Paul has not lost his mind and that it wasn't a coup. And that's the truth."

"Okay, Allen, we believe you," replied Winks.

The PR pair later met briefly with Ely around noon before breaking for lunch and reassembling at 3:00 P.M. for the telephone board meeting with Larry Sonsini. But this was a sad, emotionally-stirring session as well. No champagne corks were popped. The board members—some of whom tried to convince Michels not to surrender his control—now cast their votes. And Michels experienced those same mixed feelings of sorrow, joy and relief that consumed Ely only 24 hours earlier when he told David Packard his H-P career was over. The vote was unanimous. Sonsini nonchalantly slipped the $1 million bonus check into Ely's pocket. Ely accepted it without any visible excitement or pleasure.

Although they originally wanted to get the news out five days later on Wednesday, January 9, a reporter from *Electronic News* had been calling H-P and Convergent that Friday afternoon, trying to confirm a rumor that Ely was to succeed Michels. Somehow, a leak oc-

curred. Price believes it came from one of the PR firms which failed
to get the business. "After telling both of them it was super, super
confidential and that there were SEC (Securities & Exchange Commission) concerns, I identified the client and candidate," says Price.
"The ethics of these people really make me wonder."

The leak forced everyone to move the schedule up so that the news
could be announced by 8:00 A.M. in New York on Monday,
January 7, when *Electronic News* would come out and before the
stock exchange opened. "We wanted to do it properly rather than
have to respond to rumors and calls," says Price. "Everybody," adds
Winks, "had to break ass."

All day Saturday, Winks and his team began to work out the details of the release and who it would go to and to prepare a two-
page memo from Michels to Convergent's employees. The release, a
nine-paragraph notice, was carefully crafted so that it contained
quotations from both Michels and Ely and made clear that it was
Michels, not the board, who "initiated an extensive search for a chief
executive to lead the company."

Winks, with 33 years of experience in public relations behind him,
knew all the tricks. And in writing the release, he skillfully skirted
the issue of Wegbreit's obvious demotion. "Ben Wegbreit, 39, also
a founder and a key figure in the growth of the company, has been
elected executive vice-president," he wrote in the fifth paragraph of
the release. Winks did not note that Wegbreit had been named president less than four months earlier and that he was effectively being
demoted since Ely would be named both president and chief
executive.

Ely, comfortable dealing with the press over his H-P days, displayed an innate sense for the public relations game. Over the weekend, he was on the phone virtually day and night, calling stock
analysts who followed Convergent's shares on the stock market. He
wanted to alert them to what was happening so that when reporters
called on Monday they could respond the "right" way. "What we
were trying to do," says Winks, "is give the analyst the chance to
say, 'As a matter of fact, I talked to Paul the other day and here's
what he told me.'"

At 10:00 A.M. on Sunday, the team met at Michels's house to ap-
prove the release and prepare for questions the media would likely
ask both Michels and Ely. Price was there along with Winks, Stark
and Nariman Karanjia, Hill & Knowlton's San Jose office manager.

Over coffee and warm danish, they laid out the strategy. Michels would stay by the phone at Convergent on Monday, taking calls from the media. Ely would do the same at H-P where Roy Verly, a Hewlett-Packard PR guy, would answer general queries and make it clear that H-P had not kicked Ely out.

Michels wanted the meeting to occur that afternoon at 2:30, but Ely insisted it be scheduled for earlier in the day. He wanted to watch the San Francisco 49ers tackle the Chicago Bears in the National Conference championship at Candlestick Park in San Francisco. Television coverage of the event was to begin at 1:00 P.M., and they didn't want to miss the kickoff.

"How come this afternoon was no good?" Michels asked.

"Well, the 49ers are in the playoffs this afternoon," said Ely.

"Is it that important?" asked Michels, not the greatest sports fan alive. "Hell, I've got these Super Bowl tickets, and I'm not going to use them. Would you like them, Paul?"

"Sure, I'll take my son," said Ely as he grabbed the tickets from Michels. A broad smile stretched across Ely's face—a smile far more expressive than when the $1 million check was placed in his pocket two days before. Those Super Bowl XIX passes, after all, were golden, too. They would entitle the new chief executive officer of Convergent seats to the 49ers' 38-16 rout of the Miami Dolphins at Palo Alto's Stanford Stadium. But Ely gave the tickets to his sons because he had to play host to a Super Bowl party at his home.

On Monday, January 7, 61 days after Price first met Michels, the announcement went out. Winks sent the three-page release by messenger to nine key editors and reporters and also had it telecopied to Hill & Knowlton's New York office for delivery to *The New York Times* and to its Los Angeles office for the *Los Angeles Times*. Hill & Knowlton's San Jose office personally contacted 44 securities analysts and reporters to inform them of the news. The release also was mass mailed to major trade and business editors. None of the reports which followed mentioned that Wegbreit had been ousted as president. And Price even won an important plug for his search firm when the *San Francisco Chronicle* reported on Tuesday that Ely "was 'found' by the executive searchers at Russell Reynolds Associates."

By week's end, Convergent's stock had risen by nearly 30 percent to $8.25 a share, increasing the market value of the company by over $72 million. Was Ely worth all the money he was getting? At least Wall Street thought so. The increase made Ely's Convergent stock options immediately worth nearly $2.5 million on paper. Certain that the stock would climb, Price wanted to buy Convergent shares during his search but had been informed by Reynolds's general counsel that he would qualify as an "insider" and needed to wait at least three days after the announcement of Ely's appointment.

Old French taxicab horns, acquired by Reynolds on a trip to Paris one year, are affixed to the walls of each of his offices. They are ceremoniously sounded everytime a headhunter completes an assignment. When Price returned to his San Francisco office that day, he grasped in his hand the horn's black bulb and squeezed as hard as he could. Gostyla, who had been looking for a successor to Willits, never got to blast the horn. Ely eventually cancelled that search, later recruiting by himself John M. Russell, an 18-year H-P veteran and a friend with whom Ely frequently had played racquetball. Two months after Ely came aboard, Russell replaced Willits, who says he and Ely did not see "eye-to-eye on many things."

Michels and his longtime friend Eliot Wegbreit would last much longer. But they, too, would depart the company they created. Less than one year after Ely joined Convergent, Michels, Wegbreit and two other key executives quit the company in October, 1985, with plans for a new upstart computer firm. The parting appeared amicable. "I want to feel the wind in my face again," Michels told reporters.

Nonetheless, Price's sounding of the French horn signalled not only just another completed job, but more importantly what likely was the largest fee ever collected by a search firm on a single assignment.

Reynolds charged his standard one-third of first year compensation: $433,300 on Ely's $1.3 million. Most headhunters would discount that fee because it was so large. Not Reynolds. When Gerry Roche, chairman of Heidrick & Struggles, raised eyebrows for scooping up a third of a million dollars for helping to recruit Pepsi-Cola's John Sculley to Apple Computer, Reynolds was privately grousing that Roche should have gotten double that amount. That's because Roche based his fee on Sculley's $1 million annual salary. He thought it would have been too greedy to touch Sculley's additional $1 million sign-on bonus. "Russell Reynolds," smirches William Wilkinson, who has been doing search work for 28 years in California, "has never been known to leave a nickel on the table."

The Convergent fee, in fact, was so hefty that the company ostensibly felt the need to later explain it in a tersely worded sentence buried in its annual report: "The general administrative expense increase reflects bonus and recruiting fees of approximately $1.5 million related to the employment of the company's new president." Subtract Ely's $1 million sign-on bonus, then add Reynolds's expenses to his $433,000 fee and it totals nearly half a million dollars.

Michels, for one, didn't complain. "I would never hassle their fees," he says. "For what Tony did we received excellent value. I had never done this before. Paul had never done this before. Left to me, I think it would have been bungled. God, he was skillful."

Reynolds, of course, was elated. Calls and letters streamed into Price's office from his colleagues around the firm. "We are a team-oriented organization," says Price. "We share in the glories and sorrows together, and I don't think anything meant more to me than the messages and congratulations."

But one message, arriving over the office telecopier from Reynolds's office in Boston, meant more to him than any other. On the flimsy telecopier paper, his colleagues had drawn an ornamented plaque with the words "1984 Recruiter of the Year." Beneath the accolade was the name "Gerry Roche." It had been crossed out, however, and replaced with "Tony Price."

Headhunting's Grand Acquisitor

"My son will grow up an executive recruiter."

GERARD R. ROCHE, the most eminent headhunter in the world, the man who has put more presidents and chief executive officers into major American corporations than anyone else, is standing on the steel step of a rising escalator in New York's Pan Am Building. The grand acquisitor of executive talent is on his way to lunch at his table in the Sky Club.

But Roche abruptly stops speaking to his guest about the business which provides him with an estimated annual salary of $500,000 and which has made him a multimillionaire. Something else has captured his gaze. Roche's blue eyes are ogling the marvelously shaped rears of two young women rising on the same escalator only a dozen steps ahead.

"You're a bit old for that aren't you," his guest jokes.

The 53-year-old man in a well-pressed dark suit smiles.

"My wife says she doesn't mind where I work up my appetite as long as I come home to eat."

Roche—a man who once seriously entertained the notion of joining the priesthood—delivers the line with the panache of a comedian on a Las Vegas stage. A master of charming small talk, Roche's mind is a depository for the one-liner, the mini-speech, the ice-breaking phrase, the metaphor that lends him an exceptional ability to secure the attention and devotion of some of the most powerful people in corporate America.

The Sky Club captain, in a gaudy green-and-yellow uniform, again welcomes Roche to his table next to the plate glass window affording a panoramic view of New York City reserved for the elite. But Roche, told of Price's recruiting coup at Convergent Technologies, seems perturbed.

"Why didn't we get the Convergent job," he wants to know. "Damn it, I should have had that search.

"If some guy in San Francisco is claiming that he's got the biggest fee ever recorded, fine," says Roche, clearly rankled.

"Let him. I mean it. It doesn't bother me. If somebody in San Francisco was saying he is the best executive recruiter in the world then he's got a problem.

"I'd say, 'Tony, did you say that, you fart?' " laughs Roche, picking up an imaginary phone to tell Price off.

Modesty is not one of Roche's virtues. But the man speaks the truth. Dubbed by some the high priest of headhunters, Roche is the best of the bunch. Of the more than 200 executives he has helped place in power during some 23 years of headhunting, over a quarter are presidents and chief executives. It is an astonishing record, a tribute and a claim that has turned the name Gerry Roche into a figure of speech which connotes success. Headhunters use his name as a synonym for the best.

Yet Roche, a gregarious raconteur of good humor, can curiously act downright humble in other ways. He can just as easily speak in gee-whiz awe with an almost childhood reverence about some of the people he personally knows.

"I'm a hero worshipper," he says, drenching his smoked salmon with wine vinegar. "It was probably the biggest honor of my life to work with David Rockefeller. I still can remember our first meeting. I refused to call him David. I just couldn't bring myself to do it. Finally, we were in a meeting with the rest of the Rockefellers and I kept calling him Mr. Rockefeller."

" 'You better get specific Gerry,' " Roche relates Rockefeller's response, deepening the resonance of his voice. " 'Call me David.' "

" 'Yes David.' And from that time on it's been David."

Once Roche begins telling a story, he seldom can stop. So here Roche is segueing into how he originally connected with one of the ten richest men in America. "Here I am at home," he says. "I had just arrived and poured myself a martini. I had a very tough and difficult day. A very tough day and I was very depressed. Part of the problem with this business is it goes in high and lows. You get a Sculley saying no to you and it can ruin nine months of work. And I had one of those days. And then I get this call from David Rockefeller. The first thing I thought was it was for fund raising. I told his secretary, 'I think you have the wrong number.' "

She didn't, of course. The call was the start of a relationship which led to Roche's finding Richard A. Voell to be chief executive and president of the Rockefeller Group, just another of his many prize catches. They also include Edward Hennessy, chief executive of $17 billion Allied Signal, who was fetched from United Technologies; Robert Frederick, chief executive of RCA who Roche found at General Electric; Thomas Wyman, chief executive of CBS Corp. who left Pillsbury; John Sculley, chief executive of Apple Computer from Pepsi-Cola; Philip Beekman, president of Seagram from Colgate-Palmolive. The list goes on: John Petty, chief executive of Marine Midland Bank; Neil Austrian, chief executive of Showtime; Michael Dingman, now president of Allied Signal who Roche brought to Wheelabrator-Frye as chairman and chief executive, and Thomas Vanderslice, a GE alumnus who Roche recruited not once, but twice. First Roche put Vanderslice into GTE as president and later into Apollo Computer, Inc., one of the fastest growing companies in the computer industry, as chief executive.

Roche is a rarity among headhunters, one of the precious few who admits he lives off the failure of American management to develop its own managers in house. Quick to criticize companies for this failure, Roche is suave enough to get away with it, too. "One of the first things I ask a company is whether there is anybody inside who can do the job or that can even come close," Roche says. "If there is, I tell them you should put him in the job because promoting from within is the way to go. I don't encourage people to go outside.

"We're back surgeons and if you come to us with a back problem, we don't want to take you to the table tomorrow. We'll try to get you to do exercises, get some rest, lose some weight. And we'll hope we can avoid bringing you to the table. But if you have to go to the table, you can't do better than us. We know how to do it."

Contrary to what one might think, scavenging the executive suites of the country for corporate super heroes is a far easier task than rummaging through the ranks of middle managers in low-level searches. For the vast majority of search work at these lower levels, the universe is bigger, the people more invisible and the track records of individuals more elusive if in fact they are possible to discern at all. "By contrast," says an admiring competitor of Roche's, "if you're Apple and want to find the best consumer marketing guy in the country there are only a couple of dozen places to look. Finding him is easy; trying to get him to jump is hard."

In these high-level searches, then, the skill is in getting the job and then often persuading an executive who already is on the up to jump ship for an uncertain future in a new environment. This is undisputably Roche's forte. He juggles a half dozen or more searches at any given time, doing between 10 and 12 completions annually. That's roughly average in the headhunting business. The difference is the size of those assignments. The top producer at Heidrick & Struggles, Roche bills well over $1 million a year. Accounting for jobs which fail to result in actual placements, that means the "average executive" Roche puts in a job has a starting salary in the $300,000-to-$400,000 range.

To work in this stratospheric part of the business requires the clever cultivation of some very big-league contacts. For as Roche is quick to point out, "Do you know the number one ingredient for making rabbit stew? You've got to catch the rabbit. So the number one thing it takes to be a good recruiter is you've got to have an assignment to recruit for. You can be the best recruiter in the world, but if you don't have an assignment, where are you?"

The fact that Roche is an executive voyeur and a natural aficionado of people contributes mightily to his success. His theory of life is simple: "The most successful people are those who integrate their business and personal lives."

For Roche, that means total integration. He and his wife, Marie, regularly entertain clients and candidates at their Chappaqua, New York, home. Roche has been known to bring an executive into his teenage son's room to tinker with his computer, to give one a spin in his white Porsche Carrera, to shoot a round of golf at Sleepy Hollow in nearby Tarrytown or to go for a walk in the woods behind his home.

"There isn't anybody I meet who isn't a prospect, a candidate, a reference or a client," Roche laughs, "and all are tax-deductible."

And then there are his annual, and sometimes more frequent, bashes for friends at 21, the tony New York restaurant. He calls them his ROGUES (the Royal Order of Gregarious Uplifters of Eloquence and Style) meetings. These are sit-down dinner affairs with hors d'oeuvres and lots of drinking to which, he says, "Lester [Korn] and Russ [Reynolds] will never be invited."

Guests have included William McGowan, chief executive of MCI, and his brother, Andrew McGowan, a Catholic priest who Roche describes as "the funniest man alive." One recent guest commented that it was the largest group of corporate castoffs ever assembled in one room: David Mahoney, a one-time Ward Howell recruit and former head of Norton Simon who took the money and ran; Tom Vanderslice, who at that time had just resigned from GTE Corp. where Roche put him; Bill Agee, a Russell Reynolds recruit who had recently pulled the ripcord on a huge golden parachute, and his wife Mary Cunningham for whom Roche had found a job at Seagram as a favor after she resigned from Bendix. Cunningham would later write in her book, *Powerplay*, that Roche "really helped me get back on my feet." Agee and Cunningham, both widely in disfavor, were blowing kisses at each other across the room.

To this particular ROGUES gathering, Roche also had invited Ed Hennessy, chief executive of Allied Corp. It was an embarrassing faux pas. Hennessy had just won a nasty public fight with Agee in a corporate takeover battle for Bendix. Roche had to call Hennessy back and inform him that Agee and his wife would be attending the event. Hennessy wisely decided that he had other things to do. "Boy was I dumb," Roche says. "But I was uptown with them, and I'll go downtown with them."

He is back in his office, two blocks away from the Sky Club, in an airy, handsomely appointed room with a view of the Chrysler Building looming in the background. He keeps a jug of ice water on top of a tall wooden stationmaster's desk—a gift from Mike Dingman—which sits in the corner of his office behind his main desk. There, he often stands to take notes and leaf through papers while on the telephone.

There also are pictures scattered about the room—his wife, son, twin daughters, clients and friends. A collection of management books line his bookshelves, which hold some unusual titles as well. Like David Frost's *Book of the World's Worst Decisions* which he'll send to those who fail to follow his advice. Time is so precious that he removes his watch from his wrist and places it in front of him atop the desk to keep track of the day. Yet, he spends hours on the tele-

87

phone each day, not conducting search work but hearing confessions and dispensing advice to friends.

A recent Roche recruit, a chief executive in a sizable New York corporation, calls to ask Roche how he should deal with the executive who was passed over in favor of him. The longtime company manager is placing significant roadblocks in the way of the new executive.

"What should I do?" he asks Roche.

"Look, take him out for a walk or lunch and explain the facts," Roche tells him over the telephone. "This happens a lot of times. If he can't understand that you're the boss, tell him he'll have to go."

The executive asks if a year's severance pay would be enough.

"That's very generous," replies Roche, volunteering the name and telephone number of a lawyer who, he advises, could put together a nice little severance package to get rid of the guy.

"The single key to this business is credibility," Roche says. "To be able to look a Sculley in the eye and have him tell you how he feels about his superiors and to have him give you his entire career plan. 'I trust that with you, Roche. You could kill my whole career. I trust you. Suppose it doesn't work out,' I'm asked. 'Two or three years down the road, where could I go, what could I do, Roche? You're in the business, tell me. Can I go back? What are you going to do with me?' So you must help them think through their total career. It is an awesome responsibility. Whether you can get it playing golf, socializing or just plain communicating doesn't make any difference."

Inevitably, Roche gets it. "Of all of them," says Arthur Taylor, former CBS president and a director on the board of competitor Korn/Ferry International, "when it comes time to sell the candidate, Gerry is the best. Gerry is fundamentally a salesperson. And his products are people. He sells candidates better than anybody I've ever seen. It's kind of a coarse thing to say, but it is the business."

Taylor was once a Roche product himself, a product who became with Roche intertwined in one of the most bizarre episodes ever played out in the corporate world. In over two decades of headhunting, there could have been no work more challenging and grippingly dramatic than Roche's work for CBS patriarch William Paley over a span of nine years from 1971 to 1980. In that time, Roche would play a hand in the recruitment of four potential successors to the CBS crown. One died, two were abruptly dismissed, the final one, Thomas Wyman, made it to the top.

Roche plucked Taylor into all this intrigue in 1972 from International Paper. An ambitious, urbane, if sometimes pompous, young man, Taylor was nothing less than a Whiz Kid. And when Roche first glanced at his resume, he couldn't have been anything but impressed. Taylor graduated magna cum laude with a B.A. from Brown University in 1957. Then, while serving as Brown's assistant director of admissions in 1961, he earned a graduate degree in American Economic History. Taylor joined First Boston Corp., spending nine years with the investment banker and becoming a director and vice-president in the process. He jumped to International Paper as its vice-president for finance in 1970. Two years later, when Taylor was chief financial officer at the age of 37, Roche's call came.

It led to what seemed like the chance of a lifetime: to become president of CBS Corp. and to work directly under Bill Paley, the unpredictable boss of the broadcasting giant. Taylor was the second president Roche would deliver to Paley, and certainly not the last.

Paley enlisted Roche after concluding that CBS no longer needed a broadcaster at its helm but rather a professional business manager. For that, he and his president, Frank Stanton, would have to look outside. Roche landed the job to find Stanton's replacement who, it was understood, also would eventually succeed Paley as chairman and chief executive.

Roche first delivered Charles "Chick" Ireland, a former secretary of the New York Central Railroad, former president of Alleghany Corp., former chairman of Investors Diversified Services and for the last four years the right-hand man to Harold S. Geneen of ITT, a favorite Roche hunting ground. Ireland was named president in September 1971, and Paley became delighted with him. "He was a strong, no-nonsense leader who brought about better financial controls, a better flow of information within the executive ranks and better analyses and predictions of what we could expect at CBS," wrote Paley in his subsequent memoirs.

After six months on the job, Ireland suffered the first of two heart attacks at CBS that eventually took his life at the age of 51. Paley turned to Roche again, although he also engaged Russell Reynolds Associates on the same job as a "consultant." Paley and Stanton interviewed "quite a few promising candidates," but settled within one month on Roche's Taylor, who joined as president in July 1972. This was despite the fact that Reynolds, who did the reference checking on Taylor, recommended against his hire.

Paley, however, was suitably impressed. "He was only 37 years old, tall, good-looking, and extremely articulate," wrote Paley, "and above all it was immediately obvious that here was a man with a very quick mind and a tremendous amount of energy and vitality."

Taylor went to work in July 1972 and by virtually all outside assessments did a terrific job. Three years into his presidency, *Forbes* magazine noted that "Wall Street is applauding Arthur Taylor, who is emerging as the strongest president in CBS history and Paley's first designated successor. Nearly everyone agrees that Taylor has restored to CBS the managerial spit and polish that Bill Paley so much admires."

Taylor became close friends with Roche, even to the point of vacationing together with their wives. Not surprisingly, then, he turned to Roche to recruit a number of outsiders into "Black Rock," as the corporation's Avenue of the Americas skyscraper is familiarly called. "While I was at CBS he must have done literally dozens on which the two of us were working," says Taylor. Taylor could not have possibly known it at the time, but one of those searches brought in the man who would unexpectedly succeed him. John D. Backe, former president of General Electric's and Time, Inc.'s ill-fated General Learning Corp., had been recruited as president of CBS's Publishing Group a year after Taylor joined CBS.

One morning in October 1976 Paley summoned Taylor to his office and in the presence of two directors fired him on the spot. Paley never publicly explained why. "He did not have all of the essential qualities to become my successor," was the line he used in his memoirs. Backe, whom Paley had begun courting a month earlier when Taylor was in Moscow negotiating network television rights for the 1980 Olympics, took over. A stunned Taylor, whose future once looked so bright and promising, never seemed to recover from the dismissal. Today, as a "consultant," he has a small, modest office in Rockefeller Center.

Roche prefers not to talk about Taylor in detail, but he somehow sounds as if he shares some blame. "A large corporation," says Roche, "can survive a mistake. An individual cannot. You can wreck an individual's life. But the company goes on. I know one executive who had a psychological mindset of saying, 'Hey, I am the hottest guy in the world. A few years later he is out and hasn't connected since. He's asking, 'What happened?' And I have to tell you the truth. I live with the question personally. No one will ever convince me that he wouldn't have been better off if he never met me. That guy would be the president of a major American corporation today if he never met me. And I still have trouble sleeping at night because of it."

The story doesn't end here. Backe lasted less than four years before Paley gave him the ax, too. The story goes that Roche was looking for a new CBS director at the same time. He found, by a suspicious "coincidence," Thomas Wyman who rather than being named just a director also copped the titles president and chief executive officer shortly after Backe was out in the street.

His most egregious mismatch, the one which many of Roche's colleagues are likely to bring up, was that of Maurice Valente. Roche plucked Valente from ITT where he was an executive vice-president and helped put him into the $600,000-a-year post as RCA president. Valente's appointment was the result of a four-month search by Roche in late 1979. The 50-year-old Valente, who once managed ITT's European operations, was known as a trouble-shooter.

Initially, he was one of 50 executives Roche considered for the job. That list was further winnowed to a dozen managers whom RCA seriously considered. Valente reportedly was Roche's third or fourth choice, but Chairman Edgar Griffiths's first. Ultimately, his hiring was approved by a four-member executive committee, whose members included Griffiths and John R. Petty, who Roche had earlier placed as president of Marine Midland Bank, Inc.

This was a match never made in heaven. Valente lasted all of 25 weeks. Griffiths was an aloof, methodical and reserved manager who reflected RCA's conservative and staid corporate environment. Valente, on the other hand, was a flamboyant, cosmopolitan and gregarious executive. "He was the wrong man in the wrong job," an ITT executive told *BusinessWeek*. When Griffiths gave him the ax, he also issued an unprecedented statement to the press which said Valente "did not meet expectations" on the job.

"My 14-year-old daughter could have told you Valente wouldn't have lasted," says Dwight Foster, head of Peat Marwick's search practice. "It was a terrible mismatch."

Valente left, but not very quietly. He gave interviews to every journalist in sight, wailing about his misfortune. Nonetheless, RCA felt obliged to pay him a $1.25 million severance. Valente formed his own investment banking firm, Maurice R. Valente & Associates, was a limited partner in the Wall Street firm of Wolsey & Co. and became chairman of the St. Louis-based Sabreliner Corp. Three years after his dismissal, however, he was found dead at an Italian resort hotel in Ladispoli, a coastal town 18 miles from Rome. A judge ruled later that he committed suicide by hanging. He was 54. Valente's wife of 29 years, Dolores, had died four months earlier after a long illness.

Was the mismatch Roche's fault? If RCA thought so, it would not have turned to him again for Valente's successor. The board eventually fired Edgar Griffiths in early 1981 and put Thornton Bradshaw, once president of Atlantic Richfield and an RCA director for nine years, in his place. Bradshaw, who had used Roche to do a director search, called him up to find a new president and eventual successor to him as chief executive and chairman. The "specs" called for a mature, experienced, low-key, nonflamboyant executive with a high energy level.

"The problem," Bradshaw told *Fortune* magazine, "was how to conduct a wide external search and still keep it quiet. We didn't want people at RCA to get upset, though it was apparent that there was no suitable successor within the organization. I knew he [Roche] had a tremendous file. More important, I knew he could keep a secret."

Roche got together an initial list of 75 names and with Bradshaw narrowed it down to a dozen candidates. Roche got each of them to meet Bradshaw for an interview over lunch, usually at Bradshaw's New York apartment so RCA regulars wouldn't get the impression the corporation was conducting an executive beauty contest. Finally, the RCA chief picked three or four finalists who were each grilled by the board's five-member executive committee.

Robert R. Frederick, executive vice-president of General Electric, emerged as the winner. "I never responded to an executive recruiter before," says Frederick, who was impressed with Roche's professionalism. "He really cared to present my strengths in the best light." But unlike other executives, Frederick never struck up a relationship with Roche. "You don't trust anyone else with your career as far as I'm concerned. You rely on Gerry to give you his observations of the firm and its position, but you have to recognize that he's not inside the company."

As soon as Frederick joined RCA, he told executives his goal was to never go outside for a president again. The transition, by all standards, has been a success. Frederick was named chief executive in 1985, and Roche considers it one of his three most successful assignments. "Bob's background was exactly what RCA needed," Roche said when Frederick won his promotion. "He was a strategic thinker without being too think-tanky or eggheady, and he had run the international sector, which cut across all GE product lines. RCA needed a strong manager who wasn't going to upstage Brad or push him out and take over."

Frederick's future, however, is less than secure due to the acquisition of RCA by General Electric to be completed at the end of 1986. But the fact that RCA turned again to Roche, after the Valente failure, takes the headhunter off the hook, he reasons. "The key point," Roche says, "is why the hell would they have Roche back in there if he didn't do the job well. 'It sure as hell wasn't his fault and we know he can keep a secret,' they said. I think it worked out magnificently. You've got to look at the end result. I have no control over the final selection."

If ever there was a man born to a profession ideally suited for him, it was Roche. "When my mother held me in her arms," he jokes, pretending to swaddle an infant, "my mother said my son will grow up to be an executive recruiter."

Roche, actually, gained his passion for people in his father's small corner grocery store on Washburn Street in Scranton, Pennsylvania. A former H. J. Heinz salesman, Joe Roche bought the place after a World War I injury deprived him of the ability to go back on the road for Heinz. Young Roche worked behind the counter with his mother, Amelia, and his sister from the age of ten, when he entered the sixth grade at St. Patrick's, until graduating from the University of Scranton in 1953, when he was 22. Roche probably spent more time behind the counter than he would have liked. His father died at the age of 49 when he was a freshman at St. Patrick's High School so he had to help his mother run the place. His father's death, Roche says, "put me in touch with reality early."

Sticking out from one of the bookshelves in his spacious office on the 32nd floor is a large metal sugar spoon, a memento taken from his dad's store, where sugar was sold scooped from a wooden barrel. "I'm in the same business today," he says, "personal service. To this day, I find the experience of working in that store helpful in meeting and servicing customers." With that in mind, Roche tried to convince his son, Paul, not to take a job as a computer programmer during a recent summer. "I will double whatever salary you can make if you do something that forces you to meet people—even if it's pumping gas or working at McDonald's," he told him. "I mean it."

After graduating from Scranton, a Jesuit institution, where Roche played football and earned good grades, he seriously entertained the thought of entering the priesthood. But he was advised by "the Jebbies" to join the Navy to get women out of his system. It did not work. Instead, Roche met the woman who was to become his wife, Marie Terotta. After serving two years as a lieutenant in the Mediterranean, Roche returned east to Philadelphia and later to New York to begin his rather brief career in the corporate world. It lasted all of seven years, a stint that would hardly seem enough time to qualify anyone to judge the worth of other proven-executives.

A job hopper of the first order, Roche worked at three different companies during that brief time and earned an M.B.A. degree at night from New York University, where he took the famous course taught by management guru Peter F. Drucker. Roche recalls interrupting the class discussions of case studies with "what if" questions. "Young man," Professor Drucker intoned one evening, "you are either an engineer or the product of a Jesuit education."

Roche spent a year as a management trainee for AT&T's office in Philadelphia; two years as an account executive in New York with ABC; and finally four years with Kordite Corporation, a plastics company in the day when plastic was the new "in" industry. Founded by Howard Samuels, the company brought the housewives of the world "Baggies." He joined the firm, located in Macedon, New York, near Rochester, as a salesman in 1959 and rose to marketing director by 1963.

That's when he got a call from Gardner Heidrick, one of the fathers of headhunting and co-founder of Heidrick & Struggles. Heidrick, former personnel director of Farmland Industries, a Kansas City dairy cooperative, had launched his firm in Chicago in 1953 after a headhunting stint with Booz, Allen & Hamilton.

He wondered if Roche would be interested in doubling his salary by taking a marketing job at Milprint, a division of Philip Morris Industries, Inc., in Milwaukee. "It was exactly the time when Jack Kennedy got his head blown off," says Roche. "I was a 31-year-old kid trying to figure out which end was up. I was disillusioned with big business, with nearly everything. He was coming at me in November of 1963, and I was shaking my head and saying I don't want to go anywhere. I don't know what I want to do. I don't even want to stay here. I just want to go and walk in the woods or something like that.

94

" 'Gee,' " Heidrick said, " 'You sound all screwed up.' "

"I probably am," retorted Roche.

" 'You'd be perfect for us.' "

"Why would I try this crazy business as opposed to a nice, solid, Philip Morris division?" he asks out loud. "Because Gardner convinced me that what it took to do this work well had to do with human beings and dealing with people, not with plastic or lettuce bags or dry cleaning bags."

Roche probably was the best head ever hunted by Heidrick in his nearly 35 years of recruiting executives. Roche joined the firm as an associate, three months after Heidrick opened its New York office in 1964. He made partner four years later when he also was named manager of the New York office, and in 1973 Roche assumed managerial responsibilities for Heidrick & Struggles's offices in the eastern part of the U.S.

He demonstrated an all-absorbing involvement and commitment to the firm through hard work and long hours, even above the workaholic norms of the business. "He drove himself like no one I have ever met," says an admiring colleague who confesses to being a workaholic himself. "He would sometimes go down to Washington at 3:00 A.M. for a breakfast meeting and would be back in his office by 11:00 A.M. to start his day's work in New York. I've seen him walk in the office with blood vessels popped in his eyes because of the strain and stress of what he was undergoing."

Roche was unlike his colleagues in another critical way. He could bend and shape the specifications for candidates like no other headhunter. Typically, a corporate client will detail what type of individual is expected in a search and hold the headhunter to the line on those specs. Roche, more than anyone else, would wriggle free, persuading the client that a man who could sell sugared water at a premium could just as easily sell computers. "Clients are generally fearful of giving us any latitude when they give you candidate specs," notes a former Heidrick & Struggles headhunter who knows Roche well. "It can be almost as specific as Princeton undergrad, Harvard M.B.A., six years with Citicorp and four years with American Express and three years running his own company. Most of us will say, 'Yes sir' and try to fill them.

"Roche would take a look at those specs and say, 'That's ridiculous, Mr. Client. Why don't you look at someone from a completely unrelated industry in an unrelated function.' If other people tried that, the reaction would be, 'You're being lazy. You don't want to find exactly what I want. You just want to throw a body at me.' Roche would convince the client and typically be right in bringing someone in from another non-allied type of business."

Yet the key to his successful hunting in the upper reaches of corporate America, surmises Heidrick, was a tendency only to work at the top. "Early on, Gerry always went for the best three or four people in the country for a job," says Heidrick. "They often were overqualified, but he made the right contacts, the people who gave him the senior-level jobs."

It was a strategy that led to much frustration as well. "The best possible people will say no more often than mediocre or average candidates," says Roche, giving away one of the profession's secrets for fast turnovers. "I'm always going after the ungettable and 90 percent of the people I approach respond in the negative."

In Heidrick, who served as his mentor and taught him the business, Roche saw a father image. Heidrick was a tall, balding man who always sported a tan, evidence of hours spent swinging clubs on golf courses every week. Heidrick adored the game, so much so that he sometimes felt guilty about playing it. He had created a workaholic haven at the firm, where the lights burnt bright late into every weeknight and often on the weekends. So he sometimes went to great lengths to cover up his frequent golf outings, recalls a close friend. One time, for example, Heidrick was hurrying out of the firm's New York office on a Thursday in the early afternoon. An associate innocently asked him where he was headed.

"West," he said sharply.

"How far west," the headhunter queried. "Back to Chicago?"

"No, just west," Heidrick barked.

After a moment of silence, Heidrick blurted that he was only going to New Jersey's Newark Airport.

"Newark? That's not very west, Gard. Where are you going after that?"

"Well, if you have to know, I'm flying down to Florida to play golf."

It wasn't all fun and games, of course. Golf is something of a prerequisite for headhunters, a tool of the trade as important as an unerring ear for nuance when screening out candidates on a telephone. The games become opportunities to develop business and to work on sources for the names of key candidates. Alan Lafley, then head of human resources for Clark Equipment Co., recalls a round of golf with Heidrick at Benton Harbor in Michigan. "Gardner was talking about General Electric and other people for different jobs he was trying to source," says Lafley. "We chatted and that was it."

Shortly after their match, though, Lafley was recruited by Russell Reynolds Associates to Chase Manhattan Bank. When Heidrick found out, he was astonished. Heidrick had the search to find Chase a vice-president for human resources at the time the two played golf. Heidrick never brought the topic up because he knew Lafley had been at Clark for only one year, and Heidrick didn't think Lafley would be interested. "What a crazy world," Heidrick told him later. "They took that search away from me at Chase because I was just having a hell of a time satisfying them."

Roche shared with Heidrick a love of the game as well. And it helped to further their relationship in a way which was not unlike that which had long ago developed between Heidrick and James A. Newman, who as head of Booz, Allen & Hamilton's search practice recruited Heidrick into the business at Booz in 1951. Heidrick would often refer to Newman as his father and teacher. Newman, in turn, liked and admired his colorful and tough-as-nails student. "He was a very aggressive and persuasive fellow," says Newman. "He was very effective in convincing a well-located executive to look at another opportunity."

Heidrick would one day speak in nearly identical words about his own pupil. Although his junior by 42 years, Roche was, like him, aggressive, persuasive and interested in the firm's continued growth. Indeed, Roche was more like him than Heidrick's own co-founder and longtime partner John E. Struggles. Struggles and he launched their business in a tiny Chicago office with their wives as secretaries. Struggles was a born and bred conservative midwesterner, a nice guy who friends say was almost ashamed of the business he was in. Salty, sincere and handsome, he had been vice-president of personnel for Montgomery Ward & Co., where he spent a dozen years of his life.

Struggles was not a risk taker. He was downright cautious, nearly fearful of expansion. He would almost have preferred the partnership to remain a local search firm with one office in Chicago. Their nip-and-tuck relationship caused limitless frustration for Heidrick, whose vision for a growing, successful enterprise was as ambitious as Struggles's was conservative. Their dramatically contrasting personalities collided often and led to endless feuds.

"Gard and John were the original odd couple," recalls one associate. "Gard would get up in the morning running with an idea. John was more like a fireplug. Gard would bump up against it and maybe it would move an inch."

The man in the middle, who often assumed the role of a soft-spoken peacemaker, was Tom Johnston. He joined the partnership in 1956 as the second employee. The first, Spencer Stuart, lasted all of ten months before running off to start his own firm. Struggles had known Johnston at Montgomery Ward where Johnston had been retail personnel manager for five years before hopping to Panelit, Inc., another Chicago company, for a two-year stay as director of personnel.

It took Heidrick & Struggles seven years before they opened a second office in 1960, and it was Johnston who was sent to Los Angeles to run it. Johnston eventually led the firm's expansion into Europe, too, with the opening of a London office in 1968 and other branches in Brussels and Paris by 1974. And the three served as equal owners, if not unequal leaders, building the premier firm in the business. When Johnston was ready to step down in 1978, Roche was the obvious choice to succeed him.

There were other contenders, but Roche was the firm's brightest star. He was a giant in New York, the capital of headhunting, and he already was the firm's biggest moneymaking producer. In the previous two years, Heidrick & Struggles had found ten presidents for corporations whose revenues were in the billion dollar or more category. Roche had a hand in many of them, recruiting Timm F. Crull from Carnation Corp. to the $375,000-a-year job as president of Norton Simon, Inc.. There were presidents for CBS Corp., Volkswagen of America, Marine Midland Banks, Northrop Corp., Seagram Co. and International Paper, too.

He had carved for himself an enviable reputation as a hunter of major miracle workers for industry. Together with Bob Gette at competitor Haley Associates, Roche stood atop the headhunting heap. Gette was planning to take early retirement in Florida, however, and Haley viewed Roche as the ideal successor to his own superstar. Roche also had lunch with Gette, a man he respected, who told him he wouldn't be with Haley much longer. "Without Gette," thought Roche, "the Haley organization isn't much."

Nonetheless, Roche went back to his boss and tried to leverage his offer from Haley into something else. Headhunters blanch when candidates entertain their offers only as weapons to gain a raise or a promotion from a current employer. They curse executives who pull off maneuvers like that, even blackball them from future jobs. But Roche wasn't about to let this opportunity pass by.

"I'm tempted to take it," he told Heidrick. Roche wanted to know what kind of future his mentor had in mind for him. "Gard put his arm around me and took me up to the altar," says Roche. "He said, 'Son, this will be all yours someday.' And I said, 'Pop, you've got me.'"

Heidrick doesn't deny this version. "I don't remember it that precisely," he says. "You know Gerry can embellish things a bit." But soon after, Roche achieved his ambition. In 1978—when Heidrick & Struggles was thought to be the largest executive search firm in the business with $13.5 million in annual billings—Roche was named president and chief executive officer. Heidrick and Johnston remained as co-chairmen.

A furious Haley felt doublecrossed and used. Haley began negotiating with Roche in September of 1977 and claims to have drawn up a contract with Heidrick's star by early December. Roche wasn't yet ready to make the move. Roche told him, Haley adds, to wait until March after he received his annual bonus from Heidrick & Struggles. Roche maintains that "nothing was ever signed, no deal was ever made."

To this day, however, 69-year-old Haley, still chairman of his firm, remains bitter and makes little effort to disguise his disdain for Roche. "That bastard knew that Gette was retiring," storms Haley. "He came up here and made a deal with us. We even wrote a contract, and then he took that contract to Heidrick & Struggles and got them to make him CEO. As a recruiter, Gerry Roche is not worth a Goddamn. Take my word for it, he really isn't. He gives this profession a terrible reputation. But he did replace us and took an awful lot of business away."

So Roche succeeded Johnston, who had had the title of president and chief executive since 1970. Heidrick, however, had given up as little authority as he had to. Wherever he was, the sheer force of his personality kept him in charge. Heidrick, says Roche, taught him to be tough-minded, tenacious and persistent. But Heidrick would often grouse that Roche was never tough enough. "He wanted to have everybody treated the way he was treated, and sometimes you can give the ranch away doing that," says Heidrick.

The two would argue often enough about things like that. Heidrick would complain that Roche was spending too much money fixing up the New York office. Roche would maintain that the search business had reached a stage of development where it was critical to have an office that would awe or at least impress visitors by its cool elegance. Both Heidrick and Struggles would tell him that "loose lips sink ships," that he shouldn't talk to the media. Roche countered that self-promotion was important for the business.

"Gerry likes publicity and sometimes clients don't like to have it known that they've used an executive recruiter," Heidrick says. "Gerry will almost always talk too much. He's not as cautious as he should be." It sometimes got him in trouble. Roche, for example, had a hand in luring Edwin A. Gee, then a senior vice-president at Du Pont, to president of International Paper in 1978. Gee eventually became chief executive and chairman and retired in 1985. But his name surfaced in an *Esquire* magazine profile on Roche. Gee was furious.

"You guys said you are supposed to operate on confidentiality, you stay in the background, you don't talk and advertise yourself to the press," Gee complained.

"And if you do you sure as hell don't get too specific."

But the arguments with Heidrick never prevented him from giving Roche his due. "He's the best high-level recruiter in the country today, without question," Heidrick says flatly. And the two remain friends. "How can you not respect a guy who has done what he has done?" asks Roche. "He's like the rest of the human race. He's got warts, but who doesn't? We fought long and hard, but we always knew why we were fighting. We were always fighting for the same objectives, the same policies, the same principles, the same ethics and the same profits. Sometimes, our tactics were different."

Roche played at the headhunting game hard, brought into the firm some of its best producers and garnered for himself and Heidrick & Struggles the kind of prominence it required to remain a leading company in the business. He became the firm's major rainmaker, the business developer who would pass on clients and work for others to handle. Roche authored a couple of long, thoughtful articles on business executives and compensation for the prestigious *Harvard Business Review*. And editors of the top business magazines often would turn to him for opinions on the latest trends in management.

No less important, Roche was at times an inspiring teacher to the new people he brought to the firm and to the business. In Peasback's first year as a headhunter, for example, the president of a small Long Island company called Triangle Pacific invited Peasback to spend a week skiing with him in Vail, where the president owned a lavish condominium. "I went to Roche, who was then New York manager, and asked him, 'What do you think about this?' " Peasback recalls. "He was euphoric. Gerry said, 'This is the kind of client networking that is good stuff.' Out I went and subsequently did seven searches for that company in about 12 or 18 months."

He taught others, like Hoke Brissenden, a former human resources executive with Becton, Dickinson who Roche brought into the firm in 1969, his business development techniques and his smooth personal presentations to potential clients. "With clients, he puts on one of the most polished presentations on stage," says Brissenden. "His ability to communicate one-on-one is outstanding, and he has a pair of exceptional antennae for business development."

Roche also earned the nearly universal, if envious, praise of his competitors. One Korn/Ferry executive acknowledged him to be the best in the business. "Gerry Roche," says Russ Reynolds, "is a first-class professional who definitely has an exceptional feel for the business. He's funny, thoughtful, egotistical, like most of us in the business, and a nice guy."

But Reynolds left out opportunist, too. It was Heidrick & Struggles, during Roche's stint as chief executive, which became the first major search firm to hike fees to 33.3 from 30 percent of an executive's first-year salary and bonus in 1980. Yet only a few years later, Roche ironically stood before a professional trade group in New York to question the search fees he himself put into effect three years earlier. No one in the audience realized that it was Heidrick & Struggles under his stewardship that stirred a controversy over fees in the first place, prompting some corporate personnel types to label the charges "obscene."

In the mid-1950s, Ward Howell, who left McKinsey to start his own recruiting firm, established what became the normal rate by pegging it at 20 percent of salary plus expenses. It jumped to about 25 percent in the mid-1960s and stayed there for more than a decade. All the while, of course, search fees more than kept up with inflation because executive salary increases were outstripping the inflation rate during most of these years.

But the business was rapidly changing, and the competitive pressures on Roche were increasing. Korn/Ferry International, Inc., a firm which had been in business fewer than the years Roche had been hunting for heads, surpassed Heidrick & Struggles in billings soon after Roche was named president. And other firms, notably Russell Reynolds and Spencer Stuart, were closing the gap on Roche. Heidrick & Struggles continued to grow fast, too, but its rapid growth strained the firm's resources and triggered complaints from conservative partners struggling through the expansion.

One critical problem for some became the search firm's client and candidate files. Many of them were out of date; and the good people in them were overworked. "One source would have been contacted a month before by a Boston consultant and the month before that by somebody else," recalls one partner. "I would call and the executive would wonder what the hell was going on." Some headhunters would horde files, keeping to themselves executives unearthed in searches that weren't hired. If an executive didn't quite fit a current assignment, maybe the headhunter could slot him into another job a month or two down the road. Why put him back into the system?

Roche had invested $100,000 in a new, computerized system to help ease some of these problems and bring the firm into the computer age. But mistakes were made and no one was yet enjoying the full benefits of that investment. Worse still, the system gradually replacing the paper files was thought by many to be far less valuable. In converting to computer, the firm condensed its more thorough paper system so that less information would be saved. Among other things, the computer files lacked the detailed comments on candidates that the paper files allowed. Typically, a headhunter would write something like: "Considered for vice-president of manufacturing at XYZ Corp. Came in second. Would be terrific in a medium-sized metal manufacturing environment." If a search for such a company could later be gained, a headhunter might have a handful of strong candidates already interviewed in some detail.

Frustrated Heidrick & Struggles consultants—some of whom thought they were not making enough money—began leaving the firm in the double digits annually by the late 1970s. Others who remained began clamoring for a piece of the action. The firm was centrally governed by a small, autocratic group of only four partners: Heidrick, Struggles, Johnston and Roche. Struggles, who had never been the dominant personality of the partnership, had sold out his stock in the firm. The other three, however, held nearly 58 percent of the stock in 1980. And because Heidrick and Johnston were now selling down their shares in the company, Roche had become the largest single shareholder with almost 30 percent. The value of the stock soared through the 1970s, compounding at rates of up to 40 percent a year through 1980.

"All of a sudden, the stock became a very important thing in the eyes and minds of the senior partners of the firm," explains one former shareholder. "Heidrick & Struggles was not known for paying the highest salaries and bonuses around, but we all knew we were going to make money on that stock. It became something worth fighting for. It became more important than growing the firm, compensating the partners and maintaining a sophisticated operation."

Not surprisingly, some of the troops were demanding both a greater share of the equity and a greater say in the governance of the company. Seeking a solution, Roche visited Dick Paget, one of the founders of management consultants Cresap, McCormick & Paget, Inc., whose offices are but a quick elevator ride away in the same building as Heidrick & Struggles's New York headquarters. Paget developed a more structured plan that would do away with the committee of four and essentially replace it with 34 partners who would control the firm and formally elect its chief executive. Paget told Roche he had, with Heidrick and Johnston, to spread their 58 percent stake in the firm over some 30 partners to gain broader ownership of the company to make it work.

"That's where you have to go," Paget told Roche, pointing to a flip-chart diagram of the proposed new structure.

"How you get from here to here, I don't know how to help you with. That's what is going to be painful. It's going to be hell and very difficult."

Heidrick was amazed. "You're going to allow those people to run the firm?" he asked Roche. "What if they don't elect you?"

Heidrick's comment wasn't exactly prophetic, but it was a harbinger of what was to come. Roche, long a witness and outside participant of the internecine warfare at major corporations, soon would be consumed by interoffice politics himself. Brewing in the hinterlands of Heidrick & Struggles's worldwide network of offices was an effort by more than a dozen of Heidrick & Struggles's consultants to openly question Roche's managerial authority and ability. The firm, founded and headquartered in Chicago, had always suf-

fered from an intellectual split of sorts. Roche represented the eastern, liberal contingent, while most of the firm remained true to its
conservative midwestern roots. The schism widened as Roche, a liberal Democrat with a natural New York bias, gained more power
and control.

"Gerry is a high-powered, dynamic New Yorker," says Law-
rence Hill, a self-described conservative southerner who ran Heidrick
& Struggles's Houston office. "He's a super, go-go-go, growth-
oriented visionary. But there were still more people in the firm
who weren't like that."

Hill, a tall, trim man in his early 50s, was one of them. He had
joined Heidrick & Struggles three months earlier than Roche in 1963.
The pair grew up in the firm together. And Hill, a man every bit as
ambitious as Roche, had become a rival of his for the leadership of
the firm. He was, along with Roche and Donald Williams, head of
the Chicago office, part of the second generation of leaders Heidrick
assembled to keep the firm at the top of the business. Soon after
Roche was named president, Williams left to found his own firm,
Donald Williams Associates, Inc., in Chicago. "But Larry stayed and
he talked and he created cabals and he was not a loyal, supportive
team member," says a former Heidrick & Struggles consultant. "He
wanted the job that Roche had and he never accepted the fact that
he didn't get it or deserve it."

Hill joined with three others who also had grown disenchanted
with Roche's management of the firm. They included John Richmond, a partner who joined Heidrick & Struggles in 1969; Steve
Garrison, a Harvard M.B.A. and friend of Hill who opened and
managed Heidrick & Struggles's Dallas office, and Jack Vernon, head
of the Boston branch. Among their concerns was the firm's money-
losing international operations. In some cases, managers were picking up searches but failing to complete them. At least one unhappy
client in Europe sued the firm. In late 1980, Roche was telling his
colleagues that its overseas offices—which accounted for 20 percent
of its revenues and little of its profits in recent years—would end the
year making $100,000 to $200,000. Instead, they piled up a loss of
$500,000, a $700,000 swing.

"I'm convinced it was the biggest single problem at Heidrick &
Struggles," says Hill. "It was symptomatic of not being attentive.
Gerry kept making apologies for it, but the problems kept occur-
ring. He took responsibility for it, but doing something about it was

a different thing. He was not able to recognize some problems. And it was hard to get Gerry's attention. I have many memos I sent to him about this. Gerry said, 'You're not forward-thinking enough,' and I said, 'If you're not careful you're going to have no money to finance that growth.' "

Roche had doubled the size of the New York office that year, just as Heidrick and Johnston were draining Heidrick & Struggles's capital by selling their shares back into the firm. And in 1980, expansion-minded Roche had opened the doors on three new offices in Greenwich, Connecticut, Atlanta and Dusseldorf. Never before in the firm's 17-year history had it attempted to establish that many new outposts in a single year.

"I don't think Gerry got a grip on what was required to manage the firm," says Richmond. "I remember telling him the engine is running too hot. We're going to have to slow it down a little bit or we're going to have trouble."

Roche's timing for the firm's expansion was awful. The economy was just about to lapse into a severe recession. Corporations were no longer hiring middle managers; they were laying them off in unprecedented numbers. Even cradle-to-grave companies, known for their paternalistic employment policies, were pruning their managerial ranks. Many of these jobs were the bread and butter of the executive search business.

Other prominent headhunting firms also were under pressure. At William H. Clark Associates, a firm which once could boast a reputation for excellence every bit as good as Heidrick & Struggles, there was severe trouble. Its New York manager, Thomas A. Byrnes, began advising his New York partners to overbill clients on expenses to improve the bottom line. In a memo dated February 2, 1981, he urged colleagues to travel coach class, but bill clients at first-class rates. And when a trip was made on behalf of two or more corporations, Byrnes instructed headhunters to charge clients anywhere from 150 percent to 300 percent over the trip's actual costs. The firm later claimed the memo was never enforced, but it reflected the business's difficulties at the time. Heidrick & Struggles, then, wasn't the only firm hit hard by the recession, but the confluence of other problems made the economic downturn far more troublesome for Roche and his partners.

A symptom of trouble occurred in August of 1980 when Roche omitted, without explanation, the midyear bonuses paid to headhunters. Typically, the firm would provide payouts, representing 15 percent to 20 percent of the total annual bonus, to its headhunters every August. For each consultant, these halfway bonuses would amount to between $5,000 and $20,000 each. Then, in March, Heidrick & Struggles would shower its headhunters with the big bonus money after tallying up figures on the fiscal year which ended January 31.

Roche's decision to defer the midyear bonuses riveted greater attention on the firm's financial instability. Even before this latest shock, Roche had been making trips to the loan window of a bank to pay its headhunters their annual bonuses. When Heidrick & Struggles's headhunters found themselves shy of thousands of dollars they had anticipated in midyear, the firm became rife with speculation about its future. "We wondered what would happen if the firm made no money and they didn't pay any bonuses," says Richmond. "We were getting bigger and bigger, but the earnings were going down. It didn't make sense. And why were we in such a condition that we had to go to the bank and borrow money to pay bonuses in a cash business?"

At the same time Roche was wrestling with the firm's mounting problems, he was, no less, trying to carry out top-level search work for several of the nation's largest corporations, including CBS and GTE. "Roche tried to be a manager simply by taking a 20-hour day and spreading it into a 28- or 30-hour day," says Garrison. "It didn't work. He didn't have the time nor the inclination to worry about the nitty-gritty detail of the European operations. So his solution to the problem was to drive the revenue side of the business. If we have a $100,000 problem in London, all we have to do is get two more searches and it will solve the problem. So we became a revenue-driven organization, but expenses were climbing. No one was watching expenses."

Many began to doubt Roche's managerial skills. Perhaps he could place, with great fanfare, some of the biggest captains of industry, but he was having his difficulties managing a small firm with under $20 million of revenues, a firm just a fraction of the size of RCA, CBS, Allied Corp.—some of the major corporations which turned to him to find its managerial maestros. Indeed, if a firm that small in size came to Roche for a chief executive he might have passed the search to a colleague. It could very well have been too small for him to handle.

"It had become abundantly clear that Gerry was a lousy CEO," contends one former Heidrick & Struggles consultant. "For an accounting major, Gerry had trouble reading an income statement, let alone a balance sheet. He had a lot of trouble with figures. Gerry's not a manager. He was just plain, flat out in the wrong job, and that was an opinion held universally throughout the firm."

Even beyond the nettlesome management problems and the nagging doubts over Roche's managerial abilities, some of his colleagues had come to resent him for his swaggering and uncontrollable ego. Roche was the best. Everyone knew it. But did he have to remind everyone all the time? "Gerry couldn't be in a room with other people without being on center stage," complained one who worked with Roche in New York. "Even in the small lunchroom at Heidrick & Struggles he would do anything to get attention."

Tapping into these sentiments, John Richmond began drafting a letter that some would interpret as a harmless call for more financial disclosure and that others would view as an attempted coup to remove Roche from office by undermining and openly questioning his authority. Richmond's secretary, who dabbled in graphology, would type up individual copies for each of the board members and would send them via Federal Express to Chicago in time for the firm's upcoming board meeting on September 23, 1980. Richmond called his colleagues, read the letter and asked if he could sign their names in support of the statement. Richmond was hoping for 20 signatures, enough he thought, to send a clear signal to the board that something was desperately wrong and the shareholders were concerned about it.

He didn't call everyone. Some Richmond did not trust. Others had only been at the firm a short time and did not know the extent of the company's troubles. Of the 25 or so colleagues he did contact, 15 agreed to have their names fixed to the letter. Another four agreed the message was timely and appropriate, but for one reason or another did not want their names visible. There were a few outright refusals as well.

John Sullivan, a tall, broad-shouldered man who headed up Heidrick & Struggles's Los Angeles office at the time, would have none of it. "I don't want you to put my name there because I don't feel that way," Sullivan told Richmond. "And you shouldn't do it. If you do it's not only bad internally, but when our competitors hear about it you're going to put a cleavage right down the middle of the firm. You could really hurt us."

Sullivan urged Richmond to meet with Roche privately and get his concerns off his chest. But he hardly could persuade Richmond to drop his campaign. He returned home that night and told his wife that Roche should at least be prepared for what he regarded as an attempted coup. The next day he decided to blow the whistle on Richmond. Sullivan told his immediate boss, western region manager David Elliott, a Harvard M.B.A. and former Peace Corps man in the 1960s, of Richmond's plans. Elliott, in turn, relayed the message to midwestern manager Bill Bowen in Chicago whose purview included the Cleveland office Richmond managed. It didn't take Bowen long to ring his Cleveland colleague and ask if he had known anything about it. Richmond had originally hoped that he could send the letter without identifying himself as the author. Now he had to fess up to the fact.

"What are you doing?" asked Bowen. "Why can't we talk about it? Is this the way to do it."

"I think we have been talking about it," responded Richmond. "But nothing seems to be happening and the problem seems to be getting worse."

"Don't worry about it," Bowen assured him. "It's not a problem."

"It is a problem," insisted Richmond. "I know it is a problem. People are telling me it's a problem. I like this firm and I don't want to see this happening. We've got a great company here. Let's make it work instead of letting it get ill and torn apart."

The letter, however, could not be retrieved. Richmond already had dispatched the individual copies to Chicago for the board meeting on Monday. But another major slip-up also had occurred. Every board member with the exception of Roche was sent a copy of the letter. Somehow by an inadvertent error, claims Richmond, he or his secretary had failed to include a copy to Roche, the chief executive whose managerial skills were being questioned. It was no less than another insult to him.

Roche and the others saw the one-page letter. And he read it over and over again. Dated September 17, 1980, and addressed to the board of directors, it read:
"Gentlemen:

"During the past eight to twelve months, various conversations among associates have indicated a deep and growing concern for the state of the firm. We have grown rapidly, we have experienced defection, we have opened new offices with some controversy, we are struggling with a support system which does not serve us with universal confidence, we have a new organizational structure, we have a growing but marginally profitable European business, and we are ahead on volume this year but way down in profit.

"In spite of growth, the depths of concern around the firm are creating an unhealthy situation. Some old timers are shrugging, turning to the comfort of their experience, doing their own thing and putting aside their wonderment of where we are going. Younger members of staff are, in many cases, left in a vacuum, feeling a lack of communication and concern from the top. With the announced abandonment of August bonuses in the face of a known cash squeeze, many eyes are focusing now, with great curiosity, on the 1980–81 year-end results.

"With profits to date down 75%–80% compared to a year ago, it is likely that one or all of the following will fall short come the fiscal finality of this year: individual overall cash compensation; profit sharing and deferred compensation contribution; stock appreciation, particularly related to the interest costs many shareholders are bearing. It is a shared and broad concern that should any or all of the foregoing materialize, the latent unrest will manifest itself in any number of undesirable forms.

"It would, therefore, seem highly desirable for the Board and senior executives of the firm to disclose to the shareholders, now, the financial picture in sufficient detail to emulate the disclosures of a public company. While the specifics may not please the shareholders, the very effort to communicate to those of us who have financial and career stakes in the firm will be far more effective now than in March 1981. We believe that an open sincerity of purpose is at least a sound step in restoring unity, and a manifestation of leadership which we know is a cornerstone of this firm."

On the surface, the letter only called for more open disclosure of the firm's finances to its shareholders. That was hardly a challenge to Roche. But between the lines one could find far more significant rumblings from some of the firm's top producers. Many of Roche's colleagues were essentially sending him the message that he had lost their confidence as the chief executive; they felt they had reason to doubt his word over the company's financial condition, and they wanted to see the real numbers themselves.

On the following page were the 15 signatures, some of them affixed by Richmond. As Roche's eyes gazed over the names, he grew stunned. But Roche was more than outraged and shocked. He was deeply wounded. For nearly 20 years he had tirelessly worked for the firm, was the best known executive headhunter ever, probably the best, too. And he had kept his firm in the public eye by placing more presidents and chief executives at major corporations than any other headhunter inside or outside the firm. He had fully committed himself. And now his very authority, his accomplishments and all that he held close were being challenged by many of the colleagues he had called his friends. Indeed, many of them were brought into the business by himself. He felt betrayed, unwanted, rejected.

"I was mortally wounded," he says slowly. For once, Gerry Roche isn't quick with a quip. He falls silent, loosens his tie and deeply exhales. "It was an enormous disappointment. I looked at the names on that letter. There were people in this office who I thought were close friends, people like Hoke Brissenden. That probably hurt me more than anything else, that Brissenden would sign that letter. Jesus."

It was to be the saddest day in Roche's professional life. For a man's whose life work was in assessing the character of people, Roche had greatly underestimated his foes. For a man who had the uncanny gift of infecting others with his own passions, he had discovered that he had failed to win over some of his most important colleagues. Roche believed he had the ability to reconcile the vast differences in the firm. They, instead, felt he was uncompromising, unwilling to listen to their concerns and their complaints.

The board, however, did not act on the letter. An incensed Heidrick believed it did not deserve a response. "Well, boys will be boys," shrugged Struggles. Roche was understandably furious. He called Richmond to find out why he, the chief executive, was the only board member not to receive the letter.

"Why didn't I get a copy?" demanded Roche. "Is there a message built into that?"

"I'm really embarrassed you didn't get one," ventured Richmond. "It was strictly an oversight."

Although the board didn't formally respond to Richmond's demands, the letter sparked lively discussion throughout the firm as word of its contents spread. "We didn't know where the money was going," says Richmond, "and not knowing gave room for suspicions." Some speculated that Roche was taking out too much money for himself and Heidrick. Whether founded or not, the rumors continued to fester. More Heidrick & Struggle partners considered leaving, and they would quietly whisper their thoughts of quitting the firm to friends and colleagues. They would wait until April, however, when the year-end bonuses would be safely in their pockets.

Alarmed by the rumors, Richmond and Hill arranged to secretly converge in Atlanta for a four-hour meeting on a Sunday afternoon to plot a mutiny. Richmond flew in from Cleveland; Vernon from Boston, and Garrison from Houston to meet up with Hill who had opened Heidrick & Struggles's Atlanta office a year earlier. Jokingly dubbed by Richmond the "April 5th Gang," they privately met at the Ionosphere Club in Atlanta's airport to ponder what to do. They kicked around the problems, ruminated about the possible solutions and speculated what risks they would assume by going to Heidrick and Roche and challenging their authority. Richmond wasn't alone in thinking that this little maneuver could cost him his job. "But I also had the support of the guys in Cleveland who said if it all blows up in everybody's face, we could turn right around and change the name on the door," says Richmond.

"We sat there with the numbers, did some projections and got scared to death about where the firm was going," recalls Garrison. "No one wanted to get Roche out of that position as leader, image maker, seller and all of the things he does so incredibly well. That would have been like cutting our wrists. We wanted a change of management so that someone would watch the operating side of the business on a day-to-day basis."

The four mulled over which of them might take Roche's place if they could convince him to resign. Garrison, the youngest of the group, had not endeared himself to many in the firm. By his own admission, he was mercurial, egotistical and arrogant. Garrison would send off memos critical of his colleagues from time to time. Vernon might have been a greater possibility. But still not as likely as Hill, whose painstaking attention to detail was well known. Hill thought he would make a good operations executive. He had told Roche so many times, and his friend Garrison considered him the best manager in the firm. But he came across as a tough, dominant and impersonal man not likely to gain the support of others in the firm. Richmond himself had often pondered what it would be like to be in charge. "I speculated on how good a job I could have done," he says, "what it would have been like. I felt I could deliver things that weren't being delivered."

None of them, however, would present himself as a successor to Roche. That was too boldly presumptuous. Rather, the four would ask for a meeting at which they would urge Roche to step up as chairman, and convince him and Heidrick to expand the board of directors who would, in turn, elect a new chief executive. Richmond called Roche to set up the meeting only four days after their secret session in Atlanta. Roche asked if he should be concerned. Richmond was vague. "We want to talk about a few things, and it all adds up to a very positive concern on our parts."

The four arrived to meet Roche on April 9 in the small anteroom off his New York office. To break the ice, Richmond reached into the pocket of his suit jacket and pulled from it a Milky Way and a roll of tape. He plopped both items down on the round marble-topped table with the brass base in front of Roche. The message was clear: Let us do the talking.

"Gerry," Richmond said facetiously, "we're going to get your mouth full of Milky Way and then we're going to tape it shut."

The group laughed. But the meeting was tense. They found a tired and weary Roche that afternoon. "He was beaten down," says Garrison. "He was killing himself. He was hurt. You could see it in his eyes." Arms folded, face impassive, Roche listened to their complaints, sometimes questioning their comments and openly speculating about their motives.

"Gerry," they told him, "the firm is going to hell. Look at the increase in expenses. Look at the profitability decline. Look at all the problems we've had in the last several years. These are problems due to the inability of anybody to give them the attention they deserve. We don't have controls in place. There has got to be a change."

"You would be happier and much more productive going back to search and occupying the chairman's position," suggested Richmond. At one point, he recalls, Roche leaned back in his chair and said, "You know, doing search work would be more fun than doing this."

After one and one-half hours of discussion, Roche gave no hint of what he likely would do. "I'll think about it," he told the group, "and talk to Gard." Nor did he reveal his true feelings to the foursome. But he understood their message clearly.

"What they did in that room was say these are the people who are going to leave this firm unless you do something," says Roche. "They will leave as a block and this will do that to your income statement and it will destroy the firm. That was the ultimatum,"

Roche says, swiveling in his high-backed chair while staring blankly out a window. "I sat in there and had these minion-minded munchkins come in and say we think something should be done. My attitude was take it. Fuck it, fuck you, fuck them. Give me my search work. Give me my wife and kids, and screw you all. I came within an eyelash of walking out."

Three days later, the four regrouped on a Sunday to meet with a reluctant Heidrick at Palm Beach Airport in Florida. Heidrick had refused to come off his vacation in Del Ray so they had to fly down to meet him. The confrontation occurred in a small, Spartan pilot's lounge in the general aviation section of the airport. Much of the conversation was a replay of their talk with Roche.

Heidrick wasn't antagonistic. He didn't even appear angry. Uncharacteristically reticent and taciturn, he sat stone-faced for over an hour as they tried to win him over. Heidrick would say nothing, would show no emotion. He thought they were a bunch of restless guys who wanted to run things themselves. If they believed he would undercut Roche, they were sorely mistaken.

"I want time to think about it," he told the group. "I came here to listen."

"We were surprised and disappointed that he didn't have more to say," says Richmond. "You could tell he would rather have not been there listening to what he was listening to."

The four wondered whether their meetings with Roche and Heidrick would suffer the same fate as Richmond's letter some eight months earlier. To insure it would not, they planned that Vernon and Hill, both members of the board, would carry the message to the next board meeting in an effort to force the issue.

Early in the morning on April 28, 1981, Heidrick & Struggles's eight board members gathered in the 32nd floor conference room of the firm's New York offices in the American Brands Building on Park Avenue. It was soon after Roche had doubled the firm's New York office space just as business "went to hell in a handbasket" as one headhunter put it. Many of the offices were empty. "It was like sitting in a mausoleum," recalls another Heidrick & Struggles consultant. Roche struck first, avoiding a likely confrontation in front of the entire board. He surprised both Vernon and Hill by abruptly resigning his position. Immediately after Roche quit as chief executive, another board member proposed that Bowen be elected president and chief executive officer.

It was an unexpected development, and both Vernon and Hill

sensed a setup. Bowen and Roche had long been close friends. An eight-year Heidrick & Struggles veteran, who was carving a niche for the firm in university president searches, Bowen had been enticed into the business by Roche himself. Back then, Bowen and Roche were neighbors who played vigorous games of paddle tennis and commuted together nearly every day on the 7:29 A.M. train from Chappaqua to New York's Grand Central Station.

Indeed, the two met one morning in the train's coffee car through a mutual friend nearly a decade earlier. Bowen, a Wall Street salesman, was introduced to Roche as the most knowledgeable baseball fanatic his friend had ever met.

"Okay," quizzed Roche, rising to the inevitable challenge, "who was Shovels Koveski?"

Roche figured he had him. Koveski was a little-known minor leaguer who never played in the majors. But Roche was in for a shock.

"He used to play third base for the Elmira Pioneers," quipped Bowen with a wide grin.

"I can't believe it," laughed Roche. "This is a setup. You put him up to this."

In fact, he hadn't. Bowen, a man hopelessly addicted to the game of baseball, had been a bat boy for the Elmira Pioneers in 1945. He has crooned "The Star-Spangled Banner" at several baseball stadiums and faithfully logs the daily scores of every professional game in a small record book he carries with him through every baseball season.

Bowen immediately won Roche over with his quick answer, and the two struck a close friendship. It later led to a headhunting call from Roche, who wondered if Bowen would be interested in leaving Shearson Hammill and Co., Inc., where he was manager of institutional sales, for a related job on the West Coast. He declined, but Roche eventually brought him aboard as a Heidrick & Struggles recruiter in 1973. When Don Williams quit the firm after Roche was tapped to succeed Heidrick as chief in 1978, Roche had dispatched Bowen out to Chicago to manage the firm's most important office in the Midwest. Two years later, Bowen's responsibilities took another jump when he was named central regional manager.

Now, Bowen was being proposed as an alternative to Roche. He was hardly a compromise candidate, and Hill would be damned if Heidrick and Roche could pull off this little maneuver. Two sides quickly emerged at the tense board meeting. In one camp were Hill,

Vernon, David Elliott and Gerard Clery-Melin, the French-born manager of Heidrick & Struggles's Paris office who had joined the firm only two years earlier from competitor Spencer Stuart. In the other camp were Roche, Heidrick, Johnston and Bowen. The vote split four–four on Bowen's election as chief executive officer.

Hill's group then brought up a motion to expand the board from eight to 13 members. The vote was deadlocked again. But each side refused to yield to the other. Quiet conversations would take place in the corners of the room. The company was without a leader. Roche already had resigned. So who would it be? "We drank a lot of coffee, ate donuts and took pee breaks," laughs one former board member. "There was a lot of talking. It was civil. Gardner would pipe up and say something pretty barbed at times. But it was not angry. It was intense."

As the hours wore on and the clock approached noon, a compromise was reached: Hill's group would accept Bowen if Roche's group would agree to expand the board. At least Roche had quietly acquiesced without a fight. He became chairman and went back to doing what he had always done best—search work.

"They got Gerry, they took him out as CEO," says John Sullivan, who had been running Heidrick & Struggles's Los Angeles office. "He enjoyed the job and it was heart wrenching for him to give it up. But when he did, he did it with a great deal of class and graciousness. He said things like 'I really want to get back into search.' But I saw him up close. It was a terribly tough time for him."

Roche, a religiously devout man who attends church several mornings each week, sought strength during that period through his faith. "Someone once said that Christ thinks so much of us that he allows us to participate in the redemptive process," philosophizes Roche. "I think when the Guy said pick up your cross and follow me he meant it. We get our load of crosses. Anyone who tries to get through his life by avoiding the cross is missing a hell of an opportunity."

But the power struggle led to even greater defections. In one 13-month period, encompassing 1981 when Roche resigned as chief executive officer, more than 25 professionals left the firm, nearly a third of its staff. One of the biggest hits was the departure in April 1981, the same month in which Roche stepped down, of Brissenden, Richard McFarland and Robert Knapp who left as a trio to start their own firm in Stamford, Connecticut, taking with them many of the clients they had cultivated while at Heidrick & Struggles and over $1 million in annual billings. A fourth Heidrick & Struggles headhunter, Carl Fuccella, a former Procter & Gamble executive, later joined them as a partner. The following year, placements fell to an estimated 500, from about 600 in 1981.

Of the four who led the revolt, only Richmond remained. Hill quit in 1981 to found his own firm, but eventually enlisted with Russell Reynolds's Houston office. Vernon was fired. Garrison left in 1982, taking nearly all of Heidrick & Struggles's Dallas office with him to competitor Ward Howell International, Inc. The move spurred a lawsuit which has since been settled out of court, but it took Heidrick & Struggles nearly four years to reopen a Dallas branch.

Among the departures was none other than Gardner Heidrick, the guiding founder and irascible boss himself, who left in 1982. Heidrick realized he could no longer impose his forceful personality on the firm as control and ownership became more dispersed. No less important, however, he felt cast aside as an outsider in his own firm. "The young guys wanted me off the board," he says. "I said I'd get off if you buy me out lock, stock and barrel."

After the firm agreed to buy his last 15 percent stake in the company, he stepped down from the board in the fall of 1981 but remained as a search consultant. Heidrick demanded control over the firm's search work for directors of boards, a specialty of his own, as well as authority over the firm's public relations activities. But relations between Heidrick and the younger managers of the firm had long been strained. He would fly into a city, visit the local Heidrick & Struggles office and commonly undermine the authority of the branch manager, the regional officer and chief executive Roche. Resentful over his interference through the years, the exasperated board members refused his request.

" 'I look at you as someone I respect," Bowen told Heidrick. "And I will always seek counsel with you even if I don't always follow your advice.' That wasn't good enough for Gard."

Powerless and embittered, Heidrick resigned from the firm he created in the spring of 1982. "They pulled the shade down," he says. "They blocked me out and I said the hell with it. I just don't think they wanted me around. I didn't want to leave. I didn't have to leave. But I'm an independent thinker and an operating executive. When you cease to be a part of things, what the hell?"

His departure, however, did little to bolster the firm's troubled image because Heidrick, although 71 years old at the time, did not quit to retire. He joined his son, Bob, in founding a new search firm, The Heidrick Partners, Inc., in Chicago in direct competition with Heidrick & Struggles.

Even many who stayed, including some of the firm's top producers, wondered whether they should take off as well. "I laid awake at nights asking myself, 'What are you Brenda, asleep?'"recalls Brenda Ruello, one of the leading women in the business and another Roche recruit. "But I never saw it being a benefit for me to leave."

It was people like Ruello who helped hold the firm together, who helped to take up the slack, enabling it to post record billings of $28 million by fiscal year 1986. But Heidrick & Struggles was no longer the top firm in the business as it was when Roche took over as chief executive in 1978. It had now fallen behind Korn/Ferry, Spencer Stuart, Russell Reynolds and perhaps even Egon Zehnder International, the European-based firm with only a small U.S. presence.

The firm had closed or was about to shutter half its overseas offices, including Milan, Madrid, Mexico City, and Leeds, England. Heidrick & Struggles's competitive position was irreparably damaged. "Our competitors had a field day," says David Peasback, who emerged as Heidrick & Struggles's first officially elected chief executive by the new corporate structure with 32 stockholders and broader ownership and control. "We were no longer head and shoulders above them anymore." Peasback took over for Bowen as chief executive officer in September 1983.

In retrospect, Roche believes he tried too hard to accommodate and balance the firm's disparate personalities and styles. "I tried to say, 'Hey fellows, we can be both Chicago conservative and New York liberal. We can be both domestic and international. My mistake was trying to keep divergent, strong-willed people happy in one family instead of saying, 'Larry, you're not going to get the job. You're unhappy and causing friction, why don't you leave?' But I didn't have it in me to do it, and I don't have it in me to do today. I didn't have the balls to tell those guys to get out of the firm."

Roche, claiming he holds no grudges, insists he was not forced out as chief executive. "Make damn sure we understand this," he says firmly. "You mean the attempted coup. There was no coup. Where are these guys today? Look where we are today. Look where

I am. I may have lost the battle, but I sure won the war. I am where I want to be, doing what I want to do, having the influence I want to have on this firm and the marketplace."

It was after all these internal struggles that Roche was to gain his biggest, most highly-publicized professional victory: his skillful wooing of John Sculley, president of PepsiCo, into the entrepreneurial company of the 1980s, Apple Computer. It was to earn him and the firm what was at that time the highest single fee ever paid to a search firm, a cool one-third of a million dollars plus expenses.

Roche landed the assignment in the fall of 1982. His orders—from then Apple Chairman Steven Jobs and then President A. C. "Mike" Markkula—were to deliver a top corporate marketing executive with broad domestic and international management experience who could fit into Apple's rather loose uncorporate working environment.

Roche placed his first call to John Sculley in December. It wasn't very productive. Sculley, on a Pepsi fast track with the chance for a future stop at the top as chairman, had no interest in leaving. You don't say no to Roche easily, however, so Sculley decided he should at least take the opportunity to meet Silicon Valley's pioneering Whiz Kids.

That meeting was arranged by Roche, but still didn't spark an interest in the job. Then came another session after Christmas as well as a stream of persistent calls and meetings in January, February and March from Roche, Jobs and Markkula. Still, nothing. He resisted Roche's constant entreaties to jump ship. There was a late-night dinner at New York's Four Seasons restaurant with Sculley in January after Jobs unveiled Apple's new Lisa computer at a press conference in the city. On another occasion, Apple executives came east to tour PepsiCo's grounds in Purchase, New York, to get better-acquainted with Sculley. By early March 1983 the relentless wooing was beginning to have an impact.

Roche had spent hours with Sculley, gently moving him from the "curious" stage to the "healthily interested" stage. Invoking images of a modern-day Renaissance and Sculley's role in it, he helped to bring the Pepsi-Cola executive around. "Gerry has unusual insight," Sculley would later tell a journalist. "He was able to see inside of me and figure out what it would take to make me excited. It wasn't the money or the chance to run a company, it was the opportunity, as he put it, 'to change the world a little.'

"Roche knew of my interest in art and architecture, and he talked about what it must have been like to live in Florence during the Renaissance. He drew the comparison that today, the best minds of the age are flocking to Silicon Valley. That approach had more impact on me than anything."

The first offer from Apple came in mid-March, nearly three months after Sculley received the first phone call from Roche. It was not nearly enough to get him to leave the security of Pepsi-Cola for the unknown at Apple. Nor, Roche said, was what he abstractly calls "the comfort level with Apple" right. Roche let Sculley know it, too. "I said, 'Hey, John, here are the facts,'" says Roche. "Here's the upside and here's the downside. And there was a time when there were two major negatives where I was saying, 'Sculley, I don't think this is right. If I were in your shoes I'd steer clear. If you want to go ahead with it, go ahead. And he did, indeed, turn it down and it wasn't only money that did it. I always say it's your decision, here are the pluses and minuses and you ought to check this out yourself. Because I don't want you coming back in three years, blaming this kid if it goes wrong."

Sculley appreciated that. "Gerry has a way of becoming the best friend you'll ever have at the time you need him most," he later said. "When I was still wrestling with it, he said 'Look, John, if it doesn't feel right, don't take it.'"

Jobs flew into New York, and he and Sculley took a Sunday afternoon stroll through Manhattan's Central Park and the Metropolitan Museum of Art. Whether it was the setting or the continued persistence of both Apple and Roche, Sculley was plainly hooked.

Still, several hurdles existed. Apple would have to put a lot of money on the table to get him to leave. "If my family didn't want to move, that was a deal breaker," Sculley told *The Wall Street Journal*. And there was the close relationship he had with PepsiCo chairman Donald Kendall, Sculley's former father-in-law, who had thought of him as a potential successor.

Over dinner, Sculley shocked Kendall with the news shortly after his Sunday walk with Jobs. If Kendall wanted to keep Sculley, Apple made it difficult. The company, Kendall said, "kept putting the ante up." The PepsiCo chairman ultimately conceded to Sculley that the opportunity might be too good to pass on.

The offer that eventually would snare Sculley came two weeks later. It was an extraordinary package, giving the executive more than four times his current $500,000 salary in the first year. Dangling a carrot that large in front of someone is pretty persuasive in itself. Forget the talk about a 1980s Renaissance. The deal included a $1 million sign-up bonus, a $1 million annual salary, $1 million in guaranteed severance pay should things not work out, options on 350,000 shares of Apple stock and help in buying a $2 million house in Woodside, California. Sculley arrived at Apple's Cupertino headquarters in May 1983.

The search raised eyebrows and howls from many of Roche's competitors who were shocked to see their profession publicly exposed in such detail. This was, after all, still a profession in which client-and-candidate confidentiality was expected and demanded. Yet much of this tale was recounted in a story in *The Wall Street Journal*. So the code of secrecy was broken.

What they didn't know, however, was that publicity-minded Roche had little to do with placing the story. "I called Regis McKenna up and told him *The Journal* was banging on my door and we don't talk," Roche says. "He said, 'Talk. Tell them anything you want to.' Well," laughs Roche, "my mother's name was Amelia." McKenna, one of the brightest stars of the PR business, knew the true value of this attention. As a corporate outsider coming into the Valley for the first time, it was in Sculley's interest to make a big splash. It helped Apple's image among investors, too, because the article left the impression that Jobs recognized his company needed professional management. Sculley would eventually work to oust Jobs from the company in 1985 to assume total control of Apple.

Regardless of what founders Gardner Heidrick and John Struggles always told Roche, the publicity didn't hurt. To this day, other search firms in Silicon Valley get calls from companies seeking another John Sculley. That includes Russell Reynolds's Price, whose work in getting Paul Ely out of Hewlett-Packard and into Convergent Technologies doesn't make him a slouch. "I'm tired of people calling us up and asking me who did the John Sculley search," Price moans.

In the days immediately following the completion of the Apple search, Roche received numerous calls from potential clients wanting to hire him. "Success," Roche bellows, "breeds success. One person read that story and said, 'We want another Sculley. And I'm sure you have a list of them.' I said to myself, like hell I do. I have to go out and scour the country again because I don't know another Sculley. It takes fresh digging to do that. We will pull something out of the hat. Whether it's another Sculley or not, we don't know. But he's got to roll the dice with us. He's got to have faith and trust in us."

All true, to an extent. But when dealing in the upper reaches of the executive suite, the pool of young talented already-successful executives eager to assume the risks involved in a switch is small. Candidates for these hot, big-ticket jobs have a way of being inexhaustibly recycled by headhunters from one search to another. Robert R. Frederick had surfaced in a previous Roche search before connecting with RCA. And Sculley, for example, had been seriously considered for at least one other job by Heidrick & Struggles only a couple of months before Roche approached him with the Apple opportunity.

Sculley's name had cropped up in a meeting Roche had with Steven J. Ross, the chairman and chief executive of Warner Communications, some four months earlier. At the session, held in Ross's conference room at Warner's corporate headquarters, Roche was there along with John Ingram and Louis Gerstner of American Express to discuss a search for a chief executive and chairman of Warner Amex Cable Communications, Inc. A major cable-television concern, Warner Amex was a loss-making joint venture of Warner and American Express Co.

At first, the strategy was to comb some of the nation's slow-growing, staid businesses for skillful yet frustrated chief executives. "The idea was to look at depressed industries where CEOs may be stalled and would want to go for the glamor and sex of Warner Amex," Ingram remembers. "It didn't work. We were going to double or triple their salaries. Money was no object. But most of them were too loyal to their companies."

Mulling over the names of potential candidates at the meeting, Roche and Ingram had presented a list of 20 possibilities. That group was being narrowed down to a half dozen finalists: the six included Sculley; James Morgan, a Philip Morris marketing genius; Archie R. McCardell, who had been bounced from his job as chief executive of International Harvester in May and was now on American Express's board of directors, Norm Blake of GE Credit Corp., Drew Lewis, Reagan's Transportation Secretary, and one insider.

Ingram, a former American Express executive who had joined Heidrick & Struggles in 1980, was assigned to do the actual search work. He reached Drew Lewis through levels of Washington receptionists, and soon met him for the first of six meetings. The Transportation Secretary would send his government limousine to Washington's National Airport to pick Ingram up and bring him to his office. Ingram eventually delivered Lewis to the job in December 1982, the same time Roche began speaking with Sculley about a certain computer company in Silicon Valley.

A mere three months after Sculley left for Apple in April, Roche pulled another Sculley out of the hat. He got Morgan, another of the candidates who came up in the Warner Amex search, to take over Atari, Inc. as chairman and chief executive. Roche did it again. Morgan's departure in July 1983 surprised many of his colleagues because he had been considered a company loyalist. A 20-year veteran who joined Philip Morris straight out of Princeton University, he rose to executive vice-president of marketing at Philip Morris, Inc.'s domestic cigarette operations.

Like Sculley, Morgan had a shot at succeeding the company's chairman, George Weissman. Yet, here he was joining a deeply troubled company whose future was all but certain. "Morgan had an extremely bright future at Philip Morris," Roche says. "But you are taking someone who would have to wait four or five years to get his stop at the top versus the guarantee of becoming a CEO at a $2 billion company right now."

It proved, however, a jolting move for Morgan. The year he joined in 1983, Atari piled up losses of more than half a billion dollars. Two months after Morgan publicly said he had the company under control in May of 1984, Morgan found himself cleaning out his desk. Warner Communications, Inc., owner of Atari, sold the firm. Its new owner, Jack Tramiel, the fiery founder and former president of Commodore International, fired Morgan immediately. Roche had persuaded Morgan to give up his chance to compete for the chairmanship of one of the nation's consumer marketing giants for a job that, it turns out, lasted all of ten months. Roche says he has fixed Morgan up with a consulting job with his friend Mike Dingman, then president of Allied Signal.

Roche is the first to say there are no guarantees. He owes his loyalty to his client, who pays the bill. If things go awry, his allegiance is to the client. "Suppose," he says, "that an executive goes out there and spends nine months in the job, comes back and says, 'Hey Roche, dear buddy, it's not working out and I'm ready to run another company so let's do that.' We have to say we put you in there, but we cannot take you out. We can't lift a finger without the client's permission. Of course, you can go to Russ Reynolds or Spence Stuart or Korn/Ferry, but you can't talk to us. The first thing we'll say is, 'Hey, take it easy. You're only there nine months. What's the problem?' We'll try to put oil between the friction points."

Lubrication doesn't always work out, as Roche's Arthur Taylor, Maurice Valente and James Morgan placements show. That leads to some fairly disgruntled candidates. "His is purely a body selling service with no loyalty and an enormous amount of gossip," complained one former executive placed by Roche in a major corporation which he has since left. Neither could any fair amount of oil ease the friction that led to the resignation of another of Roche's big-name recruits in recent years, Thomas Vanderslice.

A hard-driving General Electric executive of 23 years, Vanderslice had been passed over for the top job at GE when Jack Welch got the nod to succeed former Chairman Reginald Jones. Roche brought Vanderslice to GTE as president and chief operating officer under Chairman and Chief Executive Officer Theodore F. Brophy in December 1979. It was a fabulous deal: a five-year employment contract at a minimum of $325,000 annually with a cash bonus of $124,000 the first year plus another $200,000 worth of "phantom stock" to make up for lost benefits at General Electric. Not to mention the most enticing prospect of all—the possibility of succeeding Brophy as chief executive. Only three years after taking the job, Vanderslice pulled down $726,560 in cash alone at GTE. Then he left abruptly, four years to the day he joined, when Brophy, 60, made it clear he was going to stick around.

In a shocking revelation, *The Wall Street Journal* reported that "GTE veterans also were irked that Mr. Vanderslice had sought some top jobs outside the company. He applied for the presidents' slots at RCA Corp. and CBS, Inc., both of which eventually went to other candidates." Both these searches, of course, were being conducted by Roche, who could not ethically have considered Vanderslice for either of them because GTE was his client.

When Vanderslice left, however, he was again up for grabs. He could be recycled. Eight months later, in August 1984, he was named chief executive and president of Apollo Computer Corp. in Chelmsford, Massachusetts. Impatient Vanderslice was finally a chief executive officer. But at a company whose sales were under $100 million in the previous year, far below GTE's $13 billion total.

Still, his compensation package was nothing to sniff at. Apollo agreed to pay him $250,000 a year, along with a guaranteed first-year bonus of $90,000 and a second-year bonus of $258,000. The big bonanza, though, came in the form of Apollo equity. The company handed to him 200,000 shares of its stock, then valued at $4.4 million, in return for a token payment of $4,000. It amounted to a $4.4 million sign-up bonus.

Interviewed by *The Wall Street Journal*, Vanderslice said he and Apollo founder J. William Poduska were referred to each other by mutual friends, including John Cunningham, president of Wang Laboratories, Inc., and Kenneth G. Fisher, chairman and president of Encore Computer Co., who once worked for Vanderslice at GE and was Poduska's boss at Prime Computer.

What? No Gerry Roche? A visitor asked Roche recently if he knows who placed Vanderslice into Apollo.

"Who put Vanderslice in Apollo?" he shouts. "I absolutely did, without any question whatsoever. The fact that you asked me that question pisses me off. Why the hell did that son of a bitch tell *The Wall Street Journal* that someone else did it? If you think that doesn't irritate me, it does. And I've told him so. I called him on that and he said, 'Oh, they misunderstood.' Hmm."

Wanted: A Muscle–bound
Exec with Brains

"I want another me, without the faults."

IN THE MIDST of an icy Detroit winter, it was to be another brisk though brilliant January day. The sun was shining brightly barely two weeks after the Christmas holidays, and John F. Johnson was sitting in the back seat of a yellow cab that sorely needed a wash.

This was a familiar trek for Johnson, a 41-year-old man in a blue pinstripe suit with a flashy gold diamond ring on his right hand. Speeding east on Interstate 94 from the Detroit Airport, past all those roadside symbols of what Detroit was all about, the cab zipped by Goodyear Tire's tall, looming sign that keeps track of car production, past Uniroyal's monstrously huge white-walled tire, past Ford Motor Co.'s headquarters and into the heart of Detroit.

Some 25 minutes and $30 later, the cabbie would race down a rather seedy street, drive through two white gates and pass a sentry before depositing him in front of a large brick building which faced a shivering Detroit River, with chunks of ice bobbing in the water. It was 100 River Place, the new corporate headquarters for The Stroh Brewing Co., the nation's third largest brewer. The building was planted on the spacious grounds of Le Cote Du Nord-Est, a historic site that was the corporate headquarters of Parke, Davis & Co. in 1874.

Johnson dashed out of the cab and into the building's second-floor reception room, an open space organized around a large square cocktail table littered with copies of *Packaging Digest* and *Beverage Industry*. It was an area filled with briefcase-toting salesmen in rumpled suits waiting for the chance to make a pitch.

Johnson, something of a salesman himself, wasn't there to sell today. Instead, he was to meet with Stroh President Roger Fridholm to talk about starting a search for a $250,000-a-year executive vice-president of sales and marketing. He had decided that no one inside the company boasted the general management experience necessary to fill the newly created post. Fridholm had first talked about the possibility of bringing someone in nine months earlier, but he wasn't quite ready then. Now, Fridholm wanted to move forward, to let Johnson know exactly what he wanted.

In the privacy of Fridholm's small wood-paneled office, with a small refrigerator stocked with beer in a corner, the two exchanged greetings and quickly got down to business.

"John," Fridholm said half-jokingly, "I want another me, without the faults. My own leadership style is low-key, maybe cold-blooded. I want someone with more external charisma. What I really want is a guy who has an M.B.A., good marketing skills and looks like Dick Butkus."

"Holy Christ!" laughed Johnson. It was probably tough enough to bring a top marketing executive to a privately-held, family-owned brewer located in, of all places, Detroit. But a macho football player-type, too? A Dick Butkus? The beefy six-foot-three, 245-pound defensive linebacker for the Chicago Bears? Known in his playing days for his "terrifying presence" on the line, Butkus was built like the muscle-bound bear he was.

Fridholm's remark, however, was no off-the-cuff comment. This new executive would have to wheel and deal with Stroh's distributors, a group which included a good number of ex-jocks just out of the locker room. Among Stroh's more than 1,200 wholesalers, in fact, were Willie Davis, the former all-pro end for the Green Bay Packers, and Mel Norman, a former all-pro lineman for the Kansas City Chiefs.

"Beer people are big people," explained Fridholm, himself a tall yet slender executive. "And when they get into this business, they get bigger, at least around the waist.

"Of the top guys in our sales force, there are a number who are over six-foot-four and weigh more than 300 pounds, so a certain presence would be helpful," he told Johnson.

With that in mind, the pair began developing what, in headhunting parlance, is known as "the spec." Typically, it comes in the form of a two-page outline, detailing the job and the desired attributes of candidates. Stroh's, obviously, wanted much more than mere "presence." Johnson's marching orders, among others, were to find an executive with at least 15 years of consumer-packaged-goods marketing and sales experience. Fridholm knew the beer industry well, and he doubted that his ideal candidate would be plucked out of it. So he asked Johnson to look over marketing executives in both beverage and consumer packaging companies. All of these needs would be committed to paper and sent to Fridholm later for approval.

A cab was called, and Johnson made the journey back to the airport to board a plane for the half-hour return flight to Cleveland, where he is based. Over the past six years, Johnson has made this trip dozens of times. This 1984 search for brilliant brawn would be booked in Lamalie Associates' files as #203–16, the last two digits indicating that it was the 16th search Lamalie would perform for Stroh's since Johnson's first visit here in late 1977 (the 203 stands for Stroh's). A lot had changed since then, for him and Stroh's.

A former General Electric group manager, Johnson was then a relative neophyte to the search business. He joined Lamalie Associates' Cleveland office as the third man on the totem pole in 1976 and in 13 months had completed fewer than half a dozen searches, none of them in the beverage business. He was a 35-year-old man who looked more like 28 despite the long sideburns which framed his boyish-looking face. Eyebrows were raised, too, when Johnson told Stroh's executives that as an active Christian Scientist he didn't drink a sip of beer and kept no alcoholic beverages in his home. "The question my wife had was, 'Are you going to represent a brewery?' " says Johnson.

Business, of course, is business, and Stroh's was a small, family-run outfit mainly in the business of quenching local thirsts. Peter Stroh, the sixth generation brewer, was president of the company, which had less than a 4 percent share of the beer market. But Peter, as he is known, was intent on remaking the conservative regional brewer into a marketing dynamo. Central to this transformation would be Stroh's aggressive pursuit of acquisitions, not only of other beer companies such as Joseph Schlitz Brewing Co. and F. & M. Schaefer Brewing Co., but of human assets, too, professional managers from the consumer marketing giants.

Stroh's was then headquartered in offices attached to a classic brewhouse of copper kettles, brass fittings and hand-fired tiles built in 1912 on Elizabeth and Gratiot in Detroit. The building, about two miles from the company's new quarters, had all the trappings of Stroh's Old World origins. "You went back in time when you walked into their offices," says Johnson, who recalls the overpowering pungent aroma of hops in the air. "They were wood-paneled offices, decorated with old pictures of the Stroh family, and each office had a private bathroom. There was a certain awe and respect it generated."

Johnson's initial visit in September 1977 resulted in his first assignment for Stroh's. The delivered product? Roger Fridholm, a former McKinsey & Co. consultant who had been working as a vice-president in Heublein's international division. Fridholm's placement was an unqualified success story, and Stroh's became an excellent case study of how an executive headhunter can play a critical role in rejuvenating the management of a company.

Fridholm joined Stroh's as vice-president for planning and development in April 1978. Three promotions and four years later, he was named president and chief operating officer, only the second nonfamily member to hold the post in the company's 200-year history. With this 16th job, Johnson would have installed 20 percent of the company's senior management team of 25 executives. It was an impressive, skillfully wooed, lineup which included senior vice-president John H. Bissell from General Mills, group vice-president Kenneth A. Tippery from Insilco Corp. and vice-president William L. Henry from Ford Motor Corp. Meantime, the company had quadrupled its production of beer, established a market share three times greater than when Johnson first arrived and had emerged as the third largest brewer after Anheuser-Busch and Miller. "He has been the main implement in helping us build the organization and bring in professional management," says Fridholm.

Johnson was no longer a green tenderfoot in the business, either. Named president of Lamalie, the sixth largest executive search firm, he now had to his credit some 115 completed assignments over seven strenuous years of crisscrossing the country. During that time, he tallied up thousands of hours interviewing nearly 1,500 executives in person in becoming Lamalie's number one producer. And this year, 1984, he was well on his way toward establishing a firm record in billings—$616,333, nearly double the Lamalie average of $339,868 per consultant.

Johnson, a highly-driven and intense workhorse, knew this latest job would not be easy. No search for Stroh's is a piece of cake. Because it's a privately-held company, Johnson cannot dangle the prospect of lucrative stock options before his candidates, nor are all executives eager to move their families to Detroit. Indeed, many can seldom restrain their scorn when Johnson gets to the point of mentioning the exact location. Fridholm was one of them.

When Johnson first called Fridholm at Heublein, the marketing executive listened, not entirely willingly, to his pitch. Johnson had abstractly described his client as a "regional midwestern brewer." Fridholm guessed blindly but correctly which company it was. Far from tempting him, however, it put him off.

"You don't mean Stroh's?" he asked Johnson.

"Well, I suppose I can tell you. It's Stroh's."

"In Detroit?"

"Yeah."

Fridholm laughed aloud. "You're out of your mind! Why would I want to join a regional brewer in Detroit?"

Pursued relentlessly by Johnson who ploddingly aroused his interest, however, Fridholm eventually made the move from tranquil Simsbury, Connecticut. "He's very persistent," says Fridholm. "It's the telephone calls I remember most about John. He'll call anywhere up to 10:00 or 11:00 at night. And if you're not at home, he'll talk to your wife. He's a real fanatic. He'll take no for an answer, but he'll never take maybe. And once he gets close to the kill, he's all over you like a blanket. He's one of the best I've ever seen."

Fridholm doesn't make that statement without perspective. During his nine years in New York, three with advertising agency Benton & Bowles and six with McKinsey & Co., he would get lots of calls from headhunters. One primary reason was his association with McKinsey, the most prestigious management consulting house in the country. Headhunters make it their business to keep track of McKinsey people because they are on many corporations' "Most Wanted" lists. The small, blue McKinsey alumni book, holding the personal phone numbers and addresses of ex-McKinsey people, is a must for every headhunting library.

"In those years in New York, I met more executive search people than the average person by about a 100-to-1 ratio," Fridholm says. "Some of my best friends are search people, as they say." Lonsdale Stowell, an eccentric independent headhunter in New York, put Fridholm in Heublein, in fact. And at Heublein, where he would average a body-snatching call once every three months, Arlington, Texas-based James C. Orr Associates presented him as a finalist on a search for an important slot with a major financial institution.

But Johnson, who possesses a clean-cut, ever-youthful appearance, boasts a self-involved style that deviates from the headhunting norm. Many recruiters swear that you can't be a success in this business without inextricably mixing together both your professional and personal lives. Not Johnson. He and Fridholm, a loyal bedrock client, have never been together on a social occasion. "In my town," he says, "I'm known as Mrs. Johnson's husband. My wife taught first grade. She's the focal point. I keep a very low profile. I'm not like Gerry Roche or Russell Reynolds. I don't have a high ego need. I don't have a limousine to pick me up. The firm is built on the basis of good work, not who you know, who you drink with and who you play golf with."

In a business dominated by gabby, gregarious glad handers, Johnson is something of a paradox. Although respected for his aggressiveness and insight, he has neither the personal warmth nor social presence of many executive search consultants. Bob Lamalie, a former Booz, Allen & Hamilton consultant who founded Lamalie Associates in 1967, had once hired a psychologist to dissect Johnson's psyche to find out what makes him tick. The firm requires that its consultants undergo a chat on the couch before they are hired. Some executive recruiters, by one count as many as 20 percent, use psychological testing to screen candidates. But Lamalie is not one of them.

The psychologist's report on Johnson, however, removes some of the mystique over his success in an essentially social business. "It is not at all necessary for him to have people around him all of the time, especially those who travel the cocktail circuit and enjoy engaging in social chit-chat," the psychologist wrote. "Though Johnson falls short of being a 'cold fish,' it is nevertheless true that he prefers to limit his acquaintances to a select few. To be sure, he is no social joiner. Were it not for his ability to act interested in people, Johnson might conceivably alienate clients and/or candidates who do not like to be treated impersonally and who very much enjoy being wined and dined to the hilt."

Like a savvy salesman, he is a chameleon, whose flexibility in varying his personality allows him to succeed in the business. "Johnson is an exceptionally hard-driving, results-oriented and achievement-minded individual with a strong sense of urgency," the psychologist concluded. "He is energized by a fear of failure."

Johnson, who has kept the psychologist's five-page evaluation tucked away in a drawer at home as something of a joke, laughs about many of its findings. But he concedes that some of them are perceptively on target. "As Bob Lamalie once put it," he says, 'A good search man is driven by greed and fear of failure.' I haven't learned how to throttle back and smell the flowers. My wife would say I'm not trying very hard."

Typically, Johnson is in the office by 6:00 A.M. Breakfast? Not much more than a sugar-coated doughnut and several cups of black coffee. He usually works through lunch, eating only one meal a day. And these are 15-hour days. On Sunday afternoons, he starts the cycle again, working until late at night. It's not just the incredibly long hours he puts in, because many of his successful colleagues clock the same totals. It's how productive he makes those hours. Johnson does not squander time, his most precious resource.

To Johnson, exercise is walking through airport terminals, which he does frequently enough. Flying is a grueling reality for the head-hunter. This year, in the course of the Stroh's search, he would log between 120,000 and 140,000 miles in the air, some 225 flight segments on 16 different airlines. "If he spent more time in the air," says a colleague, "he'd have to have wings."

Traveling back to Cleveland on the steel wings of an airplane after his meeting with Fridholm, Johnson is dictating into a tiny tape recorder the specs for the Stroh's search. He knows what Stroh's wants in an executive and what type of man would mesh with the brewer's laid-back management style.

In the spec, Stroh's is described as "a major, free-standing beverage manufacturer which has grown dramatically through acquisition. The company's sales are now approaching $1.5 billion, and its distribution network spans the total United States and Puerto Rico."

The nitty-gritty of this document, however, is Johnson's description of the ideal candidate. It derives from the accumulation of his search work with Stroh's and from his conversation earlier in the day with Fridholm. Dictating into the machine, he notes that although an advanced degree is preferred, it isn't necessary. More critical is the person's mix of experience and style.

Under the heading "The Candidate Should Have," Johnson runs through a long, seemingly never-ending list of superlatives, a list no living executive could possibly meet, a list likely to provoke an uninterested yawn from any disinterested observer of search. Still, the spec establishes a mutual understanding with a client at the outset on the search's objectives, and it cements in writing the hunt's guidelines. Johnson continues to talk into his little machine.

"A minimum of 15 years' consumer-packaged-goods marketing and sales experience, preferably having held key management responsibilities in both sales and marketing functions.

"The leadership and management ability to build both strong marketing/product management and national sales organization.

"Experience in dealing with major high-volume national brands.

"Preferably dealt with a large distributor or store-door delivery network.

"The capacity to interface effectively with operations management, advertising agencies and major distributor organizations.

"Strong interpersonal skills to be able to sell ideas and strategies to top management and implement them within the headquarters and field organizations.

"Above-average intellectual capabilities so as to be able to approach long-range problems strategically.

"Excellent written and oral communications skills.

"An image which will gain him credibility with the distribution organization while, at the same time, allow for continued growth within the corporation."

That last, vaguely described attribute translated into contemporary language meant: Bring me a big, brawny jock with brains.

Under the final heading, "The Candidate Should Be," Johnson dictates another six, somewhat amorphous qualities. They comprise the equivalent of an executive's Boy Scout oath.

"A mature, results-oriented business executive who understands the consumer-packaged-goods industry.

"A person who values the building of strong relationships, both inside and outside the company.

"A quality-oriented individual who knows how to be personable but who is tough-minded enough to assure that bottom-line profits are maximized.

"Creative and conceptual in his approach to marketing issues.

"A person with people sensitivities and skills who is capable of building a strong team to continue the growth of the organization.

"Highly principled and ethical in his business conduct."

The spec is often a typical blend of the obvious. Would Fridholm expect Johnson to bring him someone who was not highly principled and ethical, someone who lacked creativity or was not quality-oriented? Of course not. Yet all these attributes, many of them seemingly obvious and insignificant, also would form the basis of a contract with the client. However doubtful that anyone could meet all those qualifications, the paper is there, like it is everywhere in our society today, to be pulled from the file when problems emerge. It is the kind of document that gets entered in court proceedings every day.

"The spec becomes Mr. Wonderful," notes Johnson. "And the chances of finding Mr. Wonderful are almost nil. So the spec becomes the target you're shooting for."

Days before this trip, Johnson began lining up some of those targets. Because he and Fridholm had spoken about the search for months, he basically knew what the Stroh's executive wanted. Before visiting with Fridholm, Johnson had called Lamalie's research department in Florida to get the search in motion even before he booked it.

A backroom intelligence-gathering outfit, the seven-member research group combs 40,000 unsolicited resumes which come in annually and peruses $30,000 worth of directories and periodicals, many of them obscure, dull, little Bibles for their respective industries. The staff scans and clips 50 publications from *The New York Times* to *Robotics Today,* tracking clients and potential candidates for Lamalie's headhunters. New files are opened on hot new people moving up the corporate ladder. And there are files on 10,000 companies, too, with annual reports, 10Ks, clips and sometimes organization charts. It is a veritable mini-CIA, keeping track of corporate hot shots. And all employed to give the firm's headhunters a quick start on a search.

Headhunters who lack such resources contend that executive recruiters are only as good as their appointment calendars and address books. But all the major headhunting firms boast sophisticated research arms such as Lamalie's, and they are vital to the successful completion of a search. Job-changing executives and managers inundate Lamalie and the other large search firms with tens of thousands of unsolicited resumes annually, all in the hope that their names will one day pop up. Indeed, one small, though highly respected search firm, Gould & McCoy, was receiving so many unsolicited resumes—a blizzard of 40,000 annually at its New York office—that it has stopped acknowledging them. Managing director Bill Gould gave up actively reading the resumes after finding too few needles in too many haystacks. "Out of the 40,000, we've kept 40 and shredded 39,960," he says. "And of the 40 people we contacted, probably 10 were interviewed in person. Of those, five executives were presented to clients as candidates, but only one ended up with a job. That's one out of 40,000. So we don't save any of them now."

That seldom occurs at the major headhunting firms. Lamalie discards most of the tens of thousands of resumes it gets in the mail each year. But in common with Lamalie's major competitors, the firm typically saves anywhere from 5 percent to 20 percent of them for their active headhunting files. Few searches are completed out of these existing files because recruiters prefer to approach people who are not actively in the job market. But a trip to the databank is among the first steps in any executive search.

Johnson had asked Nancy Clausen, a tall, cadaverous woman who is Lamalie's director of research, to run a check of the firm's databank for potential sources and candidates. Ensconced in a computer at Lamalie headquarters in Tampa are 23,600 mini-resumes of executives gathered over years of search work. The resumes include home and business addresses and telephones, base salary and bonus figures, educational and professional background, geographical preferences, when the person was last interviewed and for which searches he was considered. Some other firms boast more elaborate systems. Boyden Associates, for example, includes a rating (from 1 to 5) for candidates in its databank and ventures personal comments on some. One Boyden file, for instance, noted that an executive candidate was "not very attractive."

Clausen, a University of Chicago M.B.A. and former manager of information services for Borg-Warner Corp. and advertising agency Tracy-Locke, plugged into the computer Johnson's qualifying criteria and out came the names, hundreds of them. He wanted all general management, sales and marketing executives from consumer-packaged-goods companies as well as all consultants with marketing experience earning $100,000 or more a year. The computer spat out 302 possibilities. The likelihood that his candidate would be among these 302 executives was slim: little more than 15 percent of all Lamalie searches are filled with a candidate who orginates from the database. These contacts, however, may prove to be essential sources who might finger the person Johnson will eventually deliver to Stroh's.

After formally booking the search on January 9, 1984, when the research department cataloged it #203–16, Johnson had other demands for Diane Cardwell, the 29-year-old assistant director of research. The research strategy was to identify marketing and sales execs in the leading food and beverage companies whose experience included work with a major distribution network or store-door delivery. These executives would be added to the list compiled from the databank.

With Johnson, Cardwell developed a "target list," companies in which Johnson would prowl for executives. Obvious target companies were those in the beverage industry, so Cardwell sent along *Beverage World's* list of the top 100 companies. Also lumped in were a vast array of more than 50 consumer packaging companies from Campbell Soup Co. to Dannon Co., Inc. Only two of the firms on the list, Consolidated Foods Corp. and Dart & Kraft, Inc., were totally blocked. Johnson could not pirate executives from any division of these companies because they were recent Lamalie clients. But he could ply those client executives for suggestions on other candidates in the industry.

If Cardwell could not find the top three or four marketing executives in each of these companies in Lamalie's database, she then turned to a slew of directories to dig out their biographies. Cardwell also spent three hours telephoning a dozen companies, from A&W Beverages, Inc. to PepsiCo, Inc., to identify and confirm their top marketing executives. This way, Johnson would waste as little time as possible when he placed his calls to these managers.

The researcher put all this information in a package, along with organization charts from Lamalie files on 15 beverage firms, including Coca-Cola, PepsiCo and Heublein, and dispatched them to Johnson in Cleveland, who would begin the tedious and time-consuming job of working the phone to find Stroh's a new executive vice-president.

To help speed up the process, Johnson wrote a "sketch" letter, a one-pager, largely cribbed from the spec, which briefly yet succinctly describes the position, candidate requirements and compensation package with an unidentified midwestern company. Any upwardly-mobile executive receiving this document in the morning's mail would likely fix on the money: "Base salary, annual bonus and long-term incentive will be attractive to an individual currently earning up to $250,000 in cash compensation. Other executive perquisites include a company car and club."

Indeed, what executive wouldn't be flattered to be singled out among the thousands with what almost appears as a personal invitation to be considered for a plum job. Here you get an unsolicited opportunity dangled in front of you. If it doesn't immediately prompt a telephone call to a headhunter, it should put you in a helpful mood when he calls. And that's what Johnson is hoping. "Most individuals call me up with themselves in mind," says Johnson. "But it is a marketing tool. It opens up a door to make a contact with someone you might not know. In some cases, a guy might say I fit the spec but the dollars aren't big enough for me. I'd say yes, I recognize that. We show you were making so and so, is that accurate? So it also gives us an opportunity to update our databank files."

The executive, of course, doesn't know that on this search another 100 people—largely selected by Johnson from the batch of 302 executives culled from the Lamalie databank—also received the same letter. On another recent search by Johnson for the president of a $200 million (sales) company, the headhunter mailed out an astounding 600 sketch letters. So much for exclusivity. You've got to kiss a lot of frogs to find a prince. The sketch letter is little more than targeted classified advertising in a business in which the use of advertising is discouraged. A client, after all, could just as easily put an ad in a trade journal and get the same results as a headhunter without having to pay him a fee. Instead, he is employing the headhunter to come up with someone he otherwise would be unable to connect with.

The spec, neatly typed by Johnson's secretary, was sent to Fridholm via Federal Express to convey a sense of urgency. On January 18 Johnson would travel to Detroit again to finalize the spec and gain Fridholm's approval. Fridholm had sent a copy of the spec to Peter Stroh, the soft-spoken American aristocrat to whom he reported. It was returned by Peter with a few scribbles in blue ink. Stroh noted that there was nothing in the original spec "about the future. What would happen if something happened to you or I." So Fridholm, marking up the paper in green ink, noted that the individual would have the "potential to succeed to the president and chief operating officer responsibility." There were some other minor changes as well: instead of "above-average intellectual capabilities"

Fridholm wanted "superior"; instead of requiring "between 25 percent to 50 percent" of travel, he thought it was more like "10 percent to 20 percent."

Now it was all up to Johnson. Back in his modest, no frills office in Cleveland's National City Center, he starts working the phone. There are no English foxhunting prints here, a nearly ubiquitous feature in headhunting offices. Lamalie offices are tastefully decorated but lack the lavish elegance of a Russell Reynolds or Heidrick & Struggles branch. The difference in style is even reflected in the calling cards Lamalie consultants carry in their briefcases. It is a nondescript white card crammed with too much information in black print, not the off-white Heidrick & Struggles's model or Reynolds's understated light blue-inked cards with lots of white space.

In his office, Johnson looks like a disk jockey in a cluttered radio station studio. That's because he typically paces about the room with a telephone headset fixed atop his blond hair. The eight-foot-long cord allows him the flexibility to reach any part of his office for a crucial piece of paper. Pink-colored messages litter his desk, and stacks of paper files are laid out on his credenza, couch, windowsill, corner table, chair and desk. It is not the office of an executive Johnson would recruit. It's more like the office of a journalist, with all his papers scattered about. He never entertains clients or candidates in his office because it's so messy.

But it's here, amid the organized clutter, where Johnson rolls into the standard, nearly rehearsed monologue that should make a candidate wonder whether every executive recruiter was trained at a Headhunting University where classes are held behind potted plants in airport lounges.

"Hi," the voice would say. "This is John Johnson of Lamalie Associates, the executive search firm."

"Yes."

"I'm working on a search to locate an executive vice-president of sales and marketing for a consumer-package-goods company. The person would be coming in over an existing vice president of sales and vice president of marketing. I want someone who has worked both sides of the house, but who has demonstrated the ability to deal effectively in the marketplace."

The big difference was his last comment. "If this individual happened to have the stature of a Dick Butkus, that would be a plus," Johnson would venture. "What I was trying to get across to people is that what I'm really looking for is a man's man." And then the chuckles would come. But occasionally the remark would bring someone to mind. That occurred on January 27 when Johnson called one of the 302 executives fished from Lamalie's databank.

The contact was a management consultant with one of the major firms in the business whom Johnson had never met but whom he had spoken with as many as a hundred times over his headhunting years. He had been a valuable source, pinpointing executives whom he came in contact with on various consulting assignments. Today, the consultant gave Johnson five names, including two Coca-Cola Co. executives and one Canada Dry manager.

Sometimes, the call locates a potential candidate, not just a source, who seems to meet the specs. "You've got to start screening people out on the phone," says Johnson. "If a guy doesn't turn you on over the telephone you probably don't meet him. Normally, I'll ask the guy to send me something. If it's not well-presented, that tells you something, too."

By telephone and sketch letter, Johnson would eventually contact 155 of the 302 executives pulled from the databank, 45 other executives identified from Cardwell's research and 93 managers whose names cropped up in sourcing calls. These led to in-person interviews, typically two-and-one-half hour sessions, with 16 executives over a five-month period stretching into late May.

The first was to occur over a lunch in New York on February 7 with a top-level marketing executive for a major consumer goods corporation, Chesebrough-Pond's. Some headhunters say they can tell within 60 seconds whether a guy will make it past the first hurdle; others boast with bravado that they can tell a lot about an executive by his handshake. Johnson, though, doesn't use one-minute impressions, trick questions or gimmicks to weed out people. "I'm sure if you shook hands with a gorilla," he laughs, "he would have a very solid handshake. But I wouldn't recommend a gorilla to a client. At this level there are no schlocks in terms of dress, either. Nobody came in a mismatched sports coat and plaid tie."

Certainly not the first man Johnson met. His handshake was firm, and his sartorial appearance suggested a level of success and status that allowed Johnson to easily envision him behind an executive desk at Stroh's headquarters. The executive was an outgoing man in his late 40s, handsome and intelligent. Not only did he appear to have the right credentials, he was well over six-feet tall and had played a mean game of basketball during his college days.

Returning to Lamalie's New York office at 101 Park Avenue, he would pull out a "ratings" sheet to help guide him through an initial evaluation on the man he just met. Johnson would rate the individual on a one-to-five range (five being the highest) in six categories. Stroh's would never see this rating, but it would help Johnson decide if he would make the final slate of candidates who he would eventually present to Stroh's.

Johnson began dictating the kind of evaluation which would virtually assure that the Chesebrough-Pond's executive would get a shot at the job.

Appearance: six-foot-three, 195 pounds. Graying hair. Well-dressed executive presence. Athletic appearance. Rating: 4+.

Intelligence and alertness: reasonably smart. Strong gut feeling for advertising issues. Good grasp of business with multifunctional experience. Seems alert in questions, but I don't know how good a strategist he is? Rating: 4−.

Personality and maturity: outgoing, relaxed. Seems to be poised. Need to test his interpersonal impact at Chesebrough-Pond's. Obviously had some problems. Rating: 3+.

Drive and aggressiveness: wants to run a business or be the top marketing and sales executive. He is a pusher, a driver, aggressive in his pursuit of his goals. Wants to make sure he makes the right move. Rating: 4−.

Verbal expression: excellent presentation. Good verbal presence. Rating: 4−.

Experience in profession: on the surface has all of the pieces. Good grasp of consumer marketing. Need to test out what really went wrong at his company. Rating: 4−.

That was just one candidate evaluation. Many more were to follow as Johnson made his rounds. Later that same afternoon on February 7 Johnson met another candidate from PepsiCo. The following day, at the Stamford Marriott in Connecticut, he would interview yet another PepsiCo executive.

On February 22 Johnson flew to Louisville, Kentucky, to meet with two Brown & Williamson officials at the Executive Inn East, one in the morning, another in the afternoon. The following day, February 23, he interviewed two more candidates, an R. J. Reynolds Industries executive in New York and yet another PepsiCo executive at the Red Carpet Club in Chicago. But it wasn't until March 6 in Atlanta when he met another candidate who, he thought, could possibly fit.

The executive was no Dick Butkus. He was a soft-spoken man of 47 years, dressed in a European-cut suit, and not much taller than five feet ten. He wore half-moon spectacles, blue-stone cufflinks and a neatly-pressed white shirt. His name was Wayne Jones, and he brought to the meeting a short resume, modest academic credentials and a worldliness that only an executive seasoned abroad could have. There was only one company listed on that resume: Coca-Cola. He joined the firm in 1959 as an Oklahoma district manager, not long after graduating with a B.S. degree from the University of Florida. And he never left. Jones was named vice-president of marketing in 1983 after spending 11 years with Coke in overseas jobs in London and Tokyo.

His name had surfaced from several sources. As a senior executive of Coke, he was listed as one of 18 vice-presidents in the *Reference Book of Corporate Managements,* a four-volume gold-covered compendium which serves as the recruiter's Bible. It lists some 75,000 American executives and directors in 12,000 U.S. companies. To have arrived here, as Jones did, within the nine inches of pages of the directory, is to be guaranteed a never-ending parade of headhunting calls. More importantly, though, Jones also was one of two Coke men who had been recommended to Johnson by the management consultant five weeks earlier.

When Johnson first called him, he expressed little interest in the job. "The timing was disastrous," recalls Jones. "My wife, Patricia, and I had only returned to the U.S. a little over a year ago and had just moved into what we considered to be our dream home." It was a beautiful four-bedroom home which had been owned by an acquaintance whose tastes were nearly identical to their own. From the outside, the house looked as if it could have been perched atop a Mediterranean cliff overhanging the sea. The front doors opened to a spacious foyer confronting a soaring 20-foot-high window in English Regency style. Their seven-year-old son, Jordan, had just settled into school, too. So Jones suggested a few other candidates to Johnson and quickly got off the telephone. In the nearly 18 months at Coke as vice-president of marketing, Jones received some 50 calls from headhunters, giving each a polite no and then going about his work.

Unlike most of the others, however, Johnson would call back. "These people had been looking for three years for somebody they felt could do this job, and they simply haven't been able to find anyone," Johnson told Jones.

"Did you speak with any of the other people I recommended?" asked Jones.

"I've been in contact with some of them," Johnson replied, "but I think my client would be interested in you. Are you curious to know who my client is?"

"No, I'm not," retorted Jones.

Johnson laughed.

"Well, haven't you figured it out?"

"John, I really haven't given it much thought."

"Well, it's Peter Stroh at Stroh's brewery."

The information perked Jones's interest immediately. He had known of Stroh, who also was a Coca-Cola bottler in Detroit, for years. Although he never met him, Jones knew that Stroh had an excellent reputation in the business.

"The person they need will be the number three man on the management team," continued Johnson. "Peter supplies the vision. The president, Roger Fridholm, supplies the architecture. What they need is somebody to build the house."

That was an argument which Jones found both intellectually and emotionally appealing. Finally, he agreed to meet with Johnson on March 6.

The 7:30 A.M. meeting was scheduled over breakfast at the Ritz Carlton Hotel in Atlanta. Johnson and his guest tried to get seated in the hotel's restaurant, but it was too crowded. So the two made their way into Johnson's room. It was a small room that looked lived in. The bed was unmade. The fog had not yet lifted off a muggy Atlanta morning, and it made the room all the more claustrophobic.

The pair ordered up some black coffee and then began a two and one-half hour meeting.

"Take me from day one," Johnson told him. "Tell me a little about your early days growing up, family life, high school days." And Johnson often would give Jones, as he would all his candidates, a time limit of ten to 15 minutes to run through his background. "If a half hour goes by and he is only now getting around to college, it tells me he isn't well organized, isn't disciplined or maybe he just doesn't listen," says Johnson. That was not the case this time.

Jones boasted an enviable marketing background, having been involved in many of Coca-Cola's major marketing decisions over the past two decades. He was a member of the project teams which led to the introduction of Sprite in 1961, Fresca in 1962 and Tab in 1963. While in Japan from 1973 to 1977, Jones established a fruit juice business there for Coke, building it from scratch to $250 million in revenues in five years.

During his next six years in London, he helped Coke significantly improve its market share in northern Europe. And like all American executives who work for their companies abroad, he lived and savored the good life—vacationing throughout Europe, fishing for salmon in Norway, eating at the most elegant restaurants. In London, he and his wife lived in Onslow Square, just a ten-minute stroll from Harrods, where they would often shop, and five minutes from Britain's stately Victoria & Albert Museum. Since returning to Atlanta in 1983, Jones has authored the company's first worldwide marketing plan.

As Jones recorded these professional and personal high points for Johnson, the headhunter was mentally recording the man's physical appearance, personality and style. Is he articulate or not? Assertive or retiring? Well-liked or dreaded by peers? Dressed for success or dressed for failure? Straightforward or manipulative? Participative or autocratic? Johnson was feverishly scribbling notes on a white, lined pad as Jones answered his questions, one after another.

The meeting ended at 10:00 A.M. Although the room was confining and stuffy, neither man took off his jacket. And Jones, who chain-smokes cigarettes, did not light up. Johnson wasn't euphoric. Besides Jones's appearance, which didn't quite fit the job description, Jones had acquired in his years abroad a cultivated air about him —from the sophisticated veneer over his southern accent to the European-style clothes he wore. Johnson wondered if Jones, a genteel, courtly southerner with an international flavor, would be able to work well with Stroh's rough-and-tumble network of beer distributors. Still, Johnson thought that Jones could likely become another candidate he would present to his client. These were his initial impressions, laid down on a rating form shortly after the meeting:

Appearance: five-foot-ten, 175 pounds. Dark suit, wavy gray hair—little bit of the European look, not the robust executive the company described. Rating: 3.

Intelligence: deceptively smart, straightforward, direct, logical thinker. Nothing fancy, but gets to the points quickly. Good grasp of business in general as well as the specifics of marketing. Rating: 4.

Personality and maturity: relaxed, friendly, smiles a lot, animated. Always on the edge of his chair. Aggressive. Seems to be open. Rating: 4.

Drive and aggressiveness: feels he is blocked at Coke after having done an outstanding job in moving Europe. Wants to run a business but has been put in a holding pattern. Rating: 4.

Verbal expression: good grammar, articulate. Well thought out with a slight southern accent. Rating: 3+.

Experience and profession: outstanding track record of consumer-package-goods marketing. Beverage sales with international and general management profit-and-loss exposure. While his physical package isn't what Roger described, unique experiencial (sic) capabilities make him an interesting and possibly solid match. Need to check out effectiveness in the sales environment. Rating: 4.

"Experiencial capabilities." It was a curiously awkward phrase that Johnson would often employ. It simply meant experience. But like a technician who gets too close to his work, Johnson had developed a strange lingo foreign to outsiders of his profession. "Spec" was among the words in the language. So was "sketch." Or "off-spec," meaning that a candidate did not meet the desired qualifications for the job. A person could be "too staffy," perceived as lacking enough line job experience. If this candidate has "unique experiencial capabilities" that put him ahead of many others.

There were still more interviews, however. Ten days later, on March 16, Johnson met with another marketing executive in St. Louis; four days later he met with two more, one in Stamford and another at Lamalie's offices in New York. His afternoon session in New York was to be another productive meeting. He then met Benjamin J. Sottile, a personable and chunky 46-year-old executive formerly with Warner Communications, Inc.

Sottile, a 1961 Naval Academy graduate and a highly principled executive, had joined Warner as senior vice-president of consumer products in 1981. When Warner's once successful Atari video-game division proved a fast fading fad, Sottile began selling off Warner's Knickerbocker Toys and Warner Cosmetics, both units of his consumer products group, to raise cash for the company. In the process, he effectively sold himself out of a job. Warner offered him another spot in the corporation, but he decided to become a free agent. Johnson's timing was perfect.

The candidate boasted 18 years of sales and marketing experience with such companies as Colgate-Palmolive and Warner-Lambert. "The fact I'm built like a beer drinker didn't hurt my chances," says Sottile, a five-foot-eight, 200-pound man. It helped, too, that Sottile was on the board of directors of the New York Cosmos, the professional soccer team. "He was fascinated that I could apply the needed skills of the job and yet not be above the people that mattered."

The two hit it off well. "He struck me as being less of a flesh peddler and more of a philosophy matcher," says Sottile. And Johnson was sufficiently impressed to add his profile to the few he would submit to Fridholm for consideration. But Sottile warned Johnson that he had two problems with the opportunity. First, he preferred to remain in New York. Secondly, Sottile felt he had invested years of his career cultivating retail channels in consumer products. He wasn't sure he wanted to turn his back on that investment and begin anew with beer distributors.

The interviewing, meantime, continued. On April 9 Johnson met another pair of candidates, a General Mills executive at 10:30 A.M. in an airline lounge at the Minneapolis airport, the other for dinner in St. Louis. Over and over, Johnson would run through the same careful ritual, ask the same questions, take voluminous notes and dictate them for the rating sheets.

And at nearly every stop in each city Johnson also would meet with other candidates for the nearly half dozen searches he was juggling at the same time. Johnson was then searching for chief financial officers for Armco and Bausch & Lomb and the president of a small company. It is another occupational hazard, prompting one headhunter to remark that he often feels like "that little guy on the Ed Sullivan Show, the one who spun plates on the long poles, dashing from one to the other, not letting them drop." Frantically racing from one city airport to another, Johnson must have felt a sense of camaraderie with this Sunday night television juggler.

With six searches in the air, it took him three months after his January meeting with Fridholm to finally draw up a list of four candidates he would present to Stroh's. The others had been weeded out for various reasons. A few candidates clearly could not have meshed with the company's culture. One, in particular, possessed an unbounded sense of his own superiority and an uncontrolled ego which knew little restraint. A couple of other executives were, as Johnson put it, "too staffy"—they lacked experience in line jobs. Others had too much experience in sales, yet not enough in marketing. And one wasn't interested in the job.

Johnson again made the trip to Detroit on April 11 for a 9:30 A.M. meeting with Fridholm that lasted until noon. The two went over the "profiles" detailing the backgrounds of each of the four

144

candidates and how each related to Stroh, and then Fridholm ranked the executives by preference. At the top of the list was Sottile, the former Warner Communications executive in New York, immediately a problem because of location. Ranked next was the former college basketball player at Chesebrough-Pond's, the General Mills guy and finally Jones of Coca-Cola. "On the surface," recalls Fridholm, "Wayne was a bad fit. But he had so many other good characteristics that John threw him in, saying 'Here's a guy with an awful lot of talent that you should see.' I always tell John that if he finds someone who is unique or good don't hesitate to send him in even if he is off-spec."

Of the four candidates, Fridholm met first with the Chesebrough-Pond executive in Detroit only six days later on April 18. Fridholm liked him. "He was very solid, but I was looking for more spark, charisma and a little more apparent leadership," he recalls. "This person might have had it, but he didn't appear to have the zip I was looking for."

Johnson tried scheduling meetings with the first and third ranked candidates, but they already had dropped out by accepting other offers within the month they were interviewed by him. Sottile withdrew after a New York headhunter became the go-between for a job he took at Revlon in May as senior vice-president of Revlon's Beauty Group. The General Mills executive, meantime, had been lured to the Midwest to become chief executive officer and president of a sizable corporation.

If Johnson wasn't panic-stricken, he was at the very least somewhat worried. He had been at work on the search for over three months, presented four candidates and now half of them were unavailable. So Johnson kept trying to develop more candidates. On May 9 he interviewed a management consultant for Coca-Cola at the Stamford Marriott. The following night he had dinner with another PepsiCo executive at the same hotel. On May 22 he met another Coca-Cola executive in New York, and the following day a Seven-Up manager. Johnson liked the Seven-Up official enough to send Fridholm a profile on him, but by this time Stroh's interest was gravitating toward Wayne Jones of Coke.

Jones flew to Detroit from Atlanta after work on May 2, slept one night at the Westin Hotel in Detroit's Renaissance Center and met Fridholm in his office at 8:30 the next morning. The pair spoke nonstop for four or five hours, then broke for a quick lunch in the company's downstairs cafeteria where Stroh's beer is sold on tap. "It was very much a let's-feel-each-other-out meeting," remembers Jones, "like the first round of a boxing match." Fridholm must have liked what he saw because, among other things, he gave the Coke executive Stroh's marketing plans for further study and comment.

"Wayne looked very good right off the bat," says Fridholm. "I was positive on him in every way, other than the fact that he had just come back from England and had developed a very elegant manner. I wondered if he could go out and talk to beer wholesalers and work the trenches. I thought he had the leadership, but the degree of elegance concerned me. It was probably ideal for Coke. And I knew it would fit with Peter because he is a very elegant individual. So was Willie Davis (the former pro-football player) for that matter. But some beer distributors aren't.''

Meantime, Johnson had been on the phone before and after the meeting with Fridholm and Jones, giving both a mini-briefing on what to expect from each other. After the meeting, he called Fridholm for his reaction. Johnson later dialed Jones to tell him things looked good enough for a second meeting.

Johnson knew what Jones was going through. He had been on the other side of a job hunt, too. Bob Lamalie stumbled onto Johnson during a 1974 search for a vice-president of human resources for Youngstown Sheet and Tube Co. Johnson, a Columbia University M.B.A. who scraped through Tufts University with a B.A. in economics, had been organization and manpower manager for General Electric's air conditioning division in Louisville, Kentucky. Lamalie's client, which has since been acquired by LTV Corp., rejected Johnson for the job.

But Lamalie and he kept in touch and eventually Johnson joined the firm in mid-1976. "I was 34 and concluded that if I ever was going to test whether I could succeed outside the GE environment this was probably the time to do it. If I fell flat on my tail at 36, I would still be a marketable commodity." Far from falling flat, Johnson discovered his professional niche. For six of the past nine years, he had led the firm in billings, averaging as many as 18 searches a year.

Johnson relished the job's challenges, its frenetic pace and its rewards. At Lamalie, headhunters typically earn better than half of what they bill in any given year. Well on his way toward more than $600,000 in billings for 1984, Johnson could expect the kind of money he could only dream of at GE. "I liked the lifestyle, the independence, the fact that you were going to be as good as you were, that you controlled your own destiny," he says. "All the things that had frustrated me in a large organization like General Electric seemed to be gone."

Yet, he labored through new frustrations encountered by his new colleagues. Many corporate clients just wanted him to deliver a body, and many candidates were perpetual lookers who had no intention of leaving their companies. "My good clients develop a relationship in which I am truly an extension of their organization," Johnson says. "They trust me implicitly, and I trust them. We share sensitive data with each other. But other clients won't give you all the cards. They operate as if you are strictly a headhunter who brings nothing else to the party other than recruiting."

While Johnson raced around interviewing four additional candidates for Stroh's, Jones arranged to fly to Detroit for an extra two days of meetings. Those sessions didn't occur, however, until more than two months later on July 10. Few headhunters would muster the patience for such a long delay. But both executives had heavy traveling commitments and could not easily break them. This time, Jones flew in with his wife, Patricia, who would go prospecting the following day with a real estate agent in Grosse Pointe, an exclusive enclave of plush homes for many of Detroit's automobile executives. Although no job offer was yet forthcoming, they agreed that because of the long delays it would be helpful to take certain steps prematurely to speed up the process.

They arrived July 10, and Jones spent another four hours with Fridholm in his office, discussing the candidate's views on Stroh's marketing plans and the similarity between their management styles. The next day, while Patricia Jones toured the best of Detroit, Jones ran through a series of interviews with five Stroh executives, including an afternoon session with Peter. He met with the two executives who would report to him: John Bissell, group vice-president for marketing, and Kenneth Tippery, group vice-president for sales operations and market development. And he also met with Richard Lodato, senior vice-president of administration, and Arthur Tonna, executive vice-president of operations. They were courteous, but they threw the outsider some tough questions, too.

"What are you going to bring to the party here?" asked Tonna, who had behind him 35 years of experience in the beer industry and came into Stroh with its acquisition of Schlitz. "When I came here I brought a whole organization, six breweries. What are you going to bring?"

"Myself, Art," managed Jones.

Both Tonna and Lodato wanted to insure that Jones wasn't another Madison Avenue-type interested only in making pricey television commercials. "They were concerned that I would come in here and worry about making pretty television pictures," says Jones. "I assured them that I wasn't interested in spending all of Stroh's money on TV."

Mindful that the Jones's had just purchased what they considered to be their "dream home" in Atlanta, Fridholm wanted to sell the couple on Detroit. Occasionally, a courted executive or two had slipped from his grasp because of his refusal to relocate in the area. "This time, I didn't want to take any chances," he says. So Stroh's put the pair up at the lavish Country Club of Detroit in Grosse Pointe and scheduled an evening dinner at the Grosse Pointe Club, an elegant tennis and sail club on the shores of Lake St. Clair. It was a perfect, enchanting summer evening. Warm. Breezy. Sailboats gliding on the water of the lake, reflecting the day's brilliant sunset into a clear, blue sky. No better commercial for a city which has seen better times. "It tends to instantly change one's stereotype of Detroit," says Fridholm.

This was an informal gathering as well. No more hardball questions. No more carefully structured answers. Just casual conversation among the Joneses, Peter and Nicole Stroh and Roger and Henrietta Fridholm. They sipped cocktails on the club's outside deck, overlooking the picture postcard scene. Fridholm had a Stroh's Light. If Jones thought it would be an apropos move to order up a Stroh's beer, he resisted the temptation. Following Nicole Stroh's lead, Jones asked for a gin and tonic. And after their drinks they adjourned to the club's interior for a relaxing dinner. It looked like Jones had passed the test.

On this trip, however, he also discovered that Stroh routinely sent all its senior executives for an evaluation by an outside industrial psychologist. Jones would be no exception. The meeting, among other things, was to assess his "personality" fit with the organization and its top managers. The ground rules permit the shrink to tell the candidate anything he wants to know about other Stroh executives.

Unwittingly, the psychologist performed the Coke executive a great

148

favor. He would later tell Fridholm that Jones had played semi-pro baseball in northern Florida. Jones was a scrap hitter who played both as a utility infielder and left fielder in a ragtag league during his last two years in high school. ("You've heard of class D, C, B and A? Well, this was sort of Class F.") Nonetheless, it erased any nagging doubts that Fridholm had over Jones's courtly manner. "Anybody who plays baseball in the Florida League must have ridden those buses and can certainly deal with beer people," thought Fridholm. "What that told me was that Wayne was quite adaptable. What I had initially seen was his residual manner from five years in England and a high level at Coke."

While the two parties were getting closer to making a deal, Johnson was constantly on the phone with them, paving the way for an eventual offer. He was finding out how much it would take to extract Jones from Coke, and he was playing the role of a negotiator between the two. Johnson also was performing subtle reference checks on his candidate. He would call up other Coke executives, asking them for names of possible candidates. If they named Jones, he'd ask for a little more detail about him. If they didn't, he'd say someone else did. "What do you know about him?" Johnson would ask. "You do it by throwing half a dozen names at a guy and he doesn't know who you're really focusing on," explains Johnson.

The reference checks were, however, turning up some disconcerting information on Jones, the kind of intelligence that kept Johnson tossing in his bed at nights. While the executive's reviews were good, the consensus was that Jones could never be pried from Coca-Cola. "Everybody said he'll never leave Coke," says Johnson. "He just came back, his dad's on the board, his whole career has been with Coke, he's a Coke man dyed in the wool."

And Johnson, in common with every headhunter, has had his share of unexpected, last-minute dropouts. "There is," he says, "a phenomena in this business known as the wife grabbing the prospective candidate by the you-know-whats and squeezing. And it's amazing how much more pressure that can bring than money, title or anything else. If you get a surprise at the end, I'd bet that 75 percent of them are due to the wife saying, 'You want to go, go ahead, but I'm not going.' I know of situations where guys have accepted jobs and on the day they were suppose to show up they call and say I'm not coming."

That's why Johnson would often try to speak to the wives of his candidates by phone. "If you call the house and the wife casually says, 'Oh, I'll tell him you called,' you know damn well she isn't looking forward to the prospect of relocation. It's different than calling up and hearing her say, 'Hi John. Tony has told me all about you. He's not home right now, but he'll be in a little later.' What you hear is a supportive wife."

Johnson, too, correctly detected that Jones's wife was not overly enthused by the prospect of a move. So over the dozens of telephone calls with Jones he would invariably pop the question: "Are you sure you'll be able to leave Coke?" "At times, there were various degrees of confidence in the yes. Sometimes I asked twice in the same conversation," recalls Johnson. " 'Are you really prepared to leave Coke?' Because until he does you never know. The big question was would Wayne, when push came to shove, quit Coke."

It was an intriguing question. Coca-Cola Co. executives and bottlers, it is said, believe in Coke with an unabashed passion. Robert Winship Woodruff, the late patriarch responsible for making Coca-Cola one of the most widely known brand names in the world, once said he considered the company "a religion as well as a business." He was not engaging in hyperbole. E. J. Kahn, Jr., author of *The Big Drink,* a book on the company, recalls a time when Woodruff dispatched a cynical press agent to look over an assemblage of Coca-Cola men and report to him on their esprit de corps. The agent returned visibly shaken. "These boys are beyond me," he reportedly told Woodruff. "They believe in the Holy Grail."

With Jones, it was that and more. His father, Joseph, had worked for Coke since 1935, had been a longtime personal friend and secretary to Woodruff and still maintained at the age of 71 his senior vice-presidency and his seat on the Coca-Cola board of directors. As an adolescent, sitting at the dining room table, Jones would hear his father tell stories about the great company and its guiding genius Woodruff, who served as president from 1923 to 1955. Coke ran in the family's veins; it was part of the fabric of their lives. After all, Jones was a 47-year-old man who had worked his entire life for only one company.

It would prove a wrenching decision. "I had always been happy with Coke and had a very exciting career there, and every indication was that I wasn't at the end of my growth," says Jones. "I wasn't certain I wanted to give up 25 years and a future that looked bright."

Jones spent hours in seemingly endless discussion and debate. Patricia agreed she would go, but Jones clearly sensed that she would prefer to stay in Atlanta. Several of his closest friends advised him to take the opportunity, and his father—to whom he bears a remarkable resemblance—was simply supportive of any decision he made.

The courting continued. Fridholm and Jones had a long telephone conversation on July 25 which led to a dinner meeting in Detroit on a Tuesday six days later. In Jones's earlier session with the psychologist, he had taken the Meyers-Briggs personality test. It revealed that both Jones and Fridholm were similar types—commandants rather than sergeants or lieutenants. "That can be a weakness because if you put two similar people together you can have problems," says Fridholm.

"I don't know if we're going to be able to work together because we're so similar," he told Jones over dinner.

"I know you're the president and I won't forget that," Jones replied. It allayed any lingering doubts prompted by the test's results. The test itself also resolved any questions Fridholm entertained as to why Jones would consider quitting Coke.

"I couldn't see why he wanted to leave," explains Fridholm. "That was always a puzzle in my mind. But I finally realized that he would be leaving for the same reason I left Heublein. I was very well regarded there, but I wanted to get out and run my own show to a greater extent than I could at Heublein at that time. I use to say to myself that someday I'd make a good boss because I'm such a lousy middle manager. I had trouble working down very far in an organization. I guess that's what drove me. At Heublein, I was a sergeant or a colonel, but not a commandant. I realized that was what was motivating Wayne, too."

On August 1, some seven months after Fridholm's meeting with Johnson during a cold Detroit winter, the Stroh president made a formal offer to Jones over a three-hour breakfast at the Country Club of Detroit. He slipped Jones a three-by-five file card on which he scrawled in pencil the four objectives Stroh's expected of him. Fridholm wanted the candidate to "establish leadership with the sales organization; to upgrade the sales network; to translate and execute the marketing plan and to absorb marketing issues and assume a key role in marketing planning and development."

Jones convinced himself to take the offer. "Opportunity," he reasoned, "knocks just once and there are a lot of missed opportunities in the world. If I turned it down, I would constantly say to myself, 'Oh, Wayne, you should have gone.' And I didn't want to spend the rest of my life saying I should have taken it. I've watched people deny themselves opportunities and they generally end up kicking themselves later."

Jones also discovered what many of the headhunted do. Seduced by the potential of new challenges, greater autonomy and more money elsewhere, many who answer a headhunter's call are forced into a reassessment of their lives and careers. The ego receives some tender stroking, confidence shoots upward and suddenly you begin thinking about life in another environment. Once you answer the siren call, you invariably feel the need to leave. And the closer you come to winning a talent contest elsewhere, the less likely you are to remain content in your existing position. As one headhunter puts it, "Here's someone without an itch. You start the itch, and he eventually feels the need to scratch."

"Once you open the door, you open yourself to a lot of vulnerable feelings," confirms Jones. It had happened to all four of the executives Johnson initally presented by profile to Fridholm. Two were gone before Stroh's could interview them. A third left his firm within months. And now Jones was ready to ditch his newly-acquired beautiful home and move from Atlanta to Detroit to work for a beer company.

Johnson remained in contact, asking Jones whether Coke would likely make a counteroffer when he told the company of his decision to leave. If that was a possibility, Johnson would have to psychologically prepare his candidate to reject it. This was often a critical phase of closing a deal. Headhunters claim that counteroffers often can backfire on candidates because companies make them only at gunpoint, as a last resort to keep an important executive. If the company truly valued him, it would have given him the raises, promotions and attention before he was ready to leave. Johnson could save his little speech on this topic because Jones assured him a counteroffer from Coke was unlikely. "Coke has a lot of pride and never gives anyone a counteroffer," he told Johnson.

The time finally arrived when Jones would have to let Coke know he was going to leave. "It was one of the toughest days of my life," he says. After an agonizing weekend, Jones reported to work on Monday, August 20, and told Coke he was considering an offer elsewhere and wanted an opportunity to discuss it with them. In one day, he had meetings with Chairman Roberto Goizueta, President Donald R. Keough and Executive Vice-President Ira Herberto. "It came as something of a shock to all of us," recalls Jones. "The general reaction was, 'You have to make your own decision so make it. But you have a future here and you should weigh your decision carefully.' "

Before beginning work at his new job on Monday, September 17, Jones vacationed in Nantucket for ten days, walking the sandy beaches of the Massachusetts island, dumping behind his experiences at one of the world's business institutions and ruminating about his personal future. "I left 25 years of Coke on that beach," he says. "What Stroh's didn't buy or what I had to be careful not to bring was the Coca-Cola way of doing business. I came here prepared to enmesh myself in this culture."

Stroh's announced the move on September 4, and *The Wall Street Journal* carried the news the following day. When the change occurred, headhunting researchers across the country noted the top-executive shift in their files. Another head had been hunted. Like Wagnerian operas, searches do end. And back at Lamalie headquarters in Tampa, researcher Diane Cardwell closed out the half-foot-thick file on search #203-16.

The Brewing Wars Among Headhunters

"Shootout at the executive corral."

EVEN FOR A Halloween, when tricks are threatened upon those failing to offer treats, it was a nasty surprise. Storage Technology Corp., one of the highflyers of the new high-technology age, had no treats to offer that October 31, 1984. Instead, it sought protection from its jittery creditors by filing for Chapter 11 under the Bankruptcy Reform Act.

Flamboyant founder Jesse I. Aweida, a Palestinian immigrant and former IBM engineer, had guided the maker of data-storage equipment through over a decade of rapid growth. Profits and sales jumped an average 40 percent annually until 1982 when the company broke the $1 billion mark in revenues. Then, things began to unravel. Technological delays postponed deliveries of some products; price cuts on competing products by IBM eroded Storage Technology's margins. In 1983, the company posted a $41 million loss; in the first nine months of 1984, it lost another $86 million.

Now, on Halloween of all days, Storage Technology became the biggest victim of a growing shakeout in the computer industry. Chairman and chief executive Aweida likely would become a victim of the crisis, too, along with his brother, Naim, who served as president and chief operating officer. Storage Technology, meanwhile, would become a lucrative client for a sharp headhunter.

This would be a plum job, indeed. Aweida was pulling down nearly

$500,000 in salary and bonus a year. The headhunter who could capture the assignment, therefore, would capture a whopping six-figure fee in the process. No search firm could immediately stake a claim on the project. First, it would have to pass muster with Storage's directors in a competitive skirmish, or in the current vernacular, a shootout, with others.

Shootouts have become the bane of many in the headhunting business, further evidence of how hotly competitive search has become and how little loyalty exists among clients. Few corporations call a search firm today inviting a consultant over to pick up an assignment. Headhunters commonly complain that even clients for which they have successfully completed a slew of assignments still force them to engage in combat for more work. More than half the executive searches now require shootouts, estimates one major player. Five years ago, the executive hounds might have had to compete in only a third of the cases.

In the competitive arena of a shootout before a corporation's search committee, headhunters have to justify why they would be the most logical choice for a certain assignment. Few of the firms compete on price, although increasingly that is becoming a reality. One major firm recently told a top Chicago bank that it would lower its fee to 30 percent, from one-third, and place a cap on expenses if the bank could guarantee it a half dozen searches. Smaller search firms, scrapping for business, often undercut the standard one-third fee. Typically only a handful of search firms are summoned to compete on a job. But one small, hi-tech company on Boston's Route 128 once invited 21 firms to a meeting room at Logan Airport to battle it out for one presidential search.

Above all, the contests are another sign of how the business has changed, how it has become less a gentlemanly pursuit based on longstanding relationships and more a mad scramble for business. "We went over to see one of our best clients the other day, an investment banking firm," complains Russell Reynolds. "And we were asked to go through an extensive pitch on why we should be selected to do a search. They were putting two other firms through the same ordeal. We never let them down. I said, 'Have we ever disappointed you?' Every single thing we ever did for them has turned to gold."

The once-prevailing clublike camaraderie is now all but gone. The early days when firms could almost sit back and wait for clients to come to them have long since disappeared. Now search firms aggressively market their services and actively attempt to swipe competitors' clients. And they frequently steal headhunters from each other. "It used to be a club," grouses George Haley, who has been headhunting for nearly 35 years. "In the old days, we used to be like the lawyers and the accountants. We were the search firm. Now it's dog-eat-dog. There are search firms on every corner. And every corporation instead of having one firm do their business has four or five, with each division picking anyone they want to deal with."

There is, of course, a perverse irony at work here. Headhunters whose business it is to promote disloyalty among executives grumble because loyalty, in this case from clients, is often nonexistent. Longstanding relationships, commonly taken for granted in such professions as law and accounting, are hard to come by in recruiting. Most blue chip law firms can rely upon certain major corporations as bedrock clients who year in and year out help support the overhead. That is rare in executive search, partly because the assignments are smaller and shorter and partly because the business still lacks the credibility of the professions.

It used to be that the recruitment of a senior officer to a corporation would almost guarantee a firm numerous follow-up assignments. After all, that executive might in some way feel beholden to the man who helped him move into his new job. Business today, however, doesn't always follow a placement. Ward Howell, for instance, which plucked Albert Casey from Times Mirror Co. and placed him as chief executive officer of American Airlines in 1974, never received a single search from the airline company after putting him in. Gilbert Dwyer, formerly one of Ward Howell's top headhunters, couldn't understand why.

One day, he found himself sitting next to Casey on an airline. Still puzzled by American Airlines' nonuse of the firm, Dwyer seized this opportunity to ask Casey why he never came to use Ward Howell's services. "Any search firm which recruited me to be CEO of this company would never get any business from me," retorted Casey. Dumbfounded, Dwyer didn't know what to say. He simply left it at that.

Nearly everyone in the business curses the increasing use of shootouts, begrudgingly acknowledging that they have now become essential to pitch new clients or win away others from competitors. Some contend the contests are used as window dressing to demonstrate that no firm—even one whose chief executive plays rounds of golf with a favored headhunter friend—has an unfair advantage over another. "Sometimes they know perfectly well they are going to use firm X," argues Russell Reynolds, "but they need to feel they have talked to two other search firms. You don't like the feeling of being used. And very often, the people who you are meeting with really don't know enough about what we do to ask the right questions."

Sophisticated purchasers of search are few. They ask the hard questions to find out which corporations are off-limits, how much experience the consultant has in the field, how much of the work he will actually perform on the search and what approach is taken on referencing candidates. Savvy executives also press headhunters to make judgments on what's going on in their areas of expertise to find out if they're faking it.

And some ask about the firms' completion rates. These figures reflect the percentage of cases in which a search turns up a candidate hired by a client. Many headhunters believe it averages less than 70 per cent—a figure which includes assignments cancelled by clients for reasons not the fault of recruiters. Most firms refuse to divulge these numbers out of sheer embarrassment. Lamalie Associates, a top ten firm, claims a completion rate of 75 percent in 1985, up from 67 percent in 1984 and 65 percent in 1983. Peat Marwick claims a 70 percent rate in 1985, but concedes that it had fallen as low as 62.5 percent one year. Competitors of Korn/Ferry, which does not disclose such data, claim the business's giant posts completion rates no better than 60 percent.

"You have to deliver a product," says Dwight Foster of Peat Marwick. "It haunts me when we don't fill searches, and nobody really keeps good score on the searches that aren't filled. There are so many clients in the middle market who tried search and thought they were burned."

Foster once sat in on a shootout for a Peat Marwick auditing client seeking a chief executive. Peat Marwick could not perform the search itself because of a voluntary agreement not to recruit top officers for SEC-registered clients. "I had great fun," he laughs. "I sat in on the meetings, listened to the presentations. They thought I was an auditor. We interviewed five firms, and I never heard so much bullshit in my life."

Many corporations, at least, no longer hand out their business to one search firm without questions. That is a healthy trend. "You should always have an agent relationship with them," maintains Karl Pierson, the tough-minded director for personnel of ITT Telecommunications. "By that I mean if you have a moving firm, let them know you have two moving firms you work with. So you have Allied and North America. If North America screws up a move, you give two moves in a row to Allied. If North America screws up again, you drop them and you bring in Mayflower. Then you give one to each of them. Always let them know that they don't have a corner on the business and make them know I like them hungry."

Most corporations aren't as tough as that on headhunting firms, but nearly all arrange sparring matches, particularly on big jobs, like Storage Technology. The company so urgently needed a Lee Iacocca-like savior that it had no time to arrange a day of warfare at its Louisville, Colorado, headquarters. Instead, the company's board dispatched one of its longtime directors, Richard C. Steadman, to individually screen several search firms to decide which would be best for the job.

Steadman, a private investor in his early 50s who also was chairman of Houston-based National Convenience Stores, knew Storage's ins and outs extremely well. He first joined the company's board 14 years earlier when it was just a fledgling hopeful. He composed a short list of headhunters to call based largely on the recommendations of fellow directors who had employed headhunters in the past.

Included on that list were two of the largest firms in the business: Korn/Ferry International and Ward Howell International. Steadman's search led him to the New York headquarters of Ward Howell International, one of the old traditionalist firms of the business and the sixth largest. It was election day, November 5, 1985, when people were voting between President Reagan and his Democratic challenger Walter Mondale. But 20 stories above 99 Park Avenue in the wood-paneled offices where Ward Howell makes its headquarters, the discussion strayed far from the event of the day.

Gilbert Dwyer, a towering man of ample girth in a gray pinstriped suit, was trying desperately to win Steadman's business. He had with him a Ward Howell colleague who had done some of the firm's high-technology work. Dwyer, then chief executive of Ward Howell, was a headhunter with impressive credentials in the corporate world. He spent more than a decade with General Electric before founder Ward Howell got him a job at the Kennecott Copper Corp. Nine years later, in 1977, Max Ulrich, then president of Ward Howell, took him out of former client Kennecott and make him an executive recruiter.

Steadman sketched out Storage's problems, noting the urgency with which the assignment would have to be carried out. "We were pressed about how long it would take," recalls Dwyer.

"Dick," he told Steadman, "I don't know what you're going to hear from anybody else but I'm going to tell you the truth. We will start showing you candidates within two or three weeks and by the end of six weeks you will have seen just about everybody you should see. It will take two to three weeks to make a decision and another two to four weeks to get the guy extricated, so you're looking at three to four months."

That was a timetable Storage could not possibly accept. The company was in Chapter 11; its current chief executive was under heavy pressure to resign by the company's screaming creditors, and the board had to come up with a successor immediately to put Storage back on the recovery track.

Dwyer, however, felt it was not possible to deliver the best candidate that quickly. "If you're willing to compromise your standards of having the best guy in the country we could fill that search for you in two or three weeks," he told Steadman.

"There are people out there we know. But I can guarantee you that they are not the best. Even after we find these guys, selling them will be tough. I had just done two Chapter 11 searches. I could tell you I'm the world's expert on this. I know how to sell a Chapter 11 company. But I don't know how to sell a company with the market problems Storage Technology has. But I want to take some time to learn how to do that before I go out and chase some heads."

When Steadman left the meeting that day, he gave no commitment to Ward Howell that they would get the search. And in retrospect, Dwyer thinks his comments might have put Steadman off the firm. Perhaps, he was too honest. Perhaps, he was too slow. In any case, Dwyer's gut feeling served him well. Ward Howell, despite the preferential hearing it received, thanks to a Storage Technology board member, wasn't about to get the job.

Ten days later, Steadman flew to Denver and sat in a private meeting room in a red carpet lounge of the airport waiting for another headhunter. The man who would soon walk through the door that Friday night was Korn/Ferry's John Sullivan. Like Dwyer, he was a big-boned man and a former corporate executive who turned headhunter in the very same year as Dwyer. That fact would have been of little import to Steadman.

What did interest him, however, was Sullivan's rich technology background which included service with IBM, Honeywell, Memorex and ADP. He put in 13 years at IBM, joined Heidrick & Struggles's San Francisco office in 1977 and switched to Korn/Ferry's Los Angeles quarters in 1981.

The November 15 session between the two men dragged on for four hours as Steadman filled in Sullivan on what he thought was needed to turn around Storage Technology. The director told him the company was prepared to offer total compensation of up to $500,000, plus a big chunk of equity for an executive Superman. He did not ask Sullivan if he had worked on previous high-technology searches for chief executives, and he didn't have to. Given Sullivan's high-tech background, the pair immediately were on the same wavelength. The headhunter could fluently speak the lingo of the computer world, and he also demonstrated a grasp for the nuances of the company's problems.

Sullivan, like all Korn/Ferry partners, knew how to sell aggressively, too. He sold Korn/Ferry's bigness, its worldwide network of 36 offices, the background of its people and the speed with which he could deliver a savior to the troubled company. If Sullivan thought it would take him just as long as Dwyer to pull a miracle worker from his hat, he kept it to himself.

Instead, he made it clear he understood the company's urgency. "The company was trying to decide what products should be sold off and what other products should be backed with limited resources," says Sullivan. "They were paralyzed until they got someone in there who could live with their decisions. So I was willing to go at it seven days a week."

Steadman, recalls Sullivan, wanted the process speeded along, and the Korn/Ferry headhunter was happy to oblige without any excuses. "Don't wait until you get a critical mass of candidates," Steadman told Sullivan. "When you see someone who is going to be in that final group tell me about him. Don't wait. Let me see him."

Towards the end of the meeting, a wry smile appeared on Steadman's face. Sullivan felt he won the job. "I can't assure that you will get paid," he told the headhunter. "The bankruptcy court will have to rule whether your fee is justifiable."

That was okay by Sullivan. He flew back to Los Angeles that night with the job, and within 24 hours sent by Federal Express a letter confirming the assignment. "We decided on Korn/Ferry for two reasons," says Steadman. "Several of the board members had successfully worked with Dick Ferry, and their Los Angeles office had considerable experience in high-technology searches. John Sullivan had years of background in high technology and knew lots of the players in the business."

Sullivan emerged the winner because Korn/Ferry earned a chance to compete thanks to a director or two on Storage's board, because he could boast a high-tech background and because he could assure Steadman the search could be performed quickly with the help of Korn/Ferry's tremendous resources.

The rising frequency of shootouts have transformed them into crucial marketing opportunities for headhunters, many of whom boast of employing differing strategies to win the assignment. Sullivan may be a born and bred IBMer, but he doesn't sell search the way IBM sells computers. "You don't go in with flip charts and say, 'Let me tell you what it means to use a search firm,' " he says. "A doctor wouldn't do that and he wouldn't say to you, 'Gosh, you have a pain on your side? It sounds like appendicitis.' What he should say is, 'I did the mayor's appendix last week and I did 40 other ones in the last month.' That's the way you sell. You have to say 'tell me about your problem' just as the doctor will take a patient's pulse. He is gathering data to render a judgment that will be valued. If you are impressed with the way he does it and he shows concern, you won't go down the street and talk to another doctor."

Thomas Neff, Spencer Stuart & Associates' president and one of the most respected executive search consultants in the business, utilizes a rather bold approach. He has been known, at some shootouts, to take bows for the success some of his key placements have achieved over the years.

In competing for chief executive bank jobs, Neff has pulled out charts detailing the performance of companies before and after his recruits took over. One of his stars is Raymond Dempsey, who Neff found as chairman and president of Fidelity Bank in Philadelphia in 1978. When Dempsey was put into place, Neff boldly tells shootout evaluators, Fidelity lost $13.3 million and its stock traded at $9 a share. By 1983, the bank was reporting net income of $46.8 million, its shares traded at $39 each and the total market value of the company had risen fourfold to $200 million.

That strategy, Neff claims, allowed him to trounce Russell Reynolds & Associates on key bank searches in five consecutive shootouts. But his streak may have been halted when he tangled with Korn/Ferry's Windle "Win" Priem. Dempsey's performance apparently failed to turn the trick when Neff made his pitch to a search committee looking for a new chairman and chief executive for European American Bancorp. in 1984. They turned, instead, to Priem, who faced directors of the troubled bank at 6:00 P.M. after Neff and Russell Reynolds had already made their presentations.

Priem, Korn/Ferry's top biller, personally brings in an astounding $1.4 million in revenues annually—perhaps the highest revenue generator in all of search with the exception of Heidrick & Struggles's Gerry Roche. The banker-turned-headhunter is known as one of the search business's sharpest pitchmen. For this shootout, Priem assumed the all-knowing, assertive approach of a "bank doctor," which he is sometimes jokingly called.

"Look gentlemen," he intoned, "on this one you need a proven commodity. You shouldn't hire an executive vice-president who would look at this as a tremendous step up. You've got to hire a guy who has already been there before. Someone with credibility."

Priem gained instant credibility himself when he began telling the assembled directors how Korn/Ferry enticed only a year ago Richard P. Cooley to another shaky financial institution, Seafirst Corp. of Seattle, the Northwest's dominant bank. Cooley had been boss of California's Wells Fargo Bank. To clinch that assignment, Korn/Ferry put together a three-man task force composed of President Richard Ferry and managing directors Priem and Morgan Harris, who is based in Los Angeles. And they sold speed and experience, just as fellow partner Sullivan did in snatching the Storage Technology job.

"There had to be an absolute solution to that problem in a 60-day timeframe," Priem told them. "They knew we could use the team approach to get speedy results. I flew into Seattle every week to meet with the search committee. As command post leader, I talked every morning with the committee chairman. That was the sense of urgency. There was a lot at stake. The financial condition of the bank was deteriorating and the board had lost confidence in the prior CEO."

So when Priem tossed around a few names and dropped this bit of information on the search committee, he left with the belief that he picked up another big search. "I took out Neff, and I took out

Russ on that job personally," he boasts, like a victorious pugilist. Who did Priem ultimately deliver to European American Bancorp.? None other than Neff's successful old candidate at Fidelity Bank— Raymond Dempsey who was only the second person Priem had telephoned on the search. "Ray is the only guy in the country who had successfully turned around a large troubled financial institution and then moved onto another troubled institution," says Priem.

Priem's initial antics before the directors of European American Bancorp. over an hour and one-half period landed him a six-figure fee for bringing them Dempsey's head. These are the new rules of the headhunting game. And many of the old-line traditional firms have found it difficult to drop their antiquated country club connections for the more aggressive, Madison Avenue-style competitive contests. To spread the new gospel, some search firms, like Spencer Stuart, hold seminars for their staffs on selling.

Over one recent weekend, some 20 Spencer Stuart headhunters are congregated in the Goldcoast Room at Chicago's Ambassador East Hotel. With a Scotch on the rocks in one hand, Dayton Ogden is standing before them lecturing on what he calls the company's "anti-sell culture."

A former U.S. Navy lieutenant who piloted a patrol boat through Vietnam's marshy waters, Ogden has the good looks of a movie actor, the muscular arms of a competitive tennis player and the easy-going manner of a top headhunter which he is. He joined the firm in 1979 after a four-year stint with a small Washington, D.C., head-hunting shop without a national reputation where "we had to sell to eat." At Stuart, Ogden quickly established himself as one of the firm's fast-rising stars. In 1982, at the age of 37, he became the youngest managing director in the U.S., heading up Stuart's New York office, its biggest branch accounting for 23 per cent of the firm's total revenues.

Ogden cinched a reputation as a menace to opposing shootout competitors a couple of years earlier when he won a key search to find a new head of the American Council of Life Insurance in Washington, D.C. Like most trade association jobs, this one was crucial to the search firm because it offered the potential of opening up the entire life insurance market to Spencer Stuart. The executive director of a trade group would likely remember the name of the search firm which placed him when a member asked for recommendations on headhunters.

The competition was formidable. Ogden found himself a combatant against five of the major search firms in the U.S. "Most of the other firms tried to snow them on how much they knew about the business," he says. "We sold them healing." Ogden knew the interests of the mutual insurance companies were vastly different than those of the publicly-held insurance corporations. Those differences were ripping the association apart. He maintained that Stuart would use the process of selecting a new leader as the catalyst for binding the group together and for balancing the disparate interests of its membership. "We will get the members involved in the search and committed to the success of a new leader," he told them.

It worked. Ogden won the search; he successfully brought aboard a Reagan Administration official to take over the trade group; and it unlocked the doors for Stuart's headhunters to the life insurance industry. "It was like opening up a box of cookies," he says. That novel approach won him the plaudits of his colleagues. And now here he was going on stage again to give an uplifting sales talk on how to compete in shootouts—Spencer Stuart even videotaped his presentation for its library of 25 training tapes. The Jane Fonda workout has come to headhunting.

Ogden, sans pulsating aerobic music, preaches a no-nonsense, commonsensical approach to shootouts: Do advance homework to impress clients with your insight about his managerial problems; stress the firm's experience and reputation in the client's industry; toss out a few names to demonstrate you know the industry's major players; research the backgrounds of the client executives to be met to assure personal chemistry, and sell the importance of doing a search quickly.

"When I joined the firm," he says, rocking from left to right, "there were some who thought it was unclean to sell. Well, in New York, we've tried to get away from the notion that selling aggressively is unclean. We ought to position ourselves as the small firm and use more hustle in making selling a key part of our ongoing business development."

Ogden criticizes his colleagues for belittling the competition in shootouts. "We talked disparagingly about firms that were outselling us. We were smug." Instead, he advocates a more subtle competitive pressure. "If you're selling against Russell Reynolds on financial services, you can be terribly statesmanlike and say they have a good practice in financial services, but their access to companies is limited. If you're talking about Korn/Ferry, you don't have to run them down. You can say it in a nice way. Tell them you won't see the guy pitching the account anywhere. If it's Heidrick & Struggles, say they don't have the experience to do the big jobs anymore."

"Don't sell process," Ogden warns them, a reference to the firm's search methodology. "We make a tremendous mistake in thinking our system is unique. Instead, take some risks. In sessions going poorly when the glaze is setting in on their eyes, I say something shocking. I had one meeting with an entrepreneur who was practically asleep. I knew I lost him so I said, 'You know, entrepreneurs are terrible people to recruit for. They don't listen well and they're very biased.' I said nothing positive about entrepreneurs, yet we got the assignment because I got his attention."

Ogden boasts a 65 percent winning record in battling it out on some 120 shootouts during a decade of headhunting. It's the kind of record that, if a baseball player, would insure him a spot in the Hall of Fame. So he has the ears of his colleagues when he advises them to employ "disarming candor" to their advantage. "It's far more appealing to tell someone you've screwed up a few times," he says. "Show him we're human, just don't show success. If you just present the positive, you won't gain the credibility you could if you mention a few negatives."

Picking up on Neff's strategy of citing his accomplishments, Ogden also suggests talking up how certain placements have done in their jobs. "Have they had an impact on the institutions they've joined? That's a far more constructive way to talk about us than by simply mentioning the number of assignments you've done."

Neff is among the audience that night, too. And after Ogden notes the importance of advance research, Neff pipes in about how he won an assignment to find a new chief executive for Pan American World Airways in 1981. Neff was the last of six consultants to walk in and give his spiel. The search committee had tentatively decided on another firm, says Neff, who had called his airline sources in advance of the shootout to find that Pan Am's financial difficulties were worse than many had been led to believe. "We were the only ones to focus our presentation from the outset on the gravity and urgency of the problem," Neff told his colleagues. "The company was facing bankruptcy, and the new CEO would have to have instant credibility with the financial community." That appeal struck nodding heads of agreement on Pan Am's search committee: "We wanted to find someone with a track record such that employees and bankers would take heart," explained Jack S. Parker, a Pan Am director who headed up the committee. Neff captured the assignment and brought C. Edward Acker, chairman and chief executive of Air Florida and former president of Braniff, to loss-plagued Pan Am in August of 1981.

Neff's colleagues all agree it was one of the biggest assignments ever conducted in the business, and the conversation veers toward some recent shootouts lost to the competition. One Chicago-based competitor, complained a Spencer Stuart man, nabbed a vice-presidential search for a sizable corporation over Stuart by bringing the resumes of potential candidates to the shootout. The consensus is that this was beyond ethics: If the client wants some names, they'll give him some names. But to bring actual resumes to a shootout presumes there is no need to conduct a search in the first place. It reduces the business, they believed, to employment-agency-style body snatching.

"I don't like putting resumes out on the table," sniffs Ogden. "You're really manipulating your buyer by bringing in resumes before you even know the specs. Using people as benchmarks, however, can be useful. You can ask the client if he is looking for someone with a background similar to a Peter Jones. That could be valuable because it shows you know Peter Jones and you move the discussion from the general to the specific, and it gives the buyer the impression you move in the right circles."

Scattered around the room of over a dozen Stuart consultants, all intently listening to Ogden with predinner drinks in hand, are five newcomers to the firm. Two of the new faces are Joseph Griesedieck, a Russell Reynolds alumnus, and Thomas Hardy, who quit Egon Zehnder International.

Their presence underscores another aspect of the brewing wars among the major headhunting firms: the pirating of heavy-hitters from each other. One of the consequences of the lack of client loyalty in the business, besides the increasing use of shootouts, is the frequency with which headhunters themselves jump ship to competing firms. Clients indirectly fuel lots of this turnover because when they do display loyalty it is to the individual consultant and not to the firm. So good headhunters are as eagerly extracted from one firm to another as headhunters seek top execs for their own clients.

"Search firms are totally dependent upon the professional abilities of the individuals," says Alan Lafley, a Korn/Ferry partner who previously employed many search firms as a human resources executive. "The sign on the door doesn't mean a heck of a lot. If anyone of these firms lost that core of top people that would be the end of the firm. I can never recall employing a search firm, only an individual."

That's why some firms have been known to raid entire offices of others. In mid-1983, for example, Spencer Stuart welcomed with open arms the entire Los Angeles office of William H. Clark Associates. Daniel Wier, Clark's top producer, left with two other consultants and support staff. At the time, more than half a dozen other Clark consultants were already working for Stuart in New York, prompting one wag to note that Stuart now had more Clark people than Clark itself.

Shortly after the raid, however, Spencer Stuart saw its entire Brussels office of five consultants walk out in sympathy over the dismissal of flamboyant chairman Jean-Michel Beigbeder. Beigbeder switched to Korn/Ferry as did several of the Brussels consultants. There's more. The former Korn/Ferry chief in Brussels then walked across the street to rebuild an office there for Spencer Stuart.

"It's a one-product business," bemoans David Peasback, president of Heidrick & Struggles. "You bring in a guy here and within 12 to 18 months if he's any good the street knows it and that guy's phone is ringing off the hook. 'Come on over here,' they tell him."

Peasback can speak from experience. Heidrick & Struggles has been one of the most fertile and favorite hunting grounds for headhunters. In recent years, Heidrick has lost dozens of consultants to competitors. In one instance, the firm lost nearly its entire Dallas office when Stephen Garrison and his colleagues jumped ship to rival Ward Howell in May 1983. Along with Garrison came two other consultants, two secretaries and the office's director of research. Heidrick & Struggles slapped a lawsuit against Ward Howell, which was later settled out of court. But it took Heidrick & Struggles more than three years to recover, only reopening a Dallas branch in the fall of 1985.

Sullivan, the man who won the Storage Technology shootout for Korn/Ferry, was another consultant to have left Heidrick & Struggles. And now he had won one of the most important searches of the year. Heidrick, which had been known to have performed search work for Storage previously, did not have it; Spencer Stuart, which lacked the good word of a well-placed director, failed to get just a hearing; but Korn/Ferry did and won. And to make good on its pledge of speed, Sullivan had sent Steadman a four-page letter detailing his requirements for a successor to Aweida within 24 hours of his meeting with the Storage Technology director at the Denver airport.

Steadman had told Sullivan he wanted someone who could establish instant credibility with the Storage Technology creditors, customers and employees, someone who had successfully run a large operation in a crisis situation and someone who obviously could boast computer know-how. All this and more was confirmed by Sullivan in his letter.

"The individual you seek," wrote Sullivan, "will be known as a professional manager with substantial status but whose style is highly participative and involved.

"Your successful candidate will probably have general management responsibility for a company or large division of at least $250 million in sales.

"The ideal candidate will range in age from 45 to 55 years, but both younger and older individuals will be given serious consideration. Formal education is not as important a factor as a successful track record."

To track down the savior, Sullivan targeted some of the nation's best known corporations: General Electric, GTE, Hewlett-Packard, Digital Equipment Corp., Rolm Corp., IBM, Data General, Burroughs, Tandem and Texas Instruments. Inevitably the final candidate came from none of these corporations, but from little-known $330 million (sales) BMC Industries, Inc., a Minneapolis company.

Ryal R. Poppa (pronounced poppy), BMC's chief, had come to the sleepy maker of eyeglasses and metal stamped parts through executive search hound Bob Lamalie. In three years, he transformed the company into a more attractive electronics manufacturer, gaining a reputation as a turnaround specialist. Now Sullivan got him to move again.

Poppa was one of up to 30 potential candidates for the job, culled from 70 telephone calls during a frantic six-week period encompassing the Thanksgiving and Christmas holidays. Sullivan personally interviewed virtually all of these likely candidates before winnowing the list down to four finalists who would be presented to Storage Technology's board. There were a couple of unusual complications due to Storage's bankrupt status.

The company's creditors committee, headed by a Citibank executive, wielded significant power. During the last two weeks of the search, Sullivan was called to put in a performance before the committee, to patiently explain how Korn/Ferry was conducting the assignment and to review the three finalists Sullivan had thus far interested in the job. Later, the headhunter had to testify in U.S. Bankruptcy Court on Poppa's qualifications for the job and on Korn/Ferry's fee for the assignment.

Before the board actually chose Poppa, however, another dilemma had arisen. The directors liked two of the four candidates presented by Sullivan: both of them from Minneapolis-based companies. Poppa, obviously, but also Stephen G. Jerritts, international president of Lee Data Corp., whose background, like Sullivan's, included stints with IBM and Honeywell. Who should they hire?

"I sat in on two board meetings and there was a lot of deliberation," recalls Sullivan. "They kicked around the two top candidates who were very different from each other. Finally I said, 'Why don't you hire them both. Because the strengths of one are the weaknesses of the other. You will have a Mr. Inside and a Mr. Outside. Poppa is good at acquisitions, spinoffs and banking relationships. The other guy is internally oriented. With all the problems you have, why don't you get both of them. Poppa is going to be totally consumed by the creditors, and Jerritts can run the place inside.' "

A week later, the board went along with Sullivan's suggestion. The directors hired them both. As chairman and chief executive, Poppa would start at a salary of $300,000 plus a $75,000 guaranteed first-year bonus; as president and chief operating officer, Jerritts would begin at $240,000 a year with a $48,000 first-year bonus. Korn/Ferry, collecting full fees for both men in a single search, bagged more than a quarter of a million dollars with expenses on the job. The competitors who lost out to Korn/Ferry did not only lose those fees, but even another search: to find Poppa's successor at BMC.

BMC reportedly was miffed at Poppa's unexpected departure, but apparently not at Sullivan who took him out. The company instead gave him the assignment to find his successor, too. Sullivan eventually turned up Robert J. Carlson, who had resigned eight months earlier as president and heir apparent of United Technologies Corp. And yet another search was picked up from a BMC Industries director for another company.

A single shootout produced for the executive huntsman four senior-level assignments and billings approaching $350,000. The competition found yet again how formidable Korn/Ferry International had become.

The Mass Merchandiser

"We didn't meet the image of the club."

THE NATION'S CAPITAL was dressed in pageantry and dusted in snow, and John Sullivan's boss was comfortably ensconced in the warmth of a suite at Washington's Hay-Adams Hotel. He had a ticket to watch the inaugural parade from the White House reviewing stand, but it was worthless because of the arctic weather which gripped Washington. The parade had been cancelled. Outside Korn's frosted windows, the temperature was a shivering seven degrees, with the wind-chill factor making it the equivalent of 11 degrees below zero.

Lester Korn had already showered, shaved and slipped on his pants and shirt. And his eyes were riveted on the color television tube in front of him. In a ceremony rich in pomp and flourish, one of his own is on stage at the nearby Capital Center, on national television with the President and Mrs. Reagan, with the Vice-President and Mrs. Bush. Yes, right alongside the first family and the second family are the smiling Walkers. Ron Walker, the amiable 47-year-old head-hunting Texan who runs Korn/Ferry's Washington office.

"I think it was the proudest day in my life," Korn says. "Of all the people in the world it could have been, it was him. I would like to see more partners become famous. You will see more people like Ron Walker in this business. Just like the law firms. You are going to see them coming and going into government and returning to search. It really made me think: The firm and the profession have come a long way."

Indeed, it had. The night before, Korn and his wife, Carol Beth, had been whooping it up at an inaugural party at Blair House. The evening before that, on Saturday, January 19, Walker and Korn's wife could be glimpsed on nationwide television in the front row at the Frank Sinatra-organized Presidential Inaugural Gala. Korn was stretching his neck to watch the festivities from a $200-a-ticket seat behind evangelist Billy Graham. Korn and the nation watched as Sinatra sang "Fly Me to the Moon" and "One for My Baby."

It was a very good year for Lester Korn and his partner Dick Ferry. His headhunting firm would end its fiscal year at the $50 million revenue mark. Two weeks earlier, *Time* magazine named Peter Ueberroth, the man he helped place as head of the 1984 Olympics, as "Man of the Year." And here was Walker, who as chairman and chief executive of the 1985 Presidential Inaugural Committee was on stage with the President to salute all the youngsters who came to Washington to march in the parade that wasn't. Yes, Walker, the Washingtonian VIP who sent out the 70,000 coveted invitations to the inaugural events.

If one of their own had come a long way, so have Lester Korn and Dick Ferry. Their prosperous 17-year partnership, with 37 offices from Cleveland to Kuala Lumpur, helps to install more than 1,500 executives into key positions every year. Nearly 30 percent of them latch onto compensation packages ranging from the high six figures to more than $1 million annually. To stalk this corporate prey, Korn/Ferry headhunters ring the telephones of over 50,000 corporate executives the world over. It is a wild safari hunt that now generates $58 million in annual billings, a modestly-sized David in the corporate world in which they toil yet an undisputed Goliath in the fragmented business that is search.

Theirs is an impressive, enviable record by any standard. Those annual billings alone reflect nearly $200 million worth of salaries, the equivalent of populating a major corporation with executive talent. In the process of building the world's largest search machine, they have revolutionized and institutionalized the business, spawned dozens of competitors and helped to transform the way executives switch jobs.

It was a year not without trauma either, however. If this was Korn's day of glory, proof of achieving some political clout by being plugged into the Potomac power base through Walker, his saddest day occurred but ten months earlier. Then, on March 20, *The Wall Street Journal*, on its front page no less, told the world that one of Korn's fastest-rising stars listed a bogus Stanford M.B.A. degree in a biography that contained other omissions and errors as well. How could it be?, Korn wondered. David Charlson, at 36, was one of the youngest managing directors in the firm and head of his important Chicago office. The news shocked and angered Korn, who speaks only off-the-record about the affair.

Charlson hooked up with another firm, Richards Consultants, and the world went on. But as Korn says, "There have been good days and bad days in my life. That was a bad day. But there has not been a day that I have regretted getting into the search business."

Lester Korn and Dick Ferry are the odd couple of the business. Korn is a thin, small-boned man who splashes cologne on his body to excess. His heavily oiled black wavy hair is combed back with a little mound of pompadour. Korn has little physical presence, and he seldom wears a suit comfortably. Despite the apparent quality of his clothes, they never quite seem to fit the man. One writer once astutely observed that Korn "looks like someone who might have been found a century ago on a riverboat sitting behind a pile of poker chips." It is an apt description.

"He can sell sand in the middle of the Sahara Desert to Arabs," affirms Charles Murphy, a longtime friend and business associate of Korn. "Lester is the greatest salesman in the business, while Dick is the greatest performer and disgustingly honest," he adds with a shrug.

Ferry, on the other hand, looks much like the accountant he is. Large black-framed glasses dominate his face. A gold pen sticks out from the breast pocket of his white shirt, a pocket padded with notes and three-by-five ruled file cards. The same writer noted that Ferry "looks like someone you would willingly buy a used car from." A bit of a Poindexter-type, he is the internal strategist who keeps careful watch over the firm's operations. His interests extend beyond the firm: Ferry is a founding director of the First Business Bank in Los Angeles, one of the most successful banks in California, and of Jimmy's, a chi-chi Beverly Hills restaurant offering guests a French and Continental cuisine.

Both have identically-sized corner offices overlooking Santa Monica Boulevard and the Los Angeles Country Club, separated by a small conference room yet linked by an interconnecting corridor, on the eighth floor of an office building in Century City's Northrop Plaza. It is just another professional building, with a Hamburger Hamlet and a Wells Fargo Bank branch in the lobby, a concrete-and-glass rectangle packed with attorneys, real estate agents, stockbrokers and now headhunters. Modern art, including a Salvadore Dali, hangs in Korn's office, while Ferry prefers traditional English prints.

Lester Korn is Mr. Outside. It is Lester, not Dick, who is always quoted in the stories on headhunting. It is Lester who gives the speeches, the interviews and whose byline will occasionally appear under a well-placed opinion article on an editorial page. Indeed, Lester gets 20 times the number of unsolicited resumes from hopeful job seekers than Dick. And it is he, for example, who is and has been in *Who's Who in America* for years, garnering 15 lines to his background and achievements.

Mr. Inside, Dick Ferry, fails to gain a mention. It's not because he doesn't qualify. It's because Ferry, not a man who cultivates publicity, has never returned the biographical form necessary to earn an entry in the book. He isn't looking for the outside recognition nor the ego gratification that Korn seemingly thrives on. Ferry eschews personal publicity, avoids it assiduously. Korn thrives on it. It might be a sense of exclusion from places and privileges that makes Korn as driven as he is. "I felt the guy had something to prove," says a New York public relations executive who worked with Korn. "It's a Sammy Glick story. You've got all these Ivy Leaguers, and Korn was saying 'I'm as good as they are and by God, I'm going to show them.' "

Son of a California grocery store owner, Korn earned a B.S. degree with honors from UCLA in 1959 and stayed to pick up his M.B.A. from the same university in 1960. During his college years, he would work between 30 and 40 hours a week at Bank of America as something of a trouble-shooting Whiz Kid who would roam from one branch to another reviewing loans and bank documents— the work helped pay for his college education because his Austrian-born father, Raymond, died while he was a teenager. He joined the bank as a part-time teller in 1953 at the age of 17.

With visions of lecturing before classes of college business students, Korn ran off to the Harvard Business School to work on a Ph.D. in 1960. But after a year he called it quits, returned to the West Coast and in 1961 joined Peat, Marwick, Mitchell & Co., the

Big Eight accounting firm, as a management consultant. Korn saw tremendous growth potential in what was then a rather small business in California for Peat Marwick. He was right. Much of his consulting work was done for Del Webb, the leisure and construction company, which Korn had brought into Peat as a client. Korn did everything from organization studies to cost accounting to computerization for his companies. A man on a fast track, Korn passed his Certified Public Accounting (CPA) exam in one sitting and was made Peat's youngest partner ever at age 30.

In 1963, Charles Murphy, who was organizing Peat's executive search practice from New York, came to California to recruit Korn to head up the business on the West Coast. Murphy had joined Peat Marwick a year earlier to set up a search and placement division. He had done the same thing at another Big Eight accounting firm, Arthur Young, starting in 1956 before joining Booz, Allen & Hamilton's search team three years later. When Murphy came west to recruit Korn, he had, perhaps, a handful of searches under his belt in his capacity as a management consultant at Del Webb. Korn liked the work, saw it as an opportunity to manage his own team of consultants and jumped at the chance. He spent one evening thinking about it before telling Murphy on May 6 that he would do it. "I've been trying to catch the little guy ever since," jokes Murphy. "He took off like a rocket."

Korn had met Ferry in Phoenix, where Ferry was working as a controller for real estate developer David H. Murdock at one of his subsidiary firms within Murdock's public holding company, Financial Corp. of Arizona (FCA). FCA, a company riding the crest of Phoenix's postwar real-estate boom, was then a Peat accounting and consulting client. Ferry made an immediate impression as an intelligent and conscientious numbers cruncher. "He was probably the smartest guy I had seen short of anyone," recalls Korn.

Born in 1937 in Kent, Ohio, where his dad owned a machine manufacturing shop, Ferry was graduated with honors from Kent State University in 1959 with a degree in accounting. He joined Big Eight accountant Haskens & Sells as a staff accountant in 1960 and switched to FCA in 1961.

Ferry left Murdock, now one of the wealthiest men in the world with a net worth exceeding $500 million, to put together a small consulting firm in 1965 called Morgan, Tatom, Ferry & Beckley. He was less than happy with his arrangement with three other partners, however, so when Peat Marwick made him an offer he was happy to leave.

Ferry was recruited to Peat Marwick in 1965 by the late Harry Littler, who headed up Peat's West Coast consulting practice, and served as a mentor of sorts to both Korn and Ferry. At Peat, the two became good friends. Ferry consulted for a couple of years, switched to search for a year, then supervised and eventually managed Peat's acquisitions advisory consulting practice. When Korn assumed broader responsibilities for human resources consulting at Peat, Ferry succeeded him as manager of the search practice which eventually grew to boast a staff of 20 consultants.

They were a highly-driven, ambitious twosome. Their accounting partners would commonly grouse that the pair were far too aggressive and pushy. The business, too, was a stepchild within the accounting firm, reflecting a miniscule portion of its total revenues. "I'd say 650 of the 700 partners at Peat couldn't care less about the business," recalls Murphy, who headed up the practice nationwide. "We would never hear from them unless they had some drunken brother-in-law looking for a job."

Walter E. Hanson, Peat's senior partner back then, would often call Murphy on a Monday morning with the admonition: "Well Charlie, your boiler shop got us in trouble again." Once Korn approached Bendix after picking up word that the company was looking to go outside for a senior executive. Haskins & Sells, at the time the company's auditors, quickly put the company on report with the American Institute of Certified Public Accountants (AICPA) for approaching one of their clients. "We never got the job because Haskins & Sells blew the whistle on us," recalls Murphy. In the staid, polite and gentlemanly world of accounting in the 1960s, poaching was a no-no.

In another instance, Korn took the chief financial officer out of Purex, a non-Peat Marwick client, provoking a storm. "What the hell is a professional firm like yours doing stealing an employee of ours?" barked the chief executive of Purex, who also filed a report against Peat Marwick with the AICPA.

Their very proper, button-down and dull accounting partners winced when they heard such stories. Max Factor's chief executive, unhappy about Korn's handling of a search for a vice-president of marketing at the cosmetics firm, threatened to withdraw all his business, worth some $700,000 a year, from Peat. "He was going to throw all of Peat Marwick out because of it," remembers Murphy. "It scared Les."

But it also made his success at Peat Marwick all the more remarkable. Still, both Korn and Ferry fought a frustrating uphill battle in running and building the business. If they wanted to speak with an executive at a company which was a Peat Marwick client, they had to clear the contact first with the nearest Peat Marwick managing partner. And there were 50,000 Peat Marwick clients. "The managing partner would often say, 'Gee, I really prefer that you wouldn't go into that company because we're trying to develop a relationship with them and what would the CEO think if you stole one of his key employees?' " says Ferry. "So we would scratch that one off the list. We were hiring very aggressive people. It was a tough job keeping these people under control."

And there were whispers, too, about Korn's Jewish background among a world of WASPs. Indeed, when the Kuwait National Petroleum Company hired Peat Marwick's search practice to find its top 29 officials in 1966 for a fee of $1.5 million, Korn had little to do with it. "Les couldn't work on it because he was Jewish," says one former Peat Marwick partner.

Nonetheless, the pair had constructed and maintained a well-greased cash machine within the confining boundaries of a complacent accounting firm. The Los Angeles practice alone represented a full third of the firm's nationwide revenues in search at the time. Some 20 consultants strong with roughly $2 million in revenues, it also was the largest single practice on the West Coast despite the limitations of working within a public accounting firm. "We were making a lot of money," says Korn. "We were highly visible, and we were bringing in companies which became big Peat Marwick clients. So we also had a lot of support on the West Coast."

They were so successful that Peat Marwick made them both two of the youngest partners in the firm's history. Korn made partner at the age of 30 in 1966 after five years with Peat Marwick; Ferry made it at age 32 in 1969 in under five years, too. Even before earning partner status, however, Ferry had made it clear that he was somewhat unhappy. He wanted more of a say in the management of the business. Peat Marwick convinced him to hang on through the next round of promotions when he was made partner.

"They lifted the window shade up, let me look in for 30 seconds and nothing happened," says Ferry. "All I got was a new title. I was one of 660 partners. But I wanted an opportunity to run something myself, and at Peat Marwick, I wasn't going to have that opportunity for a long time. So I said, 'Hey, I'm not going to stay, partnership or not.'"

Shortly after making up his mind, he told his friend and fellow partner Korn.

"Hey, look Les, I'm leaving. It may surprise a lot of people, but I'm not staying around here," Ferry told Korn.

"God, you're thinking about leaving?" Korn replied. "I'm thinking about leaving, too. If you're going, we ought to do something together. Don't do anything until we have a chance to talk about this."

Their chat together resulted in a Peat Marwick memo dated November 10, 1969, which shocked, surprised and in some cases pleased their fellow partners at the accounting firm. "It is with regret that we announce the withdrawal from the partnership of Lester B. Korn and Richard M. Ferry, who have decided to organize a new company," wrote Murphy. "Their objective will be to assemble, through acquisitions, a nationwide affiliated group of employment agencies. Messrs. Korn and Ferry believe that their concept provides a unique opportunity for the development of a new growth-oriented company."

Murphy now says he purposely called their newly created firm an employment agency so as not to ruffle the sensitive feathers of Peat Marwick partners. But Korn and Ferry knew that executive search would at least be part of their plan. "We looked at the market and concluded there was an opportunity out there to create a new search firm," says Ferry. "The old-boy network which had in my mind been responsible for such firms as Boyden, Ward Howell and Heidrick & Struggles appeared on its way out. We saw that the leadership of these firms was getting old, that they weren't being aggressively managed and that they certainly had no marketing skills."

The pair met with an investment banking friend from Mitchum, Jones & Templeton, Henry Turner, who Korn had earlier placed as treasurer of Star-Kist Foods, Inc., and with his advice started building the foundation for a company which would provide a full range of personnel consulting services, from executive search to human resources and executive compensation consulting. Korn and Ferry each put in $5,000, opened up an office in Century City and became Korn/Ferry Enterprises, a name which quickly was changed to Korn/Ferry International.

It was a bold move. Making partner at a Big Eight firm was for many a goal unto itself. It promised a safe, secure and successful future, a comfortable upper-middle-class lifestyle. So Peat partners were incredulous to find two of their youngest partners walking out so soon after being anointed by the firm. "Both our wives were convinced that they would be eating hamburger for the rest of their lives," jokes Korn. "Dick had five children and I had two by then. And here we were at age 32 and 33, walking away from a lifetime of security."

Although Korn claims he didn't immediately steal any of Peat Marwick's clients, he didn't hesitate to recruit former colleagues from the accounting firm. Within one month, he hired Jack Quinn, a Peat Marwick headhunter in California. A mere 18 months later, the pair had the chutzpa to pirate away two of Peat's most important search partners: their old boss Charles Murphy, who had written the memo informing the partners of their departure and who was founding national partner and national director in charge of Peat's entire executive search division, and George W. Ott, who had been named to succeed Ferry at Peat when the duo left. Korn/Ferry's first employee in New York in 1971 under Murphy was another Peat Marwick alumnus, Allen Parmenter. Peat threatened to sue, recalls Murphy, but "it was an idle threat."

Their dream of building a broad personnel consulting company quickly fell by the wayside. "When we got into the marketplace in 1970, things were a little tight and we were concerned about venturing too far from search," recalls Ferry. "We knew search. It was an easy sell for us. And we never had time to get into the other services we used to think about. We worked hard. We worked around the clock. We worked seven days a week. When I wasn't doing search work, I was setting up a financial system here. We were doing everything ourselves, and the profit margins in the first year were probably the highest we ever had in the firm."

Unshackled from the annoying restraints at Peat Marwick, the pair wasted little time in showing they would be a force in what was still an infant business. Their departure from Peat as well as the subsequent recruitment of Ott, who succeeded Ferry, left the accounting firm's search business in California in disarray. That meant the West Coast remained generally open, unexplored territory with only two exceptions: a strong Heidrick & Struggles office in Los Angeles and the presence of Hergenrather & Co., the first West Coast search firm begun in 1954.

The pair landed their first assignment from Donald Beall, then chief financial officer of North American Rockwell, who needed a controller. Beall, now president of Rockwell International, still remains a client. Mattel, Revlon and Norton Simon were other early important clients, too. Korn/Ferry's first big job occurred when Korn recruited William Glavin to the presidency of Scientific Data Systems, a recently acquired Xerox subsidiary. Glavin, now vice-chairman of Xerox, also remains a client. There were some critical, and touchy, assignments, too. Like the time Korn found Alan R. Gruber to become the new head of a reorganized Equity Funding Corp. of America, the Los Angeles firm which has become a synonym for business fraud and scandal.

The early days were not totally troublefree. Ferry, hoping to pick up some quick money on a search in the first year, agreed to do one assignment on a contingency basis. That meant he would only get paid if he found an acceptable candidate for his client. Conventional executive recruiters, however, look askance at contingency work because they consider themselves professionals who, like attorneys and physicians, should earn their fees regardless of their success.

"I can remember fighting with the client about the fee when we did it," recalls Ferry. "He said, 'Gee, why should I pay you the full fee when you only worked on it for two weeks. The whole concept of your firm is time and expense.' I said, 'Yeah, but that was not the understanding we had.' We had a fight about it and I was angry." Ferry learned an important lesson, however. "It was probably a sense of greed that caused me to do it. I knew I could get the job done quickly. But you don't want to do contingency work because it's contrary to the whole concept of doing a search, of going into the marketplace and spending time trying to find the best talent available."

Within three years, Korn/Ferry employed 42 professionals in New York, Los Angeles, San Marino, Houston, Atlanta, Chicago and San Francisco, boasted revenues of $1.8 million and was on its way toward becoming a public company whose shares would be traded on the over-the-counter market. For all entrepreneurs, going public is part and parcel of the American dream of business success. It was that and more for headhunting's odd couple. Ferry envisioned using the company's stock to acquire regional search firms under the common Korn/Ferry umbrella. He thought it would also allow partners to realize the value of their own stake in the company.

In October 1972, Korn and Ferry sold a little over 25 percent of the company to outsiders, raising slightly less than $1 million in the process. The move immediately put a value of $800,000 on each of Korn and Ferry's stakes in the company and each sold about $60,000 worth of stock. All a mere pittance by today's high-stakes entrepreneurial standards.

For all this, the California upstarts were willing to give everyone a peek at their financials. Never before had a search firm bared all. By going public, the pair gave the world a glimpse of the extraordinary profits that could be made in executive search—a business few knew much about. The company's public documents revealed a firm that had never had a loss, even as a start up. And in the year Korn/Ferry went public in 1972 its net margins were an amazing 12 percent. Only two years earlier, when management consultant Booz, Allen & Hamilton, Inc. went public, observers were surprised at Booz's 6.4 percent margins, then thought to show how lucrative the consulting game had become. Now here came Korn/Ferry with double those margins as a service firm. The secret was out: You could make a killing going on a safari for executive heads.

From November 1969, when the pair opened the doors to their new business, to April 30, 1970, Korn/Ferry reported net income of $56,000 on $281,200 of billings. And that was after taking out $109,100 in salaries. In the fiscal year ending April 30, 1971, Korn/Ferry earned $116,500 on $912,800 in revenues after taking out $412,800 in salaries. The company doubled its billings the following year to $1.8 million, earning $221,900 after deducting $797,300 in salaries. This was at a time when headhunters charged 25 percent of an executive's first-year total compensation, not today's 33⅓ percent. Korn/Ferry fees on average were even slightly less than the standard 25 percent flat fee because the firm billed its clients on time-and-expense.

When the company went public in 1972, Korn, Ferry and Murphy were all drawing $40,000 annual salaries and bonuses; Korn and Ferry's employment contract also would guarantee them incentive bonuses equal to 2½ percent of the company's net income in excess of $1 million after 1976. The average bonus paid to each professional in 1972 was $3,500. Then, bonuses ranged from 5 percent to 50 percent of a professional's salary. All told, each consultant was making on average about $15,000 annually in salary and bonus. Laughable compared to today's healthy six-figure sums.

As a public company, Korn/Ferry continued to do well. In fiscal

1973, net earnings jumped to $431,200 on $3.5 million in revenues. The next year's net climbed to $560,700 on $5 million in revenues. Trouble was, the company's stock didn't reflect its true fortunes. Korn/Ferry went public at $8 a share. By mid-1974, the stock had fallen to $5.25. Korn and Ferry, no less, found themselves spending a third of their time dealing with simply being a public company. It was a costly distraction. "We couldn't get any value in the stock," says Ferry. "I came to the realization that we couldn't survive as a public company. Our personal relationships wouldn't survive and our relationships with our partners wouldn't survive because they didn't see any appreciation in their shares. It was taking time away from our clients and from the basics of the business." To regain its privacy, Korn/Ferry offered $7 a share to the outsiders who held 38 percent of its total outstanding stock in late August of 1974.

The assignments, meantime, continued to roll in. Year after year the firm racked up big gains in volumes. The pair quickened the pace of expansion by merging with London-based G. K. Dickinson Ltd. in 1972 to secure a foothold in continental Europe, with Mexico-based Hazzard y Asociados in 1977 to penetrate Latin American markets and with Sydney-based Guy Pease Associates in 1979 to gain a presence in Australia. At one point in the early 1970s, Korn flew to Frankfurt for a secret meeting with Egon Zehnder, a former Spencer Stuart consultant who had founded his own European-based firm in 1964. The two talked merger, but a marriage couldn't be arranged. Zehnder, whose tax rate was about 9 percent, wanted a merger based on after-tax revenues; Korn, who paid taxes on 50 percent of every dollar, wanted the deal based on pre-tax revenues. Egon Zehnder International, probably the world's fourth or fifth largest search firm, now boasts more than $25 million in annual billings.

If the two had consummated the merger back then, Korn/Ferry would likely be a $100 million company today. In 1969, when Korn and Ferry hung out their shingle, the leading firm was Boyden Associates with $5 million in revenues. A decade later, Korn/Ferry had surpassed Boyden and dozens of other established search firms to move ahead as the world's largest. Today, Boyden's $17 million billings is less than a third of Korn/Ferry's $58 million total. On its way to becoming the biggest, the partnership has enjoyed an enviable annual growth rate nearing 30 percent.

Nothing more impressively tells the story of the firm's dramatic growth than the half dozen or so pictures of the company's partners' meetings over the years. The prints show a small, frugal beginning and lead to the large, extravagant present. Assembled together, they are not unlike a television storyboard, each portrait a visual testament to the firm's continued growth and prosperity. They are often mounted on the office walls of Korn/Ferry partners in undistinguished wooden frames, but no one seems to have a complete collection of them, no one except Charles Murphy, a 67-year-old, red-faced Irishman who has assumed the role of in-house historian. Murphy stores them all in a desk drawer in his New York office, making copies of each with numbers on every partner's head to identify them. He gleefully pulls them out for a visitor to have a peek.

The first partners' meeting in June of 1973 did not stray far from home. The picture shows a mere 18 partners at the end of a mahogany table at Los Angeles' Century Plaza Hotel with Korn dead center wearing long, dark sideburns. The following year, when the event moved to San Diego's La Costa, the group grew to 23 and was posed on a stairwell in front of orange-red drapes.

For some reason, perhaps reflecting a touch of austerity, the next three consecutive portraits were in black and white. The group, 34-strong in June 1976, met at New York's Barclay Hotel around a horseshoe-shaped arrangement of plywood tables covered with white linen. Korn, again in the center as the orchestrator, wore a white turtleneck sweater. By August 1978 the group had grown to 47 partners, all placed under a huge glass chandelier in the Rye Hilton conference center in White Plains, New York. Korn and Ferry were seated in the second row of this picture behind a row of soldiers plopped down crosslegged atop an oriental carpet. Then came the November 1979 session in Mexico City's Camino Real Hotel, an event captured in the photo of 59 partners standing stiffly on the hotel's steps, with Korn and Ferry front and center in three-piece suits.

After Mexico something changed. The business boomed, and the pictures began to reflect the cool certitude and confidence of the group. A high-flown extravagance crept into the meetings. They became as much events, ostentatious celebrations of the firm's wild success, as they were meetings around which partners would discuss business.

That is the message communicated in the color photograph of 80 partners posed on the marble steps in front of the ornate portico of Monaco's opulent casino in October 1981. Both Prince Rainier and Princess Grace made an appearance at the meeting. The principality is a client of Korn/Ferry, which found Monaco an executive to manage its tourism and entertainment industry three years earlier.

The latest session, in late July and early August of 1984, at the Santa Barbara Biltmore on the Pacific Ocean, was a five-day affair in which the hotel became a city of Korn/Ferry people who occupied 145 rooms. There was a day at the Olympic Games in Los Angeles because the firm had placed as its head Peter Ueberroth, who later would be named *Time* magazine's "Man of the Year" for his successful handling of the event. Donald Rumsfeld, former ambassador and chairman of G. D. Searle & Co., addressed the group during a salmon luncheon in a breezy, open room overlooking Santa Barbara Channel.

During much of the day, partners would meet to speak about worldwide marketing efforts, ethics or the international political and economic outlook and to hear editors from *The Wall Street Journal,* *Fortune* and *Forbes* talk about trends in management. The wives, whose attendance also was bankrolled by the firm, would then be shuttled off to tour the Zaca Mesa Winery or to sweat at aerobics classes with instructors from Jane Fonda's Workout, Inc. One managing partner says the affair carried a price tag in excess of $500,000.

There were parties on several nights. One featured an outdoor country-and-western theme cookout followed by an evening of gambling for prizes at blackjack tables and roulette wheels. But the centerpiece of this worldwide partners' meeting was the lavish black tie dinner in the Biltmore's Coral Casino on July 31, a formal dinner dance preceded by poolside cocktails. Korn/Ferry partners and their wives sipped Gewurztraminer Trimbach 1981, Cabernet Sauvignon Jordan 1980 and Brut Classico Champagne Codorniu as the orchestra played. They dined on a sumptuous banquet of Cold Asparagus Spears in Strawberry Vinaigrette, Hot Shrimp on Cornbread, Filet of Beef Wellington and Swan Glace Aux Champagne Creme in a pool of chocolate. In the middle of it all, Korn and Ferry stood on the dance floor with microphones in hand to publicly acknowledge the contributions of the more crucial members of the partnership. Each of them would rise from their seats to the applause of their peers, shake hands with Korn and with Ferry and return to their tables with a closed envelope that contained a handsome bonus. There was even a Korn/Ferry version of Sinatra's "My Way" with lyrics recognizing the pair's accomplishments.

What largely remains of this extravaganza in almost every partner's office is a color portrait of more than 100 smiling partners, only four of them women, outfitted in tuxedos and gowns on a manicured lush green lawn in the Biltmore's recreation area. Behind the posed group are several putting greens, while the Biltmore's shuffleboard courts can be seen to the right of the group.

Despite this impressive record of achievement, professional acknowledgement from competing peers has remained surprisingly elusive for both Korn and Ferry. There has always been a lack of recognition, an unwillingness to concede that Korn/Ferry is the best, or as its literature so proudly proclaims, that it is the "world's leading executive search firm."

Competitors often grouse that Korn has only been interested in quantity, not quality, that he sometimes competes by unprofessionally discounting his fees, that his firm's success in completing assignments is among the lowest in the business and that the quality of the firm's consultants is uneven. Seldom are the accusations supported, yet the sniping has continued unabated from the start. Initally, several of the established headhunting firms took out their frustrations on Korn/Ferry through the business's trade association: the Association of Executive Recruiting Consultants (AERC), once a cozy, little club whose members would indiscriminately bar others on the basis of hearsay and personal innuendo. It was a group bogged down by egos and greed, small-minded politics and narrow thinking. "It was ridiculous," recalls John Schlueter, who served as the organization's executive director from 1973 to 1979, a period of his professional life which he bitterly regrets.

In the mid-1970s, Schlueter recalls that Dick Ferry called him about possibly joining the group. Schlueter was enthusiastic. Korn/Ferry was then emerging as one of the largest search firms in the business. Their inclusion in the membership could only help make the association more credible. He quickly assembled a group of key members, including the president and chairmen of the AERC's nominating and ethics committees, and held a meeting at New York's University Club. The exploratory session degenerated into an inquiry during which AERC officials alleged all sorts of charges against Korn/Ferry. Ferry, then legitimately interested in joining the business's association, was placed on the defensive for most of the session.

"I was frankly embarrassed the way our group talked down to him," says Schlueter, who joined Korn/Ferry as a headhunter in 1979 after leaving the association. "They said things like, after all, you're not a member and we don't know whether you're qualified. He handled it beautifully. After the meeting was over, he said 'John, why don't you give me a call when you think we would be accepted by the membership.' We shook hands, and he never called."

Ferry now shrugs when recalling the meeting. "We had a lot of myths about the firm," he says. "So you had to sit there and deal with people who said, 'Well, tell us about this or that and why you have a reputation for this?' The myths were we did contingency work. That was bullshit. That we were a production shop, only interested in selling assignments, but we never made placements. Well, anyone who looked at our repeat business couldn't say that. It was all a bunch of bullshit."

Yet, many competitors, envious at having watched the upstart Korn/Ferry surpass them in size and revenues years ago, continue to refer to the company in the most disparaging terms. One president of a major search firm claims they're in the "doorbell selling" racket, a critical reference to their emphasis on building volume. Gerry Roche of Heidrick & Struggles, drawing on an analogy from the retail world, has referred to them as the Macy's of the business while claiming that his firm is the far more tony and exclusive Bergdorf Goodman. "When I lose a search to Russell Reynolds or Heidrick & Struggles I don't like it but I understand," says Robert Lamalie whose search firm bears his name. "When I lose to Korn/Ferry, I just flinch."

The venom Korn's competitors so eagerly secrete largely derives from how their partnership has changed the business. At the top levels, it no longer is the cozy white shoe club it was when Korn and Ferry opened up shop. "We were aggressively going after the competition and aggressively trying to recruit out of our competition, so we alienated a number of people," says Ferry, prominently rooted in California's Catholic community. "We weren't clubby. Our people are from a wide range of ethnic backgrounds. We didn't meet the image at all for the club."

Someone had to bear the blame for the old establishment's decline. Why not Lester Korn and Dick Ferry? "Lester Korn is a pioneer in this business, but he obviously isn't well-liked," says Alan Tower, who had done publicity for several big executive recruiting firms starting with Boyden Associates in 1975 and most recently with

Heidrick & Struggles. "He has been accused of lowering the standards of search work. But other firms are also jealous of them. Somebody would shoot me for this, too, but he's disliked because he's Jewish and the search business was largely a WASP domain. What he did was bust up the club.

"He's not afraid to sell which was a dirty word in the business. In the early days, the other firms looked at him with curiosity. Some traditionalists were actually thinking about sponsoring polo matches when Korn was talking to *The Wall Street Journal* on what kind of lunch you should buy a prospect. It wasn't until later when he started getting their clients that they looked at marketing differently. He forced the business out into the public. He also sensed his weakness was quality, not quantity, so he tried to stress quality in his marketing. He is a mass merchandiser."

Most headhunters feared reporters. Almost never willing to talk about their clients or their assignments, they worried that even meeting journalists could lead to a violation of their rule of confidence. Not Korn. His appetite for publicity was insatiable. He devoured the interviews, insisted upon them and recognized that his success was directly tied to the publicity he could generate for the company.

His marketing strategy was twofold: to keep the firm visible to potential clients and to insure that when an executive received an unsolicited telephone call from a Korn/Ferry headhunter he would at least know what the firm did and what it was all about. That could make the difference in his willingness to answer personal questions posed by a perfect stranger on a telephone. "Our objective was to get the story out on Korn/Ferry," says Ferry. "We knew we were going to be a public enterprise, and we also knew we had to be recognized by outsiders in order to have access to candidates and contacts and build the inventory."

Korn hired some of the top public relations talent available, from Kekst and Co., Inc. to Ruder, Finn & Rotman, Inc., Hill & Knowlton and Burson-Marstellar. And he was relentlessly demanding of them. Korn's first advisor was Gershon Kekst, a New York public relations maven who has since carved a niche in handling communications in corporate takeover battles. The pair knew Kekst from their Peat Marwick days, and Kekst had advised them on how best to break away from the accounting firm. But when a Kekst PR client, Shareholders Capital Corp., acquired competitor Boyden Associates in 1971, Korn insisted that Kekst resign the account. Kekst maintained there was no conflict of interest because he wasn't directly representing Boyden. Korn vehemently disagreed.

"We had a big fight over it and to punish me he took his business to Ruder, Finn & Rotman," recalls Kekst. "He [Korn] thought he was pouring salt over the wound by going from one firm to another." Korn eventually returned back to Kekst, but not before showing several other firms how central he believed public relations were to his business. When Hill & Knowlton had the account in the mid-1970s and word arrived that he was on his way to New York, "the cry at Hill & Knowlton from account people running down the hall was 'He's coming back!' "

He would scrutinize the firm's monthly activity reports, which tallied placements in publications, and would quickly complain when Korn/Ferry didn't get its share of mentions. "A meeting with Lester was tedious, anxiety-producing and sometimes volatile," says one former public relations executive at Hill & Knowlton. "The first thought I would have when I heard the name Lester Korn was to hide under my desk."

Korn had a similar effect at other agencies, too. "Everytime he came to New York he'd expect to stand in front of a room full of journalists," says another former public relations executive who worked with Korn. "He thought he was the Secretary of State. Lester would rant, rave and scream. He'd say, 'Look, you still haven't gotten me the story I want: How two guys started in this business and created the largest executive search firm.' Lester didn't care about anything except making money and promoting his company. There was a singular purpose to what he did."

All the more surprising, according to those who worked on his account at several agencies, was Korn's ability to eke out far more productivity than other clients in return for lower fees. Public relations agents, believing they could gain from his connections in the corporate world, treated his account much differently than that of the average client. "If the monthly minimum was $3,000, Lester was paying $2,000 and getting $10,000 worth of work a month," explains one PR agent.

What helped to keep Korn/Ferry in the press on a fairly regular basis was its "National Index of Executive Vacancies," a questionable pseudo-survey based on the firm's poll of its domestic clients which Korn began promoting as a legitimate economic indicator in

1972. Before a firm buys plant and equipment, Korn would say, it buys managers. So, he would argue, that made the index a leading indicator of economic activity every bit as relevant as plans for capital investment. "The press bought it because it was new and sexy," says a PR executive.

Korn not only put out one of these every three months, he had the survey structured so that it reported on five different regions, 11 major industry sectors and nine managerial functions, such as finance and marketing, to maximize his coverage. That way, local newspapers and trade publications could tailor the release specifically to their audiences. It became a widely duplicated gimmick by most of Korn's competitors from Heidrick's "Executrend" study of executive-openings display advertising in major publications to Boyden's own "Boyden Index" based on its business. Arthur Young, Lamalie Associates and the Association of Executive Search Consultants still publish similar surveys along with Korn/Ferry despite embarrassing disparities in the results, making the validity of them questionable.

Korn, however, also began underwriting exhaustive studies on senior executives and management issues at UCLA's Graduate School of Management and Yale University's School of Organization and Management. And he began publishing an annual study in 1973 on the boards of directors at the nation's major corporations, projects which lent his firm not only more newspaper clippings but prestige and credibility.

One public relations agency ruled out television for Korn because it didn't think he was charismatic enough for the tube. "He looks, at times, like Dracula," explained one adviser. "He does have a scary look to him. He doesn't smile often and he doesn't evoke a sense of comfort or pleasure."

But it didn't hinder his ability to consistently appear in print. A glimpse of Korn/Ferry's incredible success at generating news came from a cursory review of how many times the firm's name has appeared in the businessman's daily Bible, *The Wall Street Journal*, over the 12-year period from 1973 to 1984. The newspaper quoted Korn on everything from face lifts for executives to management succession. Korn's publicity machine earned his firm 64 mentions, more than five times greater than Spencer Stuart, three times more than Boyden, twice as many as Russell Reynolds and 50 percent greater than Heidrick & Struggles.

Yet, those figures say nothing of the tremendous publicity Korn/Ferry garnered for itself elsewhere, in esoteric trade journals and small daily newspapers. In one single year, 1979, a press clipping service dredged up 282 articles in which the firm had wangled at least a mention. One public relations agency developed an inch-thick list of more than 800 media contacts for Korn, from *Travel Management Daily* and *Textile Industries* to *The Harrisburg Patriot* (in Pennsylvania) and *The Shreveport Times* (in Louisiana). Public relations fluff was sent to as many as six editors at *Business Week* and five editors and reporters at *The New York Times,* which published an op-ed article by Korn on the million dollar executive and made only one alteration to his story. A *Times* editor inserted the word "orthodontic" before the word "braces."

Korn's relentless marketing efforts had an impact well beyond what his competitors could ever have imagined. In 1980, a privately-sponsored study by the opinion research firm Yankelovich, Skelly & White found that Korn/Ferry was identified as "the most prestigious search firm" in the business by Fortune 500 executives. Close behind were Heidrick & Struggles, followed by Spencer Stuart and Russell Reynolds.

Inside, Ferry was busy creating the systems to run the business like a business and unlike other executive search firms. Most of them were and are loose collections of egos under one umbrella or roof. The salaries and bonuses of each headhunter in a firm is based almost entirely on the billings he brings in. There is generally little teamwork and certainly little incentive to participate in the management of the firm or to enhance the firm's image on the outside. Most firms have little idea of how much it costs to complete a single search, either. In short, they lack even the most simplistic management and financial controls of a legitimate business. The greatest irony of the business is that men and women who recruit some of the nation's most important corporate leaders are themselves mediocre managers.

Borrowing heavily from their experiences at Peat Marwick, Korn and Ferry imposed the controls and structure of a business that other firms find incomprehensible. Among other things, its consultants turn in timesheets every two weeks that list the number of hours spent on every engagement. The firm uses this information to evaluate how effectively its employees use their time. "If you spend 100 hours doing something when the person next to you can do it in only 50 hours, then obviously the other person is more efficient," notes David Smith, one of four managing partners at Korn/Ferry. Smith, a former controller for an insurance company, is yet another Peat Marwick alumnus who jumped ship in 1979. "We're run as a business, not a club."

Every three months, a computer spits out report cards on each consultant, letting him or her know exactly where each stands, so when the annual bonus is paid out at the end of the fiscal year in April there are few surprises. Excellent performers typically earn a bonus equal to their base salary, although the up side for a bonus is triple the base pay. Powerful incentive to bring in the goods.

No less crucial, Korn and Ferry carefully assembled a structured hierarchy to do the business, a system better able to efficiently handle the sheer volume and regularity of its client's needs. With the single exception of Russell Reynolds, no other major headhunting firm has learned how to leverage its business like Korn/Ferry. Most successful service firms, be they the blue-chip corporate law firms, management consultants or accountants, hire lower-level personnel to do the nitty-gritty of their assignments, to crunch the numbers, to delve into the case histories, to write the reports. The work of these wage slaves is then billed out at rates which far exceed their salaries. The more work a service firm can successfully push down to those levels, the greater profitability it can squeeze from its operations. Seasoned and mature veterans are saved only for the most important chores, the crucial personal contacts with clients and the development of more business.

Headhunters have yet to learn this simple lesson. Korn/Ferry, though, is the most obvious exception. At the lowest ranks are its researchers and research directors, followed by associates, senior associates, managing associates, and finally staff vice-presidents, revenue center vice-presidents, office managers, managing directors and managing partners. There are about 106 partners, nearly 200 associates and 75 researchers. It is, unlike the team assembled by Russell Reynolds, a heterogeneous group. "What you've got here is a United Nations," says Windle Priem, one of Korn/Ferry's four managing partners. "We've got our Harvard and Yale people, but we also have a lot of hard-working, aggressive street-smart guys from all over."

The research staff, which keeps track of the candidate and client files, is strictly a backroom operation that does not interview sources or candidates by telephone or in person. It gathers from files, prior sources and cold contacts the names and telephone numbers of executives for specific assignments. This intelligence is fed to the next level.

The bottom three layers of the hierarchy—the associates—are executors of the business. They are responsible for the day-to-day orchestration of the search. They analyze the information delivered by the research department, make contact with potential candidates and sources, do initial in-person interviews with candidates and try to come up with finalists for review by the officer in charge of the search. The hours are long and the pay is low by headhunting standards. These associates, whose average age is in their late 30s, earn pre-bonus salaries of between $35,000 and $70,000 a year. They can tack on as much as 40 percent of their base in bonus money annually.

The top four layers—the vice-presidents, office managers and managing directors—generate the business, retain virtually all contact with the clients and personally interview, sometimes with an associate in tow, all final candidates before they are presented to clients. On senior-level searches, more of the day-to-day work gets pushed up the chain of command. The compensation ranges from $75,000 to $300,000 with bonus for these slots, occupied by seasoned professionals whose average age is in their early 50s. Each of Korn/Ferry's four managing partners can hit $400,000 to $450,000 in a good year, while both Korn and Ferry are in the high six figures. Increasingly, the firm is shifting the emphasis from bonus to base to better attract executives unaccustomed to loaded bonuses tied to performance.

The hierarchy does more than leverage the business. At the lower levels it provides young people with the first career track in executive search. At the higher levels it does away with the dull, frustrating grunt work so essential to the business. That is critical because it leads to lower turnover among the key business generators who at other firms would find a greater portion of their time devoted to cold telephone calling.

The system reserves its highest rewards for those who can bring in the business. Associates who show little aptitude for business development will never become partners at Korn/Ferry. "There's no question where the power lies," says Priem, one of the four managing partners. "There's no question about that. You cannot be successful here unless you're pretty aggressive and can sell. I view this as a selling job. You sell to get the work. You sell good candidates on jobs. Look at all the heavy-hitters out there and they all have superior selling skills."

Competitors of Korn/Ferry commonly argue that placing most of the search in the hands of juniors leads to shoddy work. They contend that executive search is such a "personal" business that the junior system of the corporate law firm cannot effectively be transferred to headhunting. Korn/Ferry has proved them embarrassingly wrong. The simple truth is that the endless telephone calling and repetitive questioning of sources and candidates by phone requires little skill at all. It is dull, boring work. Why intelligent, ambitious and savvy headhunters at other firms gladly do it would be a complete mystery if not for the six-figure incomes they bring in.

Korn/Ferry has shown everyone, however, that this needn't be so. "The research people are better than I ever was at research," says Smith, the firm's second highest producer. "The associates are as good as I ever was at search. So why shouldn't I reserve my time for things that I do best—the evaluation, presentation and consultation with clients."

Relieving senior people from the grunt work of the business also frees them to permit more time consulting with clients and less time simply transferring bodies. "I use the extra time to act as a sounding board for the CEO, working with him to arrive at the best solution," says Morgan Harris, a Korn/Ferry managing partner based in Los Angeles. "That's better use of my time than banging the phones all day. If my counterparts at Heidrick think they ought to be on the phone all day that's their business, but they are not getting any further ahead by doing that."

Slowly but surely, some of the other major firms are catching on. Heidrick & Struggles, Ward Howell and Spencer Stuart are all increasingly pushing down greater amounts of mundane telephone work to their researchers. "For years, I heard people call them the McDonald's of the search business," concedes Gilbert Dwyer, former chief executive of Ward Howell. "But I've got to tell you, I don't lose in this business except to Goddamn formidable people. I don't lose to turkeys. And they are good. They beat me more than I beat them. They bring slaves in and grind them into the firm. But they make up in sheer volume of effort whatever they may lack in quality. And the end result for clients is that their search work is competitive with anybody else."

In point of fact, it is often more competitive with everybody else.

Bringing to this fragmented business the discipline and structure of a Big Eight accounting firm, Korn and Ferry built their firm into the legitimate business that most other firms were not. That was an internal achievement, not readily apparent to all clients. What really beat down the headhunting traditionalists at their own game was aggressive marketing, which went well beyond the publicity getting. The pair pioneered the use of specialty divisions. Dated competitors saw it as a gimmick when it was a marketing coup. What client wouldn't want a so-called specialist in the field, one who could talk shop with him in detail, maybe even drop a bit of intelligence on the competition for starters. The first specialty was an obvious choice: real estate. Half of the top ten builders in the country were based in California, and the business was booming. Within three years of their start, Korn/Ferry boasted three national specialized divisions covering real estate, financial services and petrochemicals and energy. Some 11 specialty divisions now cast about in different industries and functions for opportunities.

"Once you did a half a dozen assignments in one field you clearly had an edge on the competition, and it was tough for them to catch up," says Ferry. "With each search you gain more knowledge and you get to know all the players in the market. The guys who run these specialty practices are preeminent in their fields nationally. And nobody can compete with them in the sense of knowing the market as well as they know it."

The most successful of these specializations is its financial services division. If the division were stripped out of Korn/Ferry it would rank as the fifth or sixth largest search firm in the U.S. The division has done more than 150 searches for Citicorp, Korn/Ferry's largest single global client, about 90 searches for Manufacturers Hanover, more than 100 searches for Security Pacific and numerous assignments for Chase Manhattan.

The architect of the business, with 20 partners and 22 associates, is Windle Priem, an intense, stern-faced man who can appear distant and uncordial. He joined Korn/Ferry in 1976 after serving as a President Nixon-appointed regional director for the Small Business Administration. Priem accumulated his banking know-how at Marine Midland Bank, where he had been vice-president in corporate banking from 1964 to 1972. So driven is Priem that he recently moved from an apartment on Manhattan's 82nd Street and the East River to 49th Street and 2nd Avenue simply to be closer to his office. Priem starts work at 7:15 A.M. and closes down at 10:00 P.M., typically after a late dinner with a client or candidate. That work ethic has allowed him to be Korn/Ferry's number one producer for four consecutive years, piling up an extraordinary $1,415,000 in billings in fiscal 1985. The fact that he has four associates working directly under him helps, too. But few search firms could boast an individual so outwardly aggressive in his approach.

"I built this business at the expense of Russell Reynolds," he says. "Because they had what I now have. I provided an alternative, and we now have a $12 million financial services business. When I came here in 1976 we had nothing. I maintain that the two of us control about 70 percent of the meaningful financial services business in the world. Okay?"

It was Priem who eased out Russell Reynolds as the major headhunter for Chase Manhattan after Reynolds's polished and admired New York manager Worthington S. Mayer was killed in an auto crash over the July 4th weekend in 1980 at the age of 46. Alan Lafley, then the highly respected executive vice-president of human resources for Chase, often used Mayer to do the bank's important search work. It was Mayer who brought Lafley to Chase in 1974 from Clark Equipment Co., Inc. After Mayer's death, Lafley says, the quality of the firm's work declined. "The candidates we brought in through Russell Reynolds weren't making it," says Lafley, who Priem recruited to Korn/Ferry after he retired from Chase in 1985. "We had a few sessions with Russ and he tried to find someone who could produce the quality we were looking for, but it was not coming along."

After Ward Howell's Gilbert Dwyer placed Steven Drotter as Lafley's successor at Chase, Dwyer thought he could finally break the bank. It wasn't so. Chase may have turned to Dwyer for a non-financial search not within Priem's expertise, but the bank continued to go to Priem for its mainstream bank executives. "Win Priem owns Chase," says Dwyer flatly. "And it's because of his very effective work there. It's not attributable to anything else. He doesn't have a magic personality."

Specialization allows Priem and other Korn/Ferry headhunters the opportunity to become more of a true consultant, gaining in the process a better foothold on a company's business. "I know the business well," maintains Priem with ego-gratifying bluster. "I know how it works, I know what it is today and what it will be in the future. So when I meet with a client, I'm adding a value well beyond just, 'Well, here's a position. Why don't you go and fill it.' I'm in a position to tell them, 'Look, from a strategic standpoint this is the way you ought to position your business. This is the way you ought to look at this position. If you go to search, this is the type of candidate you're going to find out there who is attracted to your company.' "

Priem strolls over to a slew of folders by a wall of windows which overlook the Park Plaza Atrium, where Korn/Ferry has its New York quarters. "Those are active assignments that I'm on the hook for and I guess there are 11 of them and I've got to account for them," he says. "There's not an assignment in there that's under $100,000, and there's one that's at $1.2 million."

Fingering the files, he picks one out after another. "There's a brokerage job at half a million; there's a president of a bank at $300,000; there's an exotic junk bond position at half a million; there's a presidency of a U.S. subsidiary of a worldwide bank at $400,000; there's a chief investment officer job at half a million for one of the wealthiest individuals in the world; the $1.2 million job is a mergers and acquisitions position at a balls-bracket firm."

Unbelievably, he says, two candidates had already turned down the $1.2 million job. "In my mind," he adds, "this is just another transaction. I'm looking for a hired gun, okay? And I happen to be very good at knowing who these people are and getting to them. It doesn't take long at all. In terms of effort and hours expended, I don't have that much into this project. It's high risk, high reward, just like the business they're in. They get atrocious fees for what they do relative to the value added. On my end, I'm getting big fees relative to the value added. But I know who the people are and I have access to them. Plus, I'm able to properly represent the client, articulate the situation and get the parties talking. This is a very unique window. It won't last and I'm riding it while it's here.

"This is a client that I've been working with for four years. At the end of last year this client said I was thinking about what we did last year and I'd feel better if we sent you another $50,000 because we're going to be doing some important work and I want you to be happy. That's the first time that happened. Usually they want money back. But this involves someone who had already paid me well over $400,000 in 1984."

The bonus didn't go directly into Priem's pocket, but rather to the firm. What keeps someone like Priem at Korn/Ferry? The specialty practice for one thing. Priem, in effect, has his own business at Korn/Ferry. "I am my own boss. I hire my own people. I make as much money here as I could make at any other firm. But I have resources available here that I probably wouldn't be able to have elsewhere, and I have access to major work that I would lose as a sole practitioner."

All these strengths are tightly wrapped in a culture driven by a unique partnership, by Korn, an incurable workaholic, and Ferry, a thoughtful, reflective man. "Dick is very calm and long-range," says Arthur Taylor, former CBS president who is on Korn/Ferry's board of directors. "He's not particularly interested in driving too hard, but he's there every day and very effective. Lester is right at it every second of the time. He's got hyper energy. He doesn't sleep; he doesn't eat; he doesn't do anything except work."

Korn knows how to handle the whip, too. One consultant says that after some particularly rough meetings during which Korn has lashed at him, colleagues have later come up to him to express their empathy. "Lester is the ass kicker," confides a consultant who had worked with him closely. "If you were the slightest bit weak, he'd bully the shit out of you. He pushed the shit out of those guys. When he was in New York and that was once a week, the office did a very deep intake of breath and let it out slowly."

Fear of failure pervades the atmosphere. Whether fictional or not, tales swirl about the company that enforces an unusual discipline on the troops. Korn, according to one story which has made the rounds, has been known to call his consultants at 2:00 A.M. to berate them if a corporation puts out a major search that Korn/Ferry either does not know about or fails to get. "I dislike stupidity," says Korn, who then informs a visitor he is about to "chew out" a consultant in the New York office. "There are days that I dislike the fact that we can't get the work done as efficiently as it should be done. But this is not easy work. And this is not a business without frustrations."

Ambitious, throttled and determined, Korn nas never allowed anything or anyone to hinder his or his firm's success. Murphy recalls that the worst day in his professional career occurred on February 8, 1974, when Korn came to the New York office which he managed. The recession had hit and business was severely down. The pair were traveling together in a cab to the airport during a New York snowstorm.

"Charlie, do we have any prospects at all?" Korn asked him.

"Les, no, I don't have anything. Our prospects sheet is blank. We aren't getting the assignments. The phone isn't ringing."

It was one of the few times that Murphy ever saw Korn concerned. "That was the low water mark in the firm," Murphy adds. Told this story, Korn bristles. "If he is referring to a bleak period," he says, "it would be only New York that was bleak. And it was bleak because it needed different leadership, which it got. You have to move people aside occasionally." So Murphy, the man who put Korn into the search business at Peat Marwick, who protected him from the oncoming flak at an accounting firm and who deserted Peat to join his former partner less than three years earlier, was removed as manager of the New York branch.

John Sullivan, who spent 13 years with IBM, compares the win-at-all-costs environment to that which dominated the culture of the world's largest computer company. Like IBM, which sets quotas for its salesmen, Korn/Ferry requires its partners to hit certain revenue targets and to develop specific target companies within an industry specialty. Implicit in this process is a strong commitment to further growth. Korn believes a professional service firm must grow between 18 percent to 20 percent annually or it will simply stagnate. That belief has been part of the religion of Big Blue as well. At IBM, Sullivan was, among other things, manager of education under former chief executive John Opel. Opel's orders: "Your job is to train the sales force and don't ever forget we want all the business."

"At IBM it was a mortal sin to lose business to a competitor," says Sullivan, "and when you did you just didn't want to go back to the office. It was like being in the Marine Corps or playing for the old New York Yankees. You just don't lose. Failure is anathema. There is some of that here. Like John Opel, Lester wants all the business, every bit of it. He won't get it, but that's the right attitude."

Unlike the nearly invincible Bronx Bombers of the 1950s, however, team spirit is often lacking within the culture of Korn/Ferry. Internal competition is fierce. And the specialty practices, albeit a brilliant marketing stroke, heighten the competitive tensions because they cut across the geographical offices. Overlap, therefore, is inevitable. At its best, the tense, competitive culture knocks out the competition and Korn/Ferry lands the job. At its worst, however, consultants bitterly compete against each other in one grudge match after another.

"It gets a little uncomfortable," says Gerry Riso, who quit

Korn/Ferry in 1985 after a 14-month stint as a New York vice-president in its health care division. "In one case, one of my partners simply had his secretary write a letter to a potential client. I followed up and did the whole damn thing, brought the job in, but he arbitrarily took all the credit himself. That's nonsense."

However disquieting to those who labor under it, the tension is inevitable and important. It is part of Korn/Ferry's success, too. Like the "creative tension" deliberately cultivated in the newsroom of *The Washington Post*. The pressure forces the best efforts from its people just as the internal tension at Korn/Ferry reminds everyone of the need for continued growth. Korn, the demanding taskmaster, maintains the tension, but he has shown the ability to entertain the criticism of partners as well with uncharacteristic patience and understanding.

Morgan Harris, who had headed up Russell Reynolds's Los Angeles operations before joining Korn/Ferry in 1980, recalls a three-hour airplane trip with Korn during which surfaced a number of complaints he had about the firm. "I went over a litany of things I thought were wrong with the firm, with him and with Dick, and he took it all in," says Harris. "I told him that in the early years we had a Korn/Ferry that was correctly accused of having too mechanistic a product, of having poor internal communications and of living in a divide-and-conquer world where people got too powerful and played off other people. Generally it stopped, but there were still a few wires sticking out and some of them were real close to home. I laid it on him pretty heavy and he took it nicely.

"Frankly," adds Harris, "I've come on pretty strong with both of them. I'm not sure how happy that makes them but they put up with it. I like an environment of candor. I once told Russ (Reynolds) that conspicuous by its absence in the firm was any semblance of leadership and conspicuous by its presence was the continuing evidence that the firm was being run for the benefit of two or three people. The goodies are spread around here."

While Korn and Ferry together own 55 percent of the firm, the remaining equity is spread among more than 100 partners. Their say in running the firm is limited, however. "It is true that we do not take a lot of votes," says Korn in a grand and wonderful understatement. "This firm is an enlightened democracy. And most enlightened democracies are very careful about the vote. They protect it."

So when Korn's partners publicly doubt that the firm can continue to grow at anywhere near the pace it has, he is quick to show his disdain. "Many of my partners disagree with me," says Korn, "but I think a professional firm must grow or else it stagnates. It must reach someplace between 18 percent and 20 percent per annum to staisfy its internal needs."

The torrid pace of that growth has presented embarrassing problems of its own. It resulted in the hiring of headhunters whose credentials were somewhat suspect. Consider the case of David H. Charlson, the Korn/Ferry managing partner who left in 1984 after it was discovered that an M.B.A. degree he claimed from Stanford University was nonexistent. Charlson not only worked for the world's largest search firm, he was managing director of its Midwest operations, a senior officer of the company and a member of its management committee. He joined Korn/Ferry nearly nine years earlier, after stints as a recruiter for General Foods Corp., Bank of America and Wells Fargo Bank. Yet his deception wasn't discovered until Charlson's biographical sketch was circulated by the Harvard Business School Club of Chicago where he was scheduled to speak at a seminar.

Jim Kennedy, the headhunting industry's news hound and watchdog, reported these and other sordid and embarrassing details about Charlson in his monthly *Executive Recruiter News*. Kennedy, who issues his widely-read newsletter from Fitzwilliam, New Hampshire, also didn't hesitate to report that other Korn/Ferry former officers and executive committee members were found with "flawed educational credentials." John B. Higgins, Korn/Ferry's former Chicago office head who left two years earlier to start his own firm, claimed a University of Notre Dame Ph.D. in finance which did not exist, while Guy H. Pullen, another recently departed Chicago headhunter for Korn/Ferry, claimed a bachelor's degree from New York University, which had no record of his attendance.

It wasn't the first time Kennedy printed such news, and it likely wouldn't be the last. The Association of Executive Search Consultants, partly due to Kennedy's reportage on headhunters with fraudulent backgrounds, now requires that new members state that they have checked the credentials of their employees. The maverick publisher goes so far as to equate recruiters who doctor their backgrounds with priests who father illegitimate children. Responding to one critic over another similar exposé, Kennedy retorted, "Is it worse for a recruiter to have a phony resume, for a priest to father an illegitimate child, for a judge to steal? Yes, I happen to think it is worse, for such people are in positions of public trust."

Korn/Ferry was so outraged over the Charlson report that it cancelled all its subscriptions to Kennedy's newsletter and said it would refuse to cooperate with him in the future. When Charlson later surfaced as a managing partner with New York-based Richards Consultants Ltd., Kennedy thought it an outrage, too. He maintained it was "like giving a convicted murderer his freedom and a new gun just 'cuz he promises never to kill again."

The feud has since died down, but it did little to bolster Korn/Ferry's image. Another prickly problem also poses a threat to Korn and Ferry's plan for growth in the future: the larger a search firm becomes, the fewer places it has available to it to discover candidates. Having too many clients in one industry shrinks the available pool of executive talent to a headhunter who agrees not to pirate executives from a client company or division for two years after an assignment. Korn/Ferry already has 1,200 corporate, government and institutional clients. Rather than significantly increasing their client roster, Korn and Ferry are trying to capture more business from existing clients who may typically employ three or more different search firms.

A critical question is how more efficient Korn and Ferry can make their machine. A clue to the future lies in the firm's Mexican operations, where consultants average between 20 and 25 searches a year, roughly double the dozen-assignment average per consultant throughout the firm. Korn/Ferry's Mexico City office is the most productive tentacle of the system. The reason: Their universe of candidates is so small and well-known that they quickly know who the candidates are for any specific search.

Ferry hopes that Korn/Ferry's computer databank will allow his troops the same advantage elsewhere. Instead of doing 12 searches a year, Korn/Ferry consultants might be able to do up to 16 if Korn/Ferry's multimillion investment in new technology pays off, says Ferry. "If you take any one field, whether it's energy, high technology or banking, there really aren't that many people you have to track to fill the assignments," he says. "If you track 2,000 people in banking, you certainly have nearly all the candidates who could be considered for any senior-level search. I don't know how far we're going to take this thing, but the potential is exciting. You really wouldn't have to track more than 50,000 people in America today to fill most of your key jobs, and that's even a large number when you think about it."

Both Korn and Ferry now have set their sights on reaching the $100 million mark by 1990, a prospect some find hard to swallow. "Our partners have always had a difficult time accepting our projections," assures Ferry. "It was difficult for them to believe that we would be at $10 million until we got there. Then we said we're going to reach $20 million and they'd say, 'God, that seems impossible.' We're over $50 million and now they are believers."

The Elitist

"A new club for a different time."

RUSSELL REYNOLDS HAD flown into a rage. When Jim Kennedy's blue-colored newsletter, blandly called *Executive Recruiter News,* arrived in the day's mail he discovered that a former client was calling him "unethical." Under the headline, "Does Russell Reynolds Associates Really Violate Client Off-Limits Canons?" was a brief, one-page story that turned his reddish face the color of a beet.

This was a nasty bit of news for the freckle-faced, blue-eyed headhunting entrepreneur. Here he was being accused of violating the cardinal rule of the business: Never raid your own clients.

It was easy enough to poach a client's managers, of course. Head-hunters promote disloyalty in comfortable anonymity. Corporations on the losing end seldom know which executive hunters have worked behind-the-scenes to lure away their corporate stars, a circumstance that makes stealing executives from clients, particularly huge, sprawling corporations, more than a temptation for some. Who would ever know?

But Russell Reynolds? The boyish, all-American, clean-cut Yalie who had put together the most elite and most grand of all the head-hunting firms? Who had himself enticed consultants with polish and good breeding to a business once considered not quite comme il faut? Whose high-browed managers variously describe the firm as the "Rolls-Royce of the industry?"

Reynolds has suppressed his anger, at least for the moment, over this latest contretemps. "I'm an inwardly positive individual despite fits of frustration and depression," he says. "We had a little scene yesterday, and if you hadn't known me better you might have wondered." But it is lunch time, after all, and Reynolds is munching a chef's salad smothered with Russian dressing at the Yale Club. The New York club has been a favorite haunt of his for years because it's only a five-minute walk from his Park Avenue office and, most importantly, because it's, well, the Yale Club. At a luncheon table in the crowded light blue room, he is sitting with two of his associates, then personal assistant Steven B. Potter and media advisor Anne Board. All three appropriately boast degrees from, where else but Yale.

If the news item about Reynolds's ungainly poaching is on his mind, he doesn't allow it to surface in conversation. Instead, he is engaged once again in a favorite sport: ego-tripping, name-dropping. Reynolds isn't the only headhunter who loves this game, but he could rightfully claim to be one of its most relentlessly adept players. Last night, Reynolds gleefully notes, he was one of only two executive headhunters at a private dinner party at 21, the tony Manhattan restaurant. The bash was thrown by Peter G. Peterson, former co-chief executive officer of Lehman Brothers Kuhn Loeb, the investment banking house, for President Reagan's budget director David Stockman.

"Pete said it would be a small dinner party. About 60 people showed up. Just like him," laughs Reynolds. Among the guests were the chairmen and chief executives of some of the largest corporations in America, including Exxon's Clifford Garvin, ex-Ford Chairman Philip Caldwell, Philbro-Salomon's John Gutfreund and American Standard's William Marquard. They were in town for a Business Roundtable meeting. Marquard chatted with Reynolds about the executive recruiter's recent trip to China. The chief executive took so much interest in the conversation, relates Reynolds with a wide toothy grin, that he thought Marquard would dash to a phone to call his people about selling toilet seats to China. Everyone laughs. Reynolds looks pleased.

This provides the perfect segue into Reynolds's next story on how he arranged his trip as an official guest of the chairman of CITIC, the China International Trust-Investment Corp., the government agency charged with attracting business investment to the country.

One of his headhunters, Eugene K. Lawson, "a very excellent person," had been deputy assistant secretary of the U.S. Commerce Department and helped to plan Reagan's trip to China in 1984.

"It was through his friendship with the Chinese Embassy in Washington that a hint was dropped that we would like to be invited," says Reynolds. "Vice-President George Bush was also nice enough to write a letter to the chairman which said he hoped that Debbie, my wife, and I would leave China with as warm a glow and feeling for the Chinese nation as he and Barbara did. I just got a handwritten letter from him, thanking me for a letter I sent to him."

Reynolds wants you to know he plays in the circles that matter, whether socially or professionally. And he takes both seriously. When a stockbroking friend once derisively offered a barbed comment about the body-snatching business that has become his professional life, Reynolds quickly barked: "I'll tell you one thing. The executives I have placed have worked out better than the stocks you've recommended." There have been failures, of course, but his remark might well be true. His firm's bagged notables, other than Convergent Technologies' Paul Ely, include First Chicago Corp. Chairman Barry Sullivan, Crocker National Bank Chairman Frank Cahouet, Prudential-Bache Securities Chief Executive George Ball, British Airways Chief Executive Colin Marshall and Black & Decker President Nolan Archibald.

There are more, much more. In a typical year, his staff of 120 headhunting professionals will conduct roughly 1,600 searches through 19 offices in the U.S., Europe, Asia and Australia. More than 10 percent of those assignments are for chairmen, presidents and chief executive officers. Well over 50 percent of those jobs pay in excess of $100,000 annually to the winning executives. A select few of those searches, which are more likely to command Reynolds's personal attention, offer compensation that, in the current vernacular, contains more than one comma. Midland Bank PLC of London, one of Reynolds's most cherished clients, has returned to his firm 74 times in the past eight years for searches in London, Hong Kong, Paris, New York and San Francisco. All those hunts have combined to provide another impressive statistic for his near $50 million-a-year business. Reynolds's firm has grown faster since 1980 than any other major search firm in the U.S., roughly a leap of 45 percent in each of the last five years.

These are all reasons why it would be difficult to believe that

Reynolds could possibly violate the ethics of a business he helped to upgrade. Quality and class have been the watchwords of his firm. Reynolds understood from the start that the business of recruiting, still considered by the fusty to be less than respectable, is a personal service just like investment banking or management consulting. It could be a business built, like investment banking, on a certain style, too.

So Reynolds did not shy from emulating other successful professional service businesses, like Morgan Stanley, McKinsey & Co. and J. P. Morgan, where he worked for nearly a decade. "At Morgan, I observed that they do things with taste," he says. "They are dignified but very aggressive. A lot of adrenalin goes through the bones."

Reynolds, of course, was not likely to duplicate the two-ton, massive chandelier in the style of Louis XV which hung in the banking room of his former employer at 23 Wall Street. But he eventually would install a grand Steinway piano beyond a pair of deep-grained solid doors leading to his Oriental-carpeted reception room.

Those who enter his 35th floor lavish Park Avenue offices in New York witness the embellishments of a true WASP establishment in the grand tradition of a Morgan Stanley. All of it is to create an aura of power, a signal to visitors and employees alike that Reynolds plays only in circles that matter. The Reynolds élan is that of an English Gentlemen's Club, updated to suit the style of the Yuppie generation.

There is, for example, in the same room with the Steinway piano which no one plays, a lit oil painting of Warren Hastings, a Governor General of India, that hangs on a wall between a pair of tall gold candlesticks. Across the room stands a flashing glass dome sensitive to touch.

Reynolds's sitting room, outside a rather modestly-sized corner office, boasts an antique drop-down writing desk with a silver inkwell. The walls are enlivened with signed letters addressed to him from Henry Ford II, President Reagan and Prince Charles. There are framed pictures, too, including one signed by Winston Churchill, and another of Reynolds's training class at Morgan Guaranty and of the 47-foot yacht called *Windsong*.

In another room is his collection of autographs: Napoleon 1808; Biddle in 1835; and O. Henry. A Winston Churchill landscape hangs in a private interviewing room which also features a ceremonial African head mask Reynolds picked up on a trip to Africa. Each office is outfitted with old French taxicab horns which are ceremoniously sounded whenever a Reynolds headhunter completes an assignment. This last touch garnered Reynolds's firm a mention in management guru Tom Peters' *A Passion for Excellence,* in which he naively noted that "even executive recruiters can celebrate!"

Yet another room is outfitted with an old-fashioned barber's chair so Reynolds can have his red hair flecked with gray clipped privately in the office. A small black man comes in to buff the leather of his shoes as he works.

In this grand environment, Russell Reynolds has carefully created the image of a firm run by privileged bluebloods, a bastion of Yuppie snobs. The typical headhunter here is white, male, and prep-school-Protestant. His firm is populated by a sea of Ivy Leaguers in neatly-pressed pinstripes and monogrammed shirts. Reynolds's elitist troops are sophisticated, conservative, trendy and, above all, credentialed. Of the 114 consultants portrayed in his 1985 annual brochure, 74 boast graduate degrees from some of the world's most distinguished universities. There are 45 M.B.A.s alone, a third of whom hold the golden passport stamped at Harvard. With the exception of European-based Egon Zehnder, Reynolds was the only search firm to interview M.B.A.s on the Harvard Business School campus last year. Among those 114, only one is black; 20 are women and seven are bald.

That latter statistic is important, too. The old traditionalists of the business, the Boyden's, Ward Howell's and Heidrick & Struggles's, tended to attract an older group of executives as headhunters. Reynolds, from the start, brought in young people and trained them. "Younger people are more valuable than older people think they are," he says. "I am a great believer that younger people can be as cool-headed and seasoned as older professionals who can be encumbered by the past. These people are the strength of our firm, and they are comparable to the people you'd find at Morgan or Goldman Sachs."

Reynolds, not unlike many of his highbrow competitors, is a modern-day Babbitt. Like Sinclair Lewis's real estate man, Reynolds knows the value of being well-known in the right circles. Babbitt had boasted of being a member in good standing of "the Rotarians, the Kiwanis or the Boosters; to the Oddfellows, Moose, Masons, Red Men, Woodmen, Owls, Eagles, Maccabees, Knights of Pythias, Knights of Columbus and other secret orders characterized by a high degree of heartiness, sound morals and reverence for the Constitution." Most importantly, noted Lewis, all this "was good for business, since lodge-brothers frequently became customers."

"Obviously," allows Reynolds, "for someone in our business, it's in their best advantage to know a lot of people. If you don't, you're probably in the wrong business." Reynolds's seemingly endless list of associations and clubs bears remarkable resemblance to Babbitt's in the 1920s. As his one-page bio dutifully notes, Reynolds is a member of the Round Hill Club, the Indian Harbor Yacht Club, the California Club, the Mill Reef Club in Antigua, the Amateur Ski Club of New York, the English-Speaking Union and the Society of Colonial Wars.

At all these venues, among friends and acquaintances, Reynolds charmingly entertains. "You know Philip Caldwell [the recently retired chairman of Ford Motor Corp.] is now on our board," he tells a guest at the Yale Club. "He made a very gracious statement at our board meeting which I will repeat because it is quite self-serving. He said that one of the great things our firm did for Ford was to recruit Peter Pistello as head of industrial relations for Ford before the big labor negotiations in 1982. Caldwell told me on the phone the other day that on his last day in the job on January 31 [1985] he was feted at a lunch at one of Ford's plants in Michigan, and they surprised him by making him an honorary member of the union. It was an awfully nice commentary on our efforts. He was honored and very flattered. I think that was the first time the head of a corporation was made an honorary member of his own union."

All this was true. Pistello, as architect of Ford's precedent-setting 1982 labor contract, saved the Detroit auto-maker millions of dollars. The contract contained wage and benefit concessions totaling some $1 billion at Ford. Caldwell was quickly credited with supporting what analysts began calling Ford's "pioneering efforts in labor relations." Only two years earlier, it had been widely rumored within the auto company that Caldwell was on thin ice with his board of directors. In some small, yet significant way, Reynolds had made a difference.

It was not the first time, and it would hardly be the last. One of the most celebrated was his firm's recruitment of Ian K. MacGregor, the retired chairman and chief executive of AMAX, Inc., as the new 67-year-old chairman of British Steel Corp. in 1980. More than 100 candidates for the job were explored in Europe, North

America, South Africa and Australia over a near ten-month period before arriving at a list of six executives.

U.S. and foreign executives often laughed at the fixed salary being offered by the British government, owner of the nationalized British Steel, which had been losing more than $2 million per day. But Reynolds's headhunters eventually worked out a deal that touched off a storm of protest in Britain's House of Commons. MacGregor would get about $110,000 a year, the same amount paid to the man he succeeded. But Lazard Freres & Co., the New York investment bank where MacGregor served as a general partner, would receive payments that could total up to $4.1 million over the next five years to compensate for his loss. Various members of Parliament termed the financial arrangement "monstrous," "farcical" and "disgraceful."

The search, conducted by then managing director of Reynolds's London office, David M. Norman, was so exhausting that Norman reportedly took a week of vacation to "recover" from the assignment. He apparently had traveled all over the world to nail down MacGregor in New York, South America and Australia to negotiate his coming aboard.

MacGregor was never able to make British Steel profitable, but he was successful in significantly reducing its losses. Prime Minister Margaret Thatcher, in fact, called upon MacGregor to run her government's National Coal Board after a stint at British Steel. MacGregor was expected to finally retire in September 1986.

It also was Reynolds's firm which sparked another big-bucks controversy when it lured Thomas D. Barrow, a senior vice-president and director of Exxon Corp., to Kennecott Corp. in late 1978 as chairman and chief executive. Barrow was viewed as a corporate savior who could save Kennecott from the clutches of T. Roland Berner, chief executive of Curtiss-Wright Corp. and a veteran corporate raider. At the time, Berner was trying to wrest control of Kennecott.

To get him to Kennecott, however, Reynolds's headhunters had to do its arm twisting with lots of dollars. "He had a compensation arrangement," recalls Reynolds, "which became the subject of quite a bit of publicity." In his first year on the job, Kennecott paid Barrow $730,000 in salary and bonus but also another $475,450 due to a controversial clause in his contract that awarded him for an increase in the price of the company's stock. "The agreement became something of an embarrassment to the company and I believe it was later renegotiated," concedes Reynolds. "But they thought that having him there was worth a great deal. What our services were worth in getting him there is another matter."

Reynolds, a man who earns in excess of $500,000 annually and whose headhunters collect between $150,000 and $400,000 a year, feels somehow underpaid. "Frankly," says Reynolds with a straight face, "I think our fees in many cases are much too low. If you compare the value of our putting a chief executive into a multibillion dollar company and the impact an individual can make. Compare that value with an aggressive investment banking firm introducing two oil companies to each other. They get $40 million in total fees and we get a third of the first-year compensation. You know, there is something out of whack here."

Reynolds envisions the day when his firm will ask to share in the success of his placements, perhaps with a final fee pegged to an executive's performance three years after he takes on the job. "If the fellow has done the job," he says, "we'd appreciate it very much if you'd consider paying us such and such. What we have got to do is to get the concept across that what happens to the company is important. In some cases, the chief executive has made the difference between life and death of a company. We put Jack Byrne in GEICO and it was really breathing its last breath. That was a search where the results had to be produced by the hour. Byrne got in there and he literally turned the thing around and the company's been a phenomenal success."

What happens when the executive fails? "The results of our work are not guaranteed," says Reynolds matter-of-factly.

Born in Greenwich, Connecticut, in 1931, he was the only child of an unsuccessful real estate agent and a dress retailer. His father was a descendant of the original potato farming settlers of Greenwich. Reynolds was a carrot-topped, roly-poly, freckle-faced boy, not very good at sports. But he was a gregarious youngster and a musically-oriented one. He more frequently dreamt about standing on the stage of the Metropolitan Opera House as a singer than standing at the plate at Yankee Stadium.

Those musical interests surfaced while at Yale, where he sang in the freshman chorus of the Glee Club, launched with a friend a singing group called the Alley Cats and crooned Cole Porter tunes in the Whiffenpoofs. Reynolds also demonstrated an aptitude for leadership at Yale as president of the university's Glee Club. "He was extremely anxious to be seen with the right people and to be successful himself," says a Yale classmate of Reynolds. The yellowing, brittle pages of Yale's 1954 Class Book contain evidence that he was a "Big Man on Campus" if not a college intellectual, given his C+ average.

"The success of the 1953–54 Glee Club season was attributable to a number of assets, particularly the efforts of Russ Reynolds as president," the book notes smugly. "His quiet, mature handling of the subtle complexities of his job was largely responsible for the club's consistently good morale." Quiet? Mature? His colleagues, who know his volatile temperament well, would scoff at that today.

While some of his Yalie friends vacationed in Europe during the summer months, Reynolds was off working. Despite his address in affluent Greenwich, his parents were neither born to great wealth nor to patrician noblesse oblige. His mother's popular dress shop, "Ginny," on East Putnam Avenue, essentially put him through Exeter and Yale. Extra pocket money had to come from a succession of summer jobs. He and a roommate once drove a two-door Ford from New York to Fairbanks, where Reynolds worked as a pipewalker in an Alaskan gold mine. Another summer Reynolds sold shirts at a men's clothing store in Greenwich. He had to borrow $400 to help finance his senior-year trip to Europe as president of the Yale Glee Club.

Reynolds was, in almost every other way, a typical Young Blue grad of the time: Republican, conservative and in step with the class on many issues. Some 78 percent of his class believed the use of the atomic bomb against Japan in 1945 was morally justified; 62 percent thought labor unions had too much power, and 53 percent thought that governmental regulation of business should decrease. Reynolds would have been safely among the majority on issues such as these.

Unlike most of his graduating classmates in 1954, however, no "future occupation" was listed in the book next to the air-brushed photo of a Reynolds with closely-cropped hair and elephant ears. The European history major ended up as a navigator-bombardier with the Strategic Air Command in El Paso, Texas. It was there that he discovered, on a blind date in a bar, the woman he eventually would marry, Deborah Toll.

After a three-year hitch in the military, Reynolds came to New

York with his new wife and in 1957 started work as a trainee at one of the most prominent addresses in the world of finance—23 Wall Street. It was the marble home of J. P. Morgan & Co., the citadel of financial acumen. Reynolds spent a year in the municipal bond department, earned a promotion as a national division lending officer and went out drumming up business in the Southeast and later Midwest.

The "House of Morgan" taught Reynolds the value of quality and detail. And Reynolds took to light J. Pierpont Morgan's long-held belief that character, not money, ruled the financial world. "A man I do not trust could not get money from me on all the bonds in Christendom," the institution's incomparable founder once said.

"I learned a great deal at Morgan Bank calling on companies, hearing why loans went bad and why they didn't," says Reynolds. "I found the ultimate determinant of whether you make a loan is the character of the person. It's not the credit. People can have the best credit in the world, but it's their intentions and desires that really matter."

But after nine years, Reynolds grew antsy and began to look for a different and new challenge. He tried but did not complete an M.B.A. degree at New York University. And one day he found himself in the office of an executive headhunter who was trying to hire him. The body snatcher was secretly taping the telephone calls of his sources and candidates in his office.

" 'This business is very easy,' " he told Reynolds. " 'All you do is record your conversations and have your secretary type them out.' "

" 'Well, God, isn't there a law against taping?' " replied Reynolds. "It sent shivers up my spine to be in his presence. The business was regarded by some as not quite up to the level of investment banking, law, accounting or management consulting. A lot of older people went into executive search out of default. They hadn't necessarily made it in the business world and this was a haven for them. I said to myself, 'What qualifications do those people have to decide who should run American industry when they haven't succeeded themselves?' "

So Reynolds began using his Yalie alumni connections to meet up with William Clark, whose New York-based executive search firm was among the elite, white-shoe headhunting shops of the time. The firm had quality clients who paid their bills and a banking relationship with Morgan Bank. Clark, a Harvard lawyer and Yale graduate, lived in Greenwich, too.

"Jesus Christ," Reynolds told him, "this is a terrible business because you people do things that are not right." Reynolds told Clark of his experience at the other firm, and Clark was, in Reynolds's words, horrified.

"Well," Clark said, "we sure as hell don't do things like that, and if you're interested in this business, you should join our firm."

Reynolds joined Clark in 1966 for a base salary of $22,500 and the potential for a bonus (which at year-end totalled $5,000). Clark put him in pursuit of executives in banking and corporate finance. One of his first clients was Oppenheimer & Co., which employed him to deliver a research director. But over a lunch at Wall Street's Delmonico's, Oppenheimer very nearly tried to lure Reynolds into its own fold.

It didn't take long for Reynolds to establish a reputation as a gutsy, tough professional who wouldn't hesitate to call up cold the most senior of executives at major corporations. But Reynolds was an impatient, arrogant fellow, too. He has told friends, for example, that he believed he was running his own firm within a firm but without the full authority of the man whose name was on the door. He had brought in so much business from the financial community that it had to be parceled out to others at Clark who knew little about finance. "There were people working on assignments which he helped generate who did not know the difference between a public offering and a private placement," Reynolds confided to a friend. Reynolds would offer to meet with his colleagues on Saturdays and in the evenings to bring them up to speed on corporate finance, and he would urge them to consider going to New York University or Columbia University Business School. With less than three years under his belt as a recruiter, Reynolds believed he was so instrumental to Clark's firm that he demanded to be named president of what was then one of the top five search firms in the business. Clark told him to take a walk.

He was making $75,000 at the time, in 1969, triple his first year headhunting income a mere three years earlier, but with a wife and three children at home he hardly felt in a position to risk going out on his own. Talking over this dilemma at lunch with his close friend, McKinseyman Donald "Obie" Clifford, Reynolds soon found a solution. Clifford, who had roomed with Reynolds at Yale and attended Exeter with him, suggested calling up a few old friends who might be persuaded to invest in a new executive search firm. The group, mainly Clifford, John Beck, of Beck, Mack & Oliver, and investor Louis Marx, agreed to commit up to $110,000 to the start up.

Reynolds asked another good friend, Lee Getz, who was graduated from Yale in 1951, three years before Reynolds, if he'd like to be his co-founder. Getz was a vice-president at Manufacturers Hanover Trust Co., where he was responsible for the corporate business and correspondent banking relationships in the Mid-Atlantic and New England states. The two knew each other well, had been introduced through in-laws who were Harvard Law School classmates and ran in the same social and civic circles. Getz had much respect for his friend and he, too, was getting bored with banking.

But Getz was less than certain about the idea. Before making the jump, he contacted both Citibank and Morgan to insure that their doors would open to him if Reynolds's firm went down the tubes. Getz's father-in-law, George Hinman, meanwhile, was none too happy when he told him he was considering quitting his respectable career at the bank. A prominent attorney, Hinman was a director of IBM Corp. and active in Republican Party politics. "My father-in-law thought I was out of my mind to give up my career in banking," recalls Getz, who sang in the freshman Glee Club just as Reynolds had at Yale. "He said, 'Who is this man Russ Reynolds?' Many considered executive recruiting a rather dubious involvement."

Reynolds wound up journeying to Edgartown on the Labor Day weekend in 1969 to meet with Hinman. The two sipped tea on a side porch and chatted about "this screwy idea" to start a headhunting firm. Not only did Reynolds win him over, he recruited his partner's father-in-law to become an outside director of the new company.

With $110,000 committed by outside investors, Reynolds and Getz together pooled $10,000 and started the firm in 1969. Unlike Lester Korn or Dick Ferry, Reynolds didn't simply want to be the largest—he wanted to be the best. He adopted Morgan's longtime approach to the business, trying to serve only first-class clients, giving first-class service and collecting classy fees.

Reynolds hasn't always succeeded in these ideals—one of his recruiters, for example, was at one point looking for editors to serve on the weekly *National Enquirer,* a tawdry tabloid that in Reynolds's way of thinking was published for the mindless. But it helped that he hitched his wagon to the burgeoning financial services business. Many of the old-guard firms—Haley Associates, Heidrick & Struggles and Ward Howell—had long relied on smokestack America for much of their business. Not surprisingly, their firms often went up and down with the economic cycles.

Most headhunters would have walked out with a few clients. Not Reynolds. "I did not take one piece of paper out of the Clark firm except my own personal belongings," he says. "No financial information, no agreements. Nothing. When I left Morgan Guaranty I vowed that I would not set foot in the place or talk to anybody in that business for a year. I didn't want to impose on that relationship. I feel very strongly that you should do things yourself."

His first search was for a leading, major bracket investment banking firm. It was cancelled within weeks, however, because "someone walked in the side door," says Reynolds. There also was an early assignment to find a chief financial officer for chicken man Frank Perdue. Reynolds's new firm didn't yet know how to "manage" a client. Perdue did most of the managing himself. The result: The firm introduced to him more than a dozen candidates for the job (versus a standard three) and it took over six months to complete. But by the end of his first year, Reynolds had handled 72 assignments and brought on 13 employees.

His first big break occurred in 1972 when a senior partner at McKinsey referred him to CBS Corp. Chairman Bill Paley, who was at the time looking for a president. Paley called and invited Reynolds to his New York apartment one evening for a two-hour visit. "With a Filipino butler serving tea, he told me the story of his life," recalls Reynolds. "It was the most fabulous experience I had ever had in business. He told me how he started a cigar company and all that."

At Paley's behest, Reynolds agreed to run the reference checks on the Gerry Roche search that turned up International Paper's Arthur Taylor. "I told him [Paley] the person he was hiring was, in my opinion, not a good candidate," says Reynolds. Paley did not heed Reynolds's warning and hired Taylor, anyway. A few weeks later, Reynolds picked up *The New York Times* and discovered a pleasant surprise. In a news story, retiring CBS President Frank Stanton was quoted as saying, "We used the services of two very fine executive recruiting firms, Heidrick & Struggles and Russell Reynolds Associates."

"Boy," beams Reynolds, "if that didn't get attention. I mean we were absolutely unknown and that was a really big breakthrough in terms of image."

Reynolds has had his share of embarrassments, too. One that he will hardly ever live down occurred in 1981 when his firm took on the job of finding an $80,000-a-year executive director to run the headhunting trade association, the Association of Executive Recruiting Consultants. First, the search dragged on for seven months, more than double the average, before Reynolds's firm found James G. Conzelman. Then, Conzelman resigned the job, citing "basic philosophical differences," after only one year. "It was an extremely poor recruiting job," says an industry insider. "You had to fault the board of directors at the time, but Russ Reynolds recruited him. The guy was terribly abrasive and out of his depth. It was a classic case of how not to do an executive search."

Reynolds, the image maker himself, is a bundle of contradictions. He bemoans the old-boy network from which the search business grew, yet plays the rep-tie circuit as the quintessential social climber. His three-page statement of corporate goals emphasize "principle above expediency," yet he has enraged some by luring away key executives from client corporations. He boasts of engendering an esprit de corps environment, yet tension and fear pervade his offices. He can, at times, be charming, yet he can be brutal, too. He grandly speaks of quality and substance, yet appears to pay as much or more attention to image.

Reynolds painstakingly attends to every detail. Each of the restrooms in the main office in New York, for instance, is equipped with a telephone, lest a weekend-working headhunter miss an important call while going about his business. "Russ sweats the details, worrying whether the receptionist in Dallas chews gum," explains an associate. During the firm's early days, each consultant would be required to surrender all his or her correspondence and memos of the week by Friday evening. The paperwork would be passed out among colleagues, partly an attempt to instill a collaborative spirit among the firm's consultants, and partly an effort to assure quality control through peer pressure. Reynolds would scrutinize each sheet of paper, often returning them with scrawled comments and circles that pointed out grammatical errors, poor syntax and misspellings. "He treated you as if he thought you were an idiot," recalls a former Reynolds office manager. "It was as if he were an English teacher in grade school."

Even the most trifling details wouldn't escape his attention. "He's like the hotel manager who spots a thread on the rug and bawls someone out for it," adds Alice C. Early, an executive director who joined Reynolds in 1979 after heading up the Harvard Business School's Alumni Placement Office. "He'd come in and give someone hell because the fresh flowers in the office were wilted or the ashtrays were not dumped. He's not called the redhead around here for nothing."

He is, in fact, regarded as a stern disciplinarian with a volatile, sometimes irrational, temperament. "Russ is quick to pounce on someone for a simple mistake," says a former Reynolds headhunter, "and not apt to pat you on the back for a job well done." Once a Christmas tree outside his personal office wasn't decorated by his chauffeur to Reynolds's satisfaction. It caused him to fly off the handle, insisting that the chauffeur, who was on his way home, be called back to the office to take the tree down immediately.

Some were surprised by Reynolds's tough reaction when one of its prized New York headhunters, Tony Thompson, decided to call it quits and go out on his own in 1982 after spending a decade with Reynolds. Thompson, a man who favors wide suspenders, called Reynolds at his house in Antigua to inform him he was resigning to start his own firm. Elizabeth Riley, who had joined the firm two years earlier and worked closely with Thompson on communications searches, also was leaving with him. Stunned and angry, Reynolds immediately began to remind him of the non-compete agreement he requires his headhunters to sign. Within 24 hours of the phone call, Reynolds's lawyers sent Thompson a four-pound tome of legal documents, which represented the lawsuit. He also changed the locks on the Stanford, Connecticut, office so that Thompson couldn't gain entrance.

Thompson's departure represented a huge loss. He had joined Reynolds in 1972 following a dozen years with Time, Inc., leaving the media giant as vice-president of marketing for its cable television unit Home Box Office. It was no coincidence that Reynolds's firm completed more than 40 searches for Home Box Office between 1972 and 1982. Thompson was one of several headhunters critical to Reynolds's plan to broaden his search business well beyond financial services. Since he joined, the firm had completed more than 400 searches in publishing, broadcast and cable television, electronics and advertising.

The dispute was quickly and quietly settled out of court. And Thompson and Riley, who have since brought their thriving communications practice to competitor Spencer Stuart & Associates,

217

prefer not to speak about the incident. But Reynolds's lightning-bolt response to Thompson's news shocked and surprised him, according to his friends. After spending ten years with Reynolds, he hardly expected a temper tantrum and a lawsuit when deciding to go out on his own.

But Reynolds doesn't take departures lightly. "We had one guy who bolted from the Dallas office and was sucked into Lamalie's sales pitch," says Reynolds. (At Lamalie Associates, headhunters typically earn a little over 50 percent of what they bill annually.) "He said, well I'm going to get X percent of the revenues. And I said what revenues? There aren't any revenues. And he said, Well, I handled so many hundreds of thousands of dollars of business last year. And I said, yes, but you didn't generate one single piece of it.

"Being the manager of one of our offices provides a person with a revenue stream simply because we exist. It doesn't matter who answers the phone. Business is going to come in over the transom. I'll never forget the time I was starting out and I was in the training program at J. P. Morgan and assigned to the municipal bond department and they sent me to Winston-Salem, North Carolina, to sell bonds to a bank and a couple of insurance companies," he says. "I was very young and had a brand-new calling card and my boss, as I walked out the door, said "Remember one thing. When you go down there and they give you an order for half a million bonds, you had nothing to do with selling those bonds. It's the Morgan name.' It was very deflating."

It was yet another important lesson Reynolds learned at Morgan. "The way you succeed in running a service business like ours is by retaining control over the compensation process," he says. Most people in this business are paid on a formula basis. They get paid more money when they bring in the General Motors business rather than on their long-range contributions to the overall quality of the firm. We've had pressure to do it. If a guy comes to us and says, 'Well, I want this or that,' I say we want you out. We want it from the point of view of the corporation and not from the individual. People say, well isn't that awfully one-sided. And we say you're Goddamn right it is and if you don't like it you don't have to be here."

He also doesn't hesitate to fire someone who has difficulty delivering the goods to his satisfaction. They often leave bitter about their experiences with him. "He's more Greenwich than Greenwich," says a former colleague who got the ax, "but he wasn't accepted as a kid because he was poor. It's very sad. I feel sorry for him. He brings in gumshoes who are to the manner born, and he loves to say he fired some Rockefeller because he couldn't make it in his firm. It makes Russ feel good about himself. He loves to take highly connected, wealthy guys into his firm and turn around and say, 'they're not good enough for me and my culture.' That's his way of reciprocating for childhood rejections."

It is another of the many contradictions in his personality. Reynolds's take-it-or-leave-it philosophy clashes with the communal spirit he attempts to instill in his troops. To stress teamwork, headhunters earn year-end credit for "assists" on colleague searches, and every Monday evening all New York associates gather to swap inside information and help each other with tips on their searches. Each headhunter's daily appointments schedule is distributed in house to his colleagues who may have a question or two for a well-placed corporate source that might aid another assignment.

"We have and are continuing to build a culture that keeps us apart from the individual mentality in the business," says Ferdinand Nadherny, president of the firm. "We dwell on teamwork." A college sports star at Yale, where he lettered in basketball and football, Nadherny had earned the nickname "Bull." Reynolds's competitors now call Nadherny, who is credited with making Reynolds the dominant search firm in the Chicago market, the "Prince of Darkness." Nadherny originally opened the Chicago branch for Reynolds in 1974 when he jumped Boyden's ship in favor of Reynolds.

But what about Kennedy's accusations in the *Executive Recruiter News?* Did Reynolds, as the tough newsletter publisher suggested, steal executives from two major corporate clients: Chase Manhattan Bank and Security Pacific Bank? "People who bring up old news irritate me," Reynolds says. "If he brought the Chase business up at the time, five years ago," he adds without completing the sentence. "All I will say is that we did not act unethically."

Chase Manhattan Bank, however, had been a steady and important client of Reynolds's when his firm captured the assignment to find a successor to autocratic chairman A. Robert Abboud at First Chicago Corp. One of the nation's largest bank holding companies, it had for years been plagued by leadership problems. In 1979, the year before Abboud's dismissal, executive officer turnover hit 12.7

percent. Abboud, it was said, erased some 200 executives from First Chicago's organizational charts, including a deputy chairman recruited from the outside only five months earlier, until he finally got the ax himself. Seeking an end to the turmoil, the board of directors named one of its members interim boss and gave him the task of finding a permanent successor.

Ben W. Heineman, chairman of Northwest Industries and an outside board director of First Chicago, temporarily took over operations and hired Reynolds. "Call me every hour if you have to," he reportedly told the headhunter. "It would be impossible for you to overcommunicate with me." By the end of the assignment, Reynolds noted, "every member of my family knew Ben Heineman's voice."

Reynolds's solution: Barry F. Sullivan, an executive vice-president at client Chase Manhattan, a bank Reynolds's headhunters knew well after completing numerous assignments there.

Typically, of course, a headhunter must wait two years before poaching a client's executives. One of the few exceptions to this rule occurs if the headhunter gains permission from his client to extract an executive. Sometimes approval is gladly given, particularly if the executive is a "problem employee" a company would prefer to see leave or if the executive is unlikely to climb further up the corporate ladder. One headhunter once proudly boasted that he had been specifically engaged by corporations to surreptitiously hunt its unwanted executives. However questionable, it was viewed as a preferable strategy to outright dismissal.

The first inkling that Reynolds's firm was ready to coax Sullivan from client Chase occurred when Chase Manhattan Chairman Willard "Bill" Butcher received an unexpected call in his New York office from a director of First Chicago's board. Butcher had been discussing other business with Chase's human resources vice-president Alan Lafley when their conversation was interrupted by the important telephone call. "He [the First Chicago director] said they had engaged Russell Reynolds to find a new CEO," recalls Lafley. "He wanted Bill Butcher's permission to talk to Barry Sullivan because Russ Reynolds said we were a client and that before he wanted Barry to take it he wanted to ask permission. So it came through the board, not Russ."

After a discussion between Butcher and Lafley, Chase called the board member and Reynolds back and said they could go. But the fact that the call came from First Chicago and not Reynolds didn't go down very well with Chase. "Russ got a fair number of calls from me about some of the things that use to happen," says Lafley. "I am damn sure that Russ Reynolds spent a lot of time talking to Barry Sullivan before he was on that sleigh. Because Barry talked to me an awful lot about whether he ought to go ahead and consider something else."

In the same year that Sullivan jumped to First Chicago, Reynolds's firm also lured fellow Yalie David O. Maxwell from California-based client Ticor Mortgage Co., where Maxwell was chairman and founder, to head up the Federal National Mortgage Association, the government-sponsored, privately-owned corporation popularly known as Fannie Mae. "We had done eight to ten searches for Ticor," says a former Reynolds associate. "Lee Getz then takes Maxwell out of there for whom all the work had been done and puts him into Fannie Mae. Is that fair? For a while I thought it was kosher, but I realized it just plain wasn't right. It's amazing what clients will put up with!"

Reynolds also put into the Chicago Board of Trade Robert K. Wilmouth, president and chief administrative officer of Crocker National Bank in San Francisco, at the very same time his firm was conducting a search for a vice-president of human resources at Crocker for Wilmouth, according to a former Reynolds consultant. The move apparently didn't create much of a stir, however, because Wilmouth's boss, Chairman Robert T. Wilcox, reportedly wasn't unhappy to lose him, and Crocker continued to work with Russell Reynolds Associates.

Reynolds's headhunting competitors, who knew of his extensive search work at Chase, seized on the Chase Manhattan incident to suggest that Reynolds's concentration in the financial services industry now posed significant blockage problems. So successful had he become as the leading headhunter to the banking industry that his access to top available talent was becoming more limited. Increasing competition and the high-level nature of the First Chicago job combined to create an issue out of it. Prospective clients began asking about the blockage problems of the larger search firms, and the business press tackled the topic without naming specifics in published articles.

Indeed, one of Russell Reynolds's major big-game hunt competitors, Spencer Stuart & Associates, soon after began to distribute private memos instructing its office managers how to deal with the "problem" in new business situations. In a memo dated September 18, 1981, Spencer Stuart President Thomas Neff acknowledged that "certain large firms may indeed have an off-limits problem (Heidrick & Struggles with its 2,000 clients, Korn/Ferry with its emphasis on volume business, and Russell Reynolds in the financial community)."

In selling the firm's services over Reynolds and other competitors, Neff urged his headhunters to tell potential clients that Spencer Stuart had pursued a deliberate strategy that precluded the off-limits problem. "By design, over half our practice is outside the U.S., thereby reducing sharply the size question regarding the U.S. market," wrote Neff. "Other large firms have the majority of their business (and client relationships) in the U.S. We have limited the number of clients that we will serve in any industry category to minimize constraints on looking into competitive companies. Among the Fortune 500 industrial companies, only 10 percent (52 companies) are off-limits at corporate headquarters."

In 1985, Reynolds's firm zeroed in on Frank V. Cahouet, moving him out of client Security Pacific Corp., where he was vice-chairman, and placing him into the chief executive's job at Crocker National Bank—where it had taken Wilmouth seven years earlier. Cahouet had been known as the architect of Security Pacific's foray into non-bank business areas such as brokerage and venture capital and as such played a crucial role on the bank's management team. So there was little surprise that the bank was none too pleased when it lost him, particularly when stolen by a firm which it had employed to bring in other executives. "We do consider their actions unethical," a company official told Kennedy's newsletter. The search, moreover, wasn't done by a novice player in the organization but by Reynolds's co-founder and vice-chairman Lee Getz. And after placing Cahouet at Crocker, the new chief executive then turned to competitor Korn-Ferry instead of Reynolds for the majority of its search work.

"I told Lee, 'You ought to do your homework,' " jokes Win Priem of Korn/Ferry. " 'Why the hell did you put Dick Ferry's next door neighbor into the job?' They both live in San Marino. We have done almost 150 searches for Security Pacific over an 11-year period. It was one of our oldest and best clients, and we are responsible in part for the new look at that bank. Russ Reynolds was a Johnny-Come-Lately to Security Pacific."

Reynolds concedes the conflict wasn't handled very carefully, if at all. "On the Security Pacific thing he [Kennedy] has more of a point. That does bother me. We could have done other things differently, and I think there was some poor communication and some misunderstanding. I'd be less than candid if I said we did everything perfectly. And I think that's a case where we probably didn't. After 15 years of doing this, I'm surprised we haven't had more problems."

Reynolds might have spoken too soon. Only a few months later, in July 1985, his firm unearthed Nolan Archibald, president of Beatrice Cos. consumer durables group, as Black & Decker Corp.'s new president and chief operating officer. But not without further raising eyebrows because Beatrice had been paying Reynolds to do executive search work only a few months earlier.

The Chicago-based conglomerate acted against Reynolds quickly. In a private memo to key executives of all Beatrice's divisions dated July 31, 1985, little more than one week after Black & Decker publicly announced Archibald's hiring, Reuben Berry, Beatrice's senior vice-president of human resources, sent out the word that Reynolds wasn't to get anymore business from the corporation.

"It has come to our attention that the executive recruiting firm of Russell Reynolds Associates was responsible for recruiting a senior officer of Beatrice Companies, Inc., Mr. Nolan Archibald, and placing him in Black & Decker. This same firm has been actively retained by Beatrice within the past several months to recruit employees for us. In our eyes, this is an obvious conflict of interest which we do not intend to overlook.

"Accepted industry practice is for a firm to abstain from recruiting executives away from a client organization for a period of two years from the date of the last recruiting assignment unless any other arrangement has been agreed to in writing by the corporate client. This was clearly not done.

"More importantly, however, our recruiting dollars are better spent with firms who will agree not to recruit from us while actively recruiting for us. You are, therefore, requested to terminate any existing relationships with this firm and refrain from retaining them for any future assignments."

Reynolds subsequently claimed that Beatrice's nonfoods business was not off-limits to his headhunters because he had not performed search work for that Beatrice sector. Still, the onus of preventing such a misunderstanding fell upon Reynolds, who ostensibly failed to clearly explain his company's off-limits policy to Beatrice.

This has always been a murky ethical area for search that has done more to undermine the business than any other single issue. "One of the most disparaging and damaging criticisms of our profession is that some firms conduct business with clients on one hand and approach employees with the other," says Robert Lamalie, chairman of Lamalie Associates, Inc. Some headhunting firms consider their entire client companies off-limits; others treat each division, group or sector separately as Reynolds did with Beatrice. Some use two years after the commencement of a search; others use two years after the completion of an assignment. "Still others do not even address the issue because they want to maintain the flexibility to do whatever seems expedient at the moment," Lamalie adds.

Indeed, Lamalie feels so strongly about the issue that he resigned as a member of the Association of Executive Search Consultants (AESC) in 1985 shortly after the group agreed to weaken a section of its code of ethics dealing with the off-limits problem. Ironically, it was the AESC's earlier and tougher code, approved in 1981, that partly led to the departure of Russell Reynolds from the group. Reynolds was not alone. Heidrick & Struggles, Boyden Associates, Ward Howell and Haley all left the same year, too. Only one firm, Ward Howell, voted against the tougher ethics code. It did so because the firm's representative believed the AESC was overstepping its boundaries.

But if Reynolds had followed that code no misunderstanding could possibly have developed between his firm and Beatrice. The new ethical standards required headhunters to define in writing what part of a client's corporation was off-limits. If Reynolds only worked for the nonfood divisions of Beatrice, he would have been obliged to tell Beatrice in writing that he would not pirate executives from the company's nonfood business. Executives in other divisions, therefore, would logically be unprotected and up for grabs by the same search firm employed elsewhere in the same corporation. In all cases, headhunters would be blocked from stealing any executives from the defined "client organization" for two full years after the completion of a search. The only exception occurs when a client agrees in writing to a change.

Reynolds and several other large firms that quit the association maintained that the rule gave smaller firms, which more readily put entire corporations off-limits rather than only divisions, a significant advantage. That's because it forced the large firms to confront

224

the issue upfront. The larger a headhunting firm gets, the smaller universe it has from which to recruit. So smaller headhunting firms often use the off-limits argument as a marketing club against Reynolds and the other large firms. By forcing members to confront this issue in writing, the AESC also handed the smaller firms a club against their larger rivals.

Some corporations have refused to do business with Reynolds because of his segmented off-limits policy. "They [Reynolds Associates] talked about it very directly with us," recalls a top official of Continental Illinois Corp., owner of Chicago's second largest bank. "There was a desire to treat separate parts of the company as separate companies. But if they bring someone into the bond department, they shouldn't take someone out of the trust department. That's not the way we operate, so we have not done any business with them."

In an attempt to again attract the large firms back into the business's trade group, the AESC weakened its code of ethics in 1984 when it allowed headhunting members to avoid defining the client organization in writing. The revised guidelines state that it should be "preferably in writing." Haley and Ward Howell returned to the trade association after the change was put into effect, but in the meantime, the group lost Lamalie.

"We are deeply disappointed that AESC has chosen to weaken its Code of Ethics in what appears to be an attempt to appease members who refuse to support the highest standards of professional executive search," Lamalie wrote in a letter in which he resigned his firm as a member of the AESC. "We consider this decision ill-advised and professionally unacceptable."

In every confirmation letter on each search, Lamalie includes a sentence: "It is our firm's policy that we will not recruit or cause to be recruited any person from the (name of division, group, sector or corporation) for a minimum of two years following the completion of this assignment unless we are authorized by you to do so." That statement is as clear as they come.

"Russ is hung up on the cosmetics of quality," claims a headhunting competitor. "He's hung up on slick brochures, rep ties and the Steinway in his reception room. Where quality counts is in the delivery of the product. So many of these cases are gray areas, but you can go the safe route or you can go the liberal route. Russ has taken the liberal view."

Back at the Yale Club, Reynolds shrugs off the problem and moves on to other things. He had spent an hour and one-half in the Pan Am Building with a real estate broker the other day to examine his options when the lease on his current New York office expires in April of 1987. The Cross & Brown broker showed him some space on the 45th floor of one of New York's largest gold-collar factories.

"This is really nice except I get acrophobia," Reynolds told him. "And what if an airplane hit this building?"

"Mr. Reynolds," he replied, "cows use to worry about steam locomotives, but they got use to it. You'd get used to it."

"It's too bad you don't have anything interesting because the Daily News building has very high ceilings and they've made a very attractive offer to us with our own private squash court."

Reynolds sits back and smiles, surveying the crowded lunch room. "It was as if I set a bomb off," he continues. "There was silence and the light went off. He said, 'Maybe you'd be interested in the 21st floor which has 19-foot-high ceilings. He's a very nice guy. Went to Yale. His name is Nelson. Class of 1980.' "

The Specialist

"They were selling nothing but bullshit."

THE ORDER OF Catholic nuns running a sizable Connecticut hospital had just lost their young managerial maestro to military service. He provided the financial acumen to keep the beds full and the bills paid. Now he was gone. A strong-willed woman in a habit who ran the hospital as its figurehead was near tears.

"Mr. Witt," sobbed the sister to the headhunting consultant, "I don't know what we'll do? We can't function without this man."

"Sister," replied Mr. Witt calmly, "all we'll do is conduct a search."

"Well, what does that mean?"

"You'll hire us and we'll find you somebody."

"Oh, Mr. Witt. You don't understand. He was a good Catholic boy."

"That's okay," the consultant shot back. "So spec number one is we want a good Catholic boy. What else? Is there anything else you want?"

"I want him to have a large family. Five children or more."

"Fine."

"I want him to have had at least a family member who is a nun so he can understand the sisters."

"Fine," the willing Witt stated, "we'll put that down."

It was John A. Witt's first executive search. The salary of the executive he discovered some seven weeks later was paltry. Nonprofit

227

hospitals didn't pay much in the mid-1960s for executives. But Witt, then a hired man with managing consultant A. T. Kearney, got a glimpse of the potential for an untapped market in executive search.

"Within seven weeks," he says, "I had not only one candidate, I had three guys for her. They were all Catholic, they all had at least five kids, and they all had at least one sister who was in a convent. And they all earned master's degrees in hospital administration."

"Oh, Mr. Witt, you're a savior!"

Witt, an animated storyteller of 50 years, recounts this tale as if it occurred yesterday. Now, some twenty years later, Mr. Witt is still finding administrators for small and large hospitals. Except he and the health care industry now call them chief executive officers, and some of them are paid far more handsomely than the good, productive Catholic boy with a nun for a sister that Witt placed nearly two decades ago.

In those years, Witt has built the most successful specialty business in executive search. In his first ten years of business, from 1969 to 1979, Witt Associates grew at a rate of 25 percent annually. With 23 professional consultants and revenues now approaching $4 million, the firm comfortably ranks as the only specialist in the business among the top 20 search firms. But Witt is less interested in that achievement than he is over some other accomplishments.

Witt has conducted more than 1,500 searches for health care executives, a third of them chief executive or chief operating officer assignments, on behalf of clients as small as a 69-bed hospital and as large as a 1,200-bed multicorporate hospital system. He has placed chief executives in 20 of the nation's 45 children's hospitals, and has put chief executive officers in 15 Jewish hospitals, a dozen Baptist hospitals and a good number of Catholic institutions thanks to that unforgettable and outrageous beginning. Some 60 times he has pirated the chief executive of an organization, only to be called later by the hospital to find it a successor. On 200 occasions, he has been called to conduct a search a second time after his first placement in a job hopped to lusher pastures.

His success mirrors a fast-growing headhunting trend. Corporations and other institutions increasingly are demanding that the huntsmen they hire boast expertise in the field they cover. Russell Reynolds splashed into headhunting by zeroing in on the financial services market, using his success there to branch out into general search. Korn/Ferry's John Sullivan sold his high-technology experience to gain the Storage Technology assignment.

Specialists have found the hunting lucrative due to two primary forces: the greater professionalism in search and the heightened influence exerted by corporate human resources execs in the selection of firms. "They tend to be dispassionate when reviewing the credentials of outside search consultants," says Herb Halbrecht, whose Stamford, Connecticut, firm under his name has placed hundreds of executives steeped in the lingo of technology.

They have cropped up in every field—high technology, real estate, Wall Street, banking, insurance, even museums. Headhunters zero in on tracking down architects, accountants, computer software nerds, university presidents, bankers, restaurateurs, and attorneys. *The American Lawyer,* a trade publication for attorneys, now publishes an annual directory listing more than 100 legal specialists. "We fill lawyers' chairs," proclaims the ads of New York Legal Search, Inc., "The partner's chair. The associates's chair. The corporate counsel's chair." Witt alone has more than 70 competitors who claim to specialize in health care services.

New York's The Cantor Concern, Inc., hunts for public relations people, San Francisco's Colton Bernard, Inc. tracks down apparel and textile executives, Boston's Daly & Co., Inc. recruits for young high-tech start ups, Philadelphia's Harry F. Twomey Associates looks for metalworking managers and Comann Associates, Inc. in Aurora, Colorado serves only the mining and mineral industry.

Several non-search companies, seeking to tap some specialized know-how, have tried to play this recruiting game as well. But some have discovered that the business of snatching specialized bodies isn't simply there for the taking. Consider Martindale-Hubbell, Inc., the staid New York publisher of the leading directory of lawyers. Headhunters who keep the elite of the legal world under their eye consider the Martindale-Hubbell directory the most comprehensive listing of national law firms and their attorneys available. So in 1983, the publisher figured it could easily diversify into the business of recruiting lawyers.

Headhunting, it turned out, was a bit tougher and coldblooded than the publishing house could stomach. A mere year later, it scurried out of the business after refusing to engage in such common tactics as "raiding" and "cold calling"—the art of aggressively luring the hunted to other firms. In an internal memorandum, the company maintained that such actions "are at odds with our corporate ethic, culture and philosophy" and "would be distasteful to the affected firms and could impair the relations of the parent company with its outstanding subscribers." The publisher scrapped the business.

Other specialist firms, tied to less lucrative or temporary trends, have disappeared like adolescent fads. The government's emphasis on affirmative action in the early 1970s spawned several of them. Management Woman, Inc., founded in 1973, focused in on the recruitment of upper- and middle-level management women. It was sold to Boyden in 1980 and then back to its original founders Anne Hyde and Janet Jones-Parker two years later. But the specialty had already outlived the changing times. Spencer Stuart also started up a subsidiary in the early 1970s to specifically recruit minority executives. That practice, headed by Rich Hanes who went on to become ambassador of Nigeria, was folded in 1974. It was, perhaps, ahead of its time.

But in fields where technical know-how is at a premium, the specialists are armed with a critical advantage. "I'm snow-proof," high-tech headhunter Halbrecht likes to say. "On technology issues, a candidate can't snow me." Halbrecht sorts out the winners and losers by knowing what questions to ask. A favorite: Identify what accomplishment you're most proud of? "If the guy says he developed a complex algorithm to discover how many angels dance on the head of a pin and won an award for it at a conference of algorithm experts, I'm ready to throw up," he bellows. "If he says he developed a system that increased data communications reliability from 90 percent to 99 percent uptime and saved the company $250,000 because of it, I'm going to want to find out more about him."

Curiously absent from Halbrecht's background, unlike many headhunting specialists, is direct experience in technology. The Bronx-born, University of Chicago M.B.A. boasts, as he puts it, "an affinity for technology" that spurred his interest as a personnel guy. Halbrecht, whose floppy ears are capped by hearing aids, is a man without pretensions. The major general search firms would consider him something of a misfit in their environments. He dresses in conservative blue pinstripes, then places a shockingly bright red satin handkerchief in his breast pocket. Before visiting client First Boston in New York, he props his briefcase atop a trash can in the lobby of a Park Avenue building. Out comes a paper towelette to wipe the sweat from his brow on a hot summer's day. "I'll take a shower in the elevator," he says.

But Halbrecht, like other specialists, is able to draw upon the specialized contacts he has cultivated over 25 years. These are relationships erected over thousands of telephone calls, personal interviews and public appearances before local chapters of esoteric trade groups, like the Society of Information Management and the International Communications Association. "You get to know who are the good guys and you become part and parcel of the crowd," says Halbrecht. "Within three to four telephone calls, I can get personal recommendations on almost anybody in the telecommunications business." The names of some 67,000 technical professionals jam his computer databank, and one of every five assignments surfaces from the candidates already in his files.

While specialty headhunting continues to flourish, however, most executive recruiters believe their instincts to judge executive acumen are as transferable as the managerial skills of their quarry. Specialization has its detractors, most notably those who have something to lose because of it. "In the recruiting business," claims Boyden Associates President Putney Westerfield, "far more important is your ability to evaluate people and know how a business operates. That's more important than having a lot of industry knowledge."

Who's kidding who? Boyden is the largest of the major firms that have failed to legitimately come up with specialty practices. But Westerfield, a tall, lean man of 55 years, contends the most successful search of his more than ten years in the business was for an executive in an industry he knew absolutely nothing about. The assignment also was his first so he didn't know much about search, either. But the man he found helped to remake the apparel industry in the U.S.

The former publisher of *Fortune* magazine from 1969 to 1973, Westerfield had been on his new job in search with Boyden less than a day when the assignment came in. It could not have been what he had in mind when considering the business, especially after spending two years in the comfy environs of Chase Manhattan Bank as president of an information subsidiary from 1973 to 1975.

To pick up the job, he walked from Boyden's New York offices at 260 Madison Avenue to 530 Seventh Avenue, where young men ploddingly push racks of dresses through Manhattan's garment district. In ten minutes, Westerfield had entered a tiny cubbyhole of an office crammed with a small desk, rows of women's dresses and a small-boned man in his 30s named Mohan B. Murjani.

Westerfield, whose knowledge of the clothing industry stopped at

Brooks Brothers' front door on Madison Avenue, didn't know very much about the mustachioed Murjani. The client had called only the day earlier, asking the search firm to send someone over who could find him an American apparel executive to run his family-owned company's U.S. business. Murjani International imported women's dresses from Hong Kong into the U.S. market. Boyden's headhunters stationed in the Hong Kong office made a few phone calls. They discovered that the swarthy skinned ragman came from a wealthy family and that he represented an important company in Hong Kong. That intelligence was relayed to Westerfield. But in New York, his firm was just another hopeful, yet tawdry, entry in a cheap selling office in the garment district.

Murjani told Westerfield that his firm was losing a million dollars a year on $5 million in gross sales. " 'Help me get a president,' " Westerfield remembers Murjani saying. " 'There's nobody here who knows what they're doing.' " This was no big-league recruiting job. The starting salary for a president of Murjani would be little more than $60,000 a year. Boyden associates in Hong Kong, no doubt, called to ascertain whether this guy could even pay their fee. But Westerfield still knew zip about either the apparel or the search business for that matter.

"When I got the assignment," he says, "I said to myself, 'I don't know anything about Seventh Avenue.' I went home to my wife that night and said, 'Tell me all you know about missy dresses and sportswear.' I knew absolutely nothing. But I talked to people in the business; I read Women's Wear Daily; I just did a crash study of the industry to know what was going on, who were the important people and which companies were successful. I had some contacts from my Fortune years who were presidents of a few companies, but it was a pure example of search strategy."

Into Boyden's files he went to dig up a roster of apparel people he could call. "I came up with a list of 20 or 30 companies where the person I was looking for might be and started talking. You just talk, talk, talk and talk and finally I was led to Warren Hirsch."

Hirsch, district sales manager for Atlanta-based Ship'N Shore, a manufacturer of women's blouses and sportswear, didn't require much arm twisting to leave. He ached to return to New York, and he viewed the job as a way to make a name for himself in the center of the industry there.

In his profile of the candidate to Murjani, Westerfield described him "as a man of very good appearance, 43 years of age, 5'9", 175 pounds, married with three children. He has excellent voice modulation with an easy gait in conversation, accelerating with inflection on points of emphasis. He is both persuasive and effective in his delivery in the sales situation."

Critical to Murjani, though, was Hirsch's record on the job. Westerfield noted that when Hirsch assumed responsibility for the southern region of Ship 'N Shore in late 1972, it produced some $6 million in sales. The same territory under Hirsch hit sales of $17 million by 1975 and was budgeted for $21 million in 1976. "The sales improvement," wrote Westerfield, "was in large part due to Mr. Hirsch's ability to gain audience with the top merchandising people. He believes that the television advertising which Ship 'N Shore has done for the past two years to be a great contributor to the merchandising success and growth of the company's sales."

As a district sales manager, Hirsch had been making $50,000 annually with a $10,000 bonus. He jumped to Murjani as president for $65,000 a year with no equity interest in the company. Boyden's fee on the search, which took six weeks to complete, was under $20,000. Not bad for someone who didn't know what a missy dress was. It turned out pretty good for Murjani, too. "It was pretty cheap for him," Westerfield says. Hirsch moved quickly, signing up Gloria Vanderbilt to lend her name to Murjani's jeans. Heavily using television advertising, he made blue jeans a status item, garnered publicity that made him the center of attention in the garment business and built Murjani into a successful company. "Hirsch rode that company up to almost $300 million in revenues," Westerfield says. "That led to a lot of searches, probably three dozen for Murjani here, in Europe and Asia." Including, adds Westerfield who still doesn't know a helluva lot about the apparel business, a search for Hirsch's successor while Hirsch still remained president in 1980.

"Warren has great talents at building small companies, but he's not the kind of person to manage an ongoing, substantial operation," contends Westerfield. That search by colleague John Foster, Boyden's New York office manager, resulted in the recruitment of Abraham & Straus retailer Alan Gilman, who has since diversified Murjani into Coca-Cola clothes.

Westerfield's success notwithstanding, all of the Big Four search firms have launched specialty boutiques in recent years as clients have come to demand specialized expertise from the headhunters. Korn/Ferry trumpets its 11 specialty divisions, Russell Reynolds boasts 11 specialty practices and Spencer Stuart has seven of them. Their motivation came from specialty shops which began chipping away at the business. Yet when Witt first pioneered the field of health care, the corporate executive hunters would sneer. They'd wonder how he could possibly rush about the country dealing with the hospital bumpkins, the nonprofit types. As a director of the business's clubby trade association, Witt would endure the snide comments.

"They looked at guys like me in the early days and said, 'Oh, you work for nonprofits. Well, we work for big steel; we work for big food, and we work for big beer' " he nearly shouts. " 'Who do you work for? Community hospitals? Oh shit, we wouldn't be interested in that.'

"It was really cutesy," Witt recalls, with a scowl on his round, puffy face. "With my simplistic Polack mind, I'm saying to myself they pay with green money and it's the same kind of money people in big steel pay with. I said to each his own. When the recession came in 1980, guess who I began to see in waiting room after waiting room around this country? The same people who were looking down their noses at me for working at nonprofit hospitals. Now they're out there trying to develop specialty practices." Witt brings his hands together in a loud clap and smiles.

He has gotten the last laugh. Among the specialists, Witt is a maverick and a loud, boisterous one at that. A recklessly outspoken, spellbinding orator, he uses his arms to make a point, as if conducting an orchestra. But Witt looks more like the foreman in a construction crew than the president and founder of a company.

In seeking clients, he successfully targeted the growing health care industry—a field in which the growth of for-profit, investor-owned hospital companies has nearly matched Silicon Valley's computer explosion. He helped change not only search but the health care field, too.

When he began his matchmaking career in the mid-1960s, the business was dominated by what Witt calls "kingmakers." These were the state hospital association directors and the academic chairmen of university health administration programs which began proliferating at the nation's graduate schools in the 1960s. The academics dispatched their graduate students to work as indentured servants at half pay for chief executives of hospitals. The chief executive officers became preceptors for the young students, watching over their progress as guardian angels. When the students completed their residencies, they were either offered jobs by their preceptors or placed by them at other institutions.

"It became a badge of honor for a director to place his resident someplace else," says Witt. "If a preceptor from the University of Minnesota got you a job somewhere and now there was a plan to add 50 beds, who do you think was running one of the most prominent consulting firms to help add those beds? Why your old course director in Minnesota, James A. Hamilton. Well what do you know. Just who do you think you'd hire? I watched some of this and said it was crazy. These kingmakers would be doing the field no favors. They were not objective in any way. They all had loyalties to others, and the alumni associations were tighter than any branch out of the Mafia."

But then entered Witt. Son of a union organizer with a sixth-grade education, he had graduated with an economics degree from Iowa's Luther College in 1957. He worked his way through college as a door-to-door salesman. Ostensibly, he was a natural. Witt had the capacity to sell air conditioners to Eskimos. "When I sold Bibles," he brags, "the first 15 homes I went to all bought a Bible. When I sold cookware, the first two gals I talked to bought cookware. Selling to me was just like stealing. It wasn't even a challenge."

Following his dad's advice to enter the business world, Witt took his college degree to old-line industrial equipment maker Allis-Chalmers in Wisconsin where he was raised. As a trainee in the personnel department, he lasted all of 18 months until he became the victim of a recession-induced layoff. Back to sales he went as a life insurance agent for Prudential. His former employment manager at Allis-Chalmers, meantime, recommended him for a personnel job to the administrator of St. Luke's Hospital in Milwaukee. Offered the post of personnel director of the 250-bed hospital, Witt quit Prudential just six months after agreeing to sell insurance.

The position at St. Luke's led four years later to another job with the American Hospital Association in Chicago, where he eventually became director of personnel services for member institutions. Traveling 90 percent of the time to conduct personnel seminars and consult with members, he had the chance to hobnob with the top executives of all the state associations and metropolitan hospitals in the country.

As Witt crisscrossed the nation, they would come up to him, asking if he knew of executives who were looking to relocate in other areas. Inevitably, he did. "In the hospital world, they would pick up the phone, call somebody I mentioned and hire him without checking any references," says Witt. "Maybe the guy was on the sauce, maybe he had a booze problem. Next time they would see me they'd say, 'John, didn't you check that fella out?'" Maybe, he was embarrassed a half dozen times or so. But the thought must have penetrated his mind that someone would make a good buck finding professional managers for the nation's hospitals.

Three and one-half years later, in 1965, Witt was on the move again. This time he hitched up with A. T. Kearney as a consultant in its health services group. He transferred to the management consultant's search group after eight months, promising his boss that a lucrative market for search existed in health care. Witt discovered so much business that he left in 1969 to put together his own firm. A former Kearney colleague, Richard C. Dolan, joined him nine months later, and in early 1971 the firm was known as Witt and Dolan.

From the start, the pair was determined not only to specialize in health care but always to remain specialists. Witt recalled the steady stream of management consultants who walked into his offices at the hospital association trying to persuade him they were experts in hospital management when they had no experience in it at all. "They were selling nothing but bullshit," charges Witt, "because wherever you said it hurt they said they did just the surgery that would help. One outfit came in wanting to put computers into hospitals. They had a slick, costly and beautiful brochure and I asked them one simple question. It blew them out of the water. I said, 'This is very impressive but can you give me the names of three hospitals where you have done this?' The Goddamn guy had all the literature printed, but he had never done anything.

"I decided I would never do that. I would do one thing and do it so well that I am going to beat the Booz, Allen & Hamiltons and the A. T. Kearneys and everybody in the business. I listened to the search consultants who said, 'What difference does it make? An executive in banking can do steel or lumber. A business is a business.' I said no. We know the jargon. We know the ins and outs of this business and we know it very well."

Utilizing his hospital contacts, he carved out a profitable niche in a still-developing field. Witt, like pioneer Thorndike Deland, emerged as a knowledgeable industry spokesman, working overtime to position his firm as the headhunting experts in medical care. His firm commissioned surveys on the business and published "how-to" hire booklets for voluntary board members, while he and his associates traveled the country speaking at state association conferences and symposiums. In one recent month in 1985 five different Witt headhunters delivered speeches in Virginia, Wisconsin, Tennessee, Kansas and Illinois on topics ranging from "Health Care in the 1990s" to "Contracts for Health Care Executives." Even within his specialty practice, he established further specialties. He broke up the firm's search activities into four regions to better cope with differing state regulations. The firm further bolstered its reputation as an industry expert by diversifying into executive compensation consulting in 1981 and management educational training in 1982 for health care only.

Witt was a maverick in other ways, too. Few search firms print a statement of ethics in their promotional brochures. Witt does and initially published beside it the Association of Executive Recruiting Consultants' code, doing the industry's guidelines one or two better. Witt, for example, would agree to keep his clients off-limits for three instead of two years. To his chagrin, he found most users didn't understand nor expressed much interest in his off-limits rule. So it is now back to two years.

Most headhunters don't evade questions about off-limits' policies. But few initiate discussions of them. It's not exactly considered the best approach to developing business. Witt's promotional literature, however, confronts the issue head on: "Clients are assured that no member of their organization will be considered by Witt Associates as a potential candidate, unless he has clearly stated his intentions to his superior, for a period of two years following an assignment with that institution or organization."

When Witt hired associates, he looked for people already credentialed in health care. Among them are former hospital administrators, a director of nursing and a registered pharmacist. John A. Lloyd, Witt's top lieutenant, was presented in 1973 by Witt as a candidate to a client who passed on him because he was only 26 years old. Too young, the client said, to work with his board of directors. "If you don't hire him, I will," vowed Witt. He brought the young Turk on staff, and today Lloyd heads up the firm's search activities as executive vice-president.

The specifications on Witt's very first search—for the nun who wanted a Catholic family man for an administrator—was a sign of what likely was to come. The specs really had little to do with the job. "Even today there are still many searches for $100 million, $200 million and $300 million businesses run by voluntary boards that start with those kinds of specifications," says Witt. "Blind prejudice on weight, dress, hairstyle, graduate school and a variety of other factors is a real force in the hiring decision."

The same, of course, is true in the corporate world. Headhunters there, however, are less candid about the discriminatory prejudices they propagate in the business. In one key search for a chief executive officer of a deeply-troubled hospital, a board disqualified candidates on the basis of height and religion. "Here was a hospital that had just had one of the biggest lawsuits in the U.S.," says Witt. "Its whole medical staff had just resigned. The hospital was down to 30 percent occupancy."

The first of Witt's three candidates was five-foot-three short. "He had experience in solving every problem they had," Witt adds. "Do you know that after they interviewed all the candidates they spent the first 45 minutes on whether a guy that short looked like a leader? Phew," Witt whistles, rolling his eyes. "With the second candidate they wondered if the community would accept a Jew running the institution? They were in the swamp, up to their assholes in alligators and they were all being picky.

"So after that I started developing a whole series of questions about height, weight, race, religion, schools and lifestyles. In this industry many of these things are far more important in getting someone to fit. All these group biases and prejudices tend to surface in this nonprofit boardroom."

Experiences such as those have given Witt little respect for many of the corporate executives who as directors on voluntary boards oversee the management of many of the hospitals for which he works. "There are an awful lot of people on these boards who do some of the dumbest, most stupid and ignorant things," he recklessly charges. "They are the captains of American industry by day and the community idiots by night when they sit on these boards."

He particularly recalls an assignment he was given to find the chief executive officer for the newly merged Catholic and Methodist hospitals. Not only did the chief executive officer have to pull off the merger in a religiously segregated community, he had to raise $15 million to build a new facility. "I found them a guy who was raised

238

a Methodist, graduated from a Catholic university and had a master's in hospital administration and in one year raised $16 million without the help of an outside consultant," Witt says.

Three years later, when Witt ran a classified ad on a search for another chief executive, the successful chief executive officer mailed in his resume. The ad, no less, promised a starting salary no larger than the starting compensation of the executive three years earlier. Witt couldn't understand what had gone wrong.

"Guess what!" Witt says. "The board forgot to look at his compensation for three years. No one was taking care of him. The board didn't give him a single raise. It's stupid, isn't it? But this was not done by the shoe clerks of the world, not by the guys who run hardware stores, but by the so-called captains of industry."

Not surprisingly, Witt—a stentorian speaker who uses sarcasm to emphasize a point—hands out few compliments for the investor-owned hospital management corporations. "Everytime I read about the geniuses at Hospital Corporation of America [HCA] or Humana I want to puke," he says. "They don't have the manual on how to run a hospital. The turkey who gets fired in Birmingham, Alabama, as likely as not surfaces running a proprietary hospital in Florida."

If a small hospital is losing money, it can pursue one of two courses to set things back on track. The board can bring in one of the large for-profit health care companies, which will then take over the management of the institution in exchange for a big consulting fee. Or the board can bring in new management itself, possibly with the help of a health care headhunter like Witt. "We go to the board and make them believe we can find someone to turn it around," Witt says, "so HCA officials unofficially consider us the biggest pain in the ass."

Why do so many small, community hospitals sign management contracts with hospital management corporations? Many of these hospitals are reluctant to pay up for sorely-needed executive talent. For the hospital with fewer than 150 beds, that chief executive officer's salary might total only $80,000 a year but it's out of the question for some voluntary boards. " '$80,000!' " yells Witt, mustering up his best southern accent, " 'We don't pay the superintendent of schools but $55,000 in this county. What you think we're gonna do? The major only makes $40,000. We ain't gonna pay nobody more than the major to run this Goddamn hospital!'

"So who do they hire? They hire a retired military type, offer him

239

$40,000 and another $15,000 under the table. He steals food and takes kickbacks and two years later they fire him. Then they hire the experts from out of town to run the place. HCA puts three or four of them on a Lear jet, flies them to Nashville and treats them like kings as if they were making the wisest decision in the world. You know what they do? They go out and hire someone for $90,000 a year. I'll bet you that you would find that every hospital which signed a contract had an administrator who got a 25 percent to 30 percent boost in pay when HCA came along."

Health care compensation, however, is still low compared to the hefty sums paid out in the corporate world. The vast majority of the firm's work is in jobs paying between $60,000 and $100,000 a year. Witt Associates lands only three or four searches annually at the $200,000 mark, the highest reported salary for a chief executive officer of a multihospital system in 1984. Virtually all major corporate vice-presidents pull down $200,000 or more in compensation annually.

So the firm's consultants must work far harder than the corporate hunters for typically less compensation. Indeed, in a recent listing by *Executive Recruiter News* of the largest U.S. search firms Witt ranked 21st of 23 firms in average billings per professional. The average consultant at Witt bills only $162,000 a year, compared to Haley's $425,000 or Korn/Ferry's $330,000. That is the price of specializing in a less lucrative profession. But Witt isn't counting numbers and dollar signs.

"Lester Korn only had one goal in the business," Witt boasts. "He wanted to be the biggest. That he got. Everything else is complete bullshit. I never said anything about having the biggest or the most profitable. I wanted to be the best at what I do."

To get there, Witt adopted some unconventional benchmarks. Looking into the future in 1972 as the head of a four-man firm, he wrote a corporate agenda that included a commitment to the personal growth, professionally and financially, of all his employees. The headhunting entrepreneur claims he spends $200,000 a year toward that purpose on tuition reimbursement, books and subscriptions for employees.

"There are some human interest stories among the staff that I am probably every bit as proud of as any professional assignment I've ever done," he says. "A professional service firm cannot grow with mirrors. It must grow its people. We've got to make it more, and we've got to make it better."

Witt practices what he preaches. In early 1984, he took a two-month sabbatical at Georgia State University, where he enlisted as a visiting senior fellow of the Institute of Health Administration. There he launched into a study of editorials in three professional trade journals for the medical profession, engaged in three different seminars on listening and struck a unique deal with his wife of 30 years. The two of them agreed to read three books together (Gail Sheehy's *Pathfinders*, Scott Peck's *The Road Less Traveled* and Michael Minton and Jean L. Bloch's *What Is a Wife Worth?*). Each night over the two-month period they would spend a minimum of one hour to "dialogue," as Witt puts it, about their readings during the day. Sometimes, the discussions would go from 5:00 P.M. to midnight.

In the aggressively driven world of headhunting this was unheard of. The Association of Executive Search Consultants, the business's trade group, invited Witt to describe his experiences at Georgia State University at a seminar to others. "An awful lot of people who do this kind of work watch people turn into animals simply to make more money this year than the year before," he says. "I looked around that room and you could see it written in their faces. There is something more in life, they thought."

241

10

An Agenda for the Future

"What next for the executive merchants?"

AT THE EXQUISITELY EXTRAVAGANT Danieli Hotel in Venice, the tiny bulbs on the crystal chandelier dim. A slide projector's bright light hits a white screen at the front of a large ornate room. The hot light bounces a glare into the group of 60 headhunters from Spencer Stuart & Associates' far-flung outposts around the world.

The largest single contingent, some 40 consultants, have flown in from Amsterdam, Brussels, London, Paris, Frankfurt, Madrid, Zurich and Milan. Another dozen have arrived from Melbourne and Sydney, Montreal and Toronto. A group of eight are over from the U.S., including the man standing before them behind a wooden lectern.

He is Thomas J. Neff, the 47-year-old icy cool, silver-haired president of Spencer Stuart. A former McKinsey & Co. consultant, Neff began pursuing executives as a search consultant in 1974 at Booz, Allen & Hamilton. He joined Spencer Stuart in 1976 and has since become the number one producer in the firm, billing in excess of $1 million last year. Neff's specialty is chief executive and board of director searches, an area which allows him a broad perspective on senior management issues.

His colleagues have come to Venice in May 1985 to, among other things, hear him speak on the outlook of the business. With a remote control button in hand, Neff begins his gaze into the future of the business, musing about the likelihood of a number of unfolding possibilities, some as promising as others are bedeviling.

(CLICK.)

"Our industry, our business is no different than that of our clients," he says. "Executive search is changing, significantly and basically. And we must face up to those changes and come to grips with them as individuals, as offices and as a firm if we are to emerge the winners."

(CLICK.)

An industry shakeout, the slide reports. "There are an increasing number of firms," Neff tells his colleagues, "the continued growth of the majors and tough competitive pressures. The Haley of the old days will never be a market leader again. When he was a leader, most firms didn't have many branch offices. Size gives you reputation and awareness. The more places you are, the more people you have and the more executives you talk to. The smaller firms are at a disadvantage."

Truth is, there will always be room in the business for a quality act whether it's a large firm, such as Spencer Stuart, or a small boutique, such as Gould & McCoy. Many major corporations, such as ITT, prefer the smaller firms if only because they still agree to keep all their U.S. operations off-limits. Those in the middle, grappling with heady egos and lacking the resources of the entrenched majors, are likely to feel the squeeze.

"You are going to see some fallout of the smaller firms," predicts Lester Korn, a Neff rival who shares his belief in a likely shakeout. "It is going to be harder for them to compete. No matter what you hear from the small firms, they just don't have the ability to do the research; they can't afford the computers and they can't afford the recordkeeping that goes with it. They can't do the depth of research that is done by a large firm whether it's this one or any other."

The Big Four search firms likely will get bigger and the gap between them and the rest of the major firms will likely grow. "I see the business being dominated some years out by a small number of very large firms with extraordinary resources, large numbers of consultants and tremendous market coverage with increasing degrees of specialization which will produce better results," thinks former Ward Howell President, Gilbert Dwyer.

"There will always be room for small firms and individuals who are highly specialized and who don't need the resources because of it. The medium-sized firm will be in trouble because they don't have the market coverage or resources to sell effectively against the big firm or the small firm. They are going to suffer in the marketplace."

(CLICK.)

Emergence of a major new force in the industry. "There have been no major new firms on the scene since Korn/Ferry and Reynolds started in 1969," Neff points out. "Why haven't there been any in an industry that is highly dynamic, growing and profitable with a low cost of entry? The possibility today of becoming a major international firm is that much more difficult because not only has the U.S. been saturated, but even internationally it's tough."

When Korn/Ferry and Reynolds launched their firms, the largest company in the business—Boyden Associates—boasted revenues of under $5 million. Today's leader, Korn/Ferry, is now a $58 million business that by decade's end could reach the $100 million mark. All newcomers face a well-entrenched Big Four with the business discipline and savvy that none of headhunting's pioneers could muster. The Old Crony network that drove the business in its early days is all but gone. Some of the smaller shops which rely on it can never hope to get big on it.

(CLICK.)

Acquisition of search firms by nonsearch firms. Neff is surmising that his two major competitors will undergo a drastic transformation when the founders leave. "Which firms might be top targets for a takeover?" he asks. "My view on that is those two which have the biggest equity problems, Korn/Ferry and Russell Reynolds. (Korn and Ferry together own 55 percent of their company; Reynolds and his co-founder Lee Getz hold roughly a 60 percent stake in their firm.) If they want to get more than book value when they cash their chips in, they will have to sell out. There might be some mergers but no one is going to get rich on them."

Neff leaves out Lamalie Associates, but of the top ten firms it is the only one in which the founder and chairman remains as sole owner of the firm. If Robert Lamalie eventually finds his consultants less than receptive to buying him out some day, he may have to turn outside to sell his company. And in 1985 he, in fact, began peddling his headhunting shop to outsiders.

(CLICK.)

Search firm mergers. "What would happen to the balance of power in the U.S. should two major search firms merge?" asks Neff. "What if Egon Zehnder acquires Lamalie or Ward Howell? We've explored smaller mergers outside the U.S. Should we continue to do so?" Neff offers no answers, only questions.

Mergers and consolidations, however, are likely prospects. In 1982, the headhunting arm of Big Eight accountant Arthur Young had agreed to a merger with TASA, Inc., a search firm especially strong in Latin America—the deal would have made the merged pair the third largest executive recruiter in the world by revenues. Arthur Young's management committee unanimously voted in favor of the marriage, but William Gladstone, AY's managing partner, vetoed the agreement. The conservative Gladstone maintained that Arthur Young never merged with any firm that it had not worked with for many years. Arthur Young has since worked out a loose joint venture with TASA, so future merger between the pair remains a strong possibility.

PA Executive Search Group, a British-based executive recruiter with 42 offices worldwide, also has been on the prowl for acquisitions. A notorious non-entity in the U.S. search market, the company lost $1.5 million in a previous drive to increase its business here. In June of 1983, PA's U.S. billings were a mere $20,000. In early 1986, however, the company's sole New York office was racking up billings of $250,000 monthly with seven headhunters. Ward Howell has had discussions with Paul Stafford Associates, Ltd., a search firm based in New York with four European branches. Boyden has chatted with Ward Howell; Russell Reynolds with Thorndike Deland.

(CLICK.)

Likelihood of a major breakthrough flashes on the screen. "It's possible," guesses Neff, "for a firm to lose a competitive edge. Should we be investing in some form of research and development that will be critical in the future? Interdatum people now walk around with a computer terminal in their briefcase and dazzle clients with real-time access to a database," says Neff. "That's impressive looking. My view is that someday in the future we'll all be doing that kind of thing. But if one of the majors is first will it give them a big advantage?"

(CLICK.)

Increasing pressure to redefine clients off-limits. This is a prickly problem. In the early days, search firms would keep every division worldwide of a client corporation off-limits for five full years after a search. Then, the period fell to two years. As the big firms grew bigger in the early 1980s, they revised their policies so that only the divisions or subsidiaries of a corporation they served, not the entire company, would be off limits. The majors also unwittingly handed their smaller competitors a marketing weapon to use against them.

Could the Big Four possibly narrow it down further? Neff, for one, thinks a one-year, off-limits rule is possible. "It would take a lot of balls for somebody to take the first step on that," he says, "but I think it is not out of the question.

"It may be that we'll end up telling our clients that 'we'll keep you off-limits as long as you are our major supplier. If you bring in another search firm, even though we just completed a search for you two months ago, we're sorry, you're no longer a client.' " Such a policy would have to be tempered by a headhunter's relationship with the client corporation. "If the client tells us about the strengths and weaknesses of his key people, it would be quite unethical to take advantage of that information," Neff tells his associates. "That's one reason you need some time to elapse before you consider a client fair game. But if you do a highly confidential and very focused search and you're not talking to other executives in the organization, I think there's more of a justification for narrowing the relationship."

Is it possible for the larger firms to continue their rapid growth without violating professional ethics by raiding their clients? Some lapses have clearly occurred. "Some of these firms are vulnerable to criticism," says Dick Ferry. "Some firms are getting sloppy in that area and it's going to cause all kinds of problems for the profession if they don't tighten them up. Abuses have taken place and we should be able to push those people out. They shouldn't be allowed to practice."

As the largest search firm in the business, however, Korn/Ferry faces the most severe blockage problem of the Big Four. To combat the problem, Korn-Ferry and its big-league competitors are trying to develop closer relationships with clients so that they can perform more of their total search needs. That way, they may be able to continue to grow within their current client base, without acquiring additional clients.

Spencer Stuart recently turned down a search from a major electronics corporation because it would not guarantee Stuart at least $300,000 in fees annually. The company was simply too important a developer of executive talent to keep off-limits. "You've got to feed that hungry gorilla bananas or he'll start rattling the cage," notes Neff's colleague, Robert Slater, managing director of Stuart's U.S. operations. Another emerging strategy is to expand more aggressively abroad.

(CLICK.)

Intensive competition to capture the multinational market, predicts the message on the screen.

Korn/Ferry, for one, expects overseas assignments to account for half of its revenues within the next several years, up from only 30 percent today. Russell Reynolds, which had only two offices abroad in 1979, today boasts eight foreign branches which account for a third of the firm's revenues. Reynolds expects further expansion in the international market, too.

"There's tremendous search potential internationally," Neff tells his colleagues. "The international growth of major search firms is continuing, and there's a competitive strategy of serving all the search needs of a client."

Foreign branches, however, tend to be far less lucrative than U.S. outposts. Executive salaries abroad are not nearly as high as those in the U.S., so average fees per assignment are lower. Spencer Stuart & Associates' total revenues of $43 million are split evenly between its U.S. and international offices. But it takes two-thirds of the firm's 120 consultants to produce the international half, while only a third in the U.S. can produce the remaining 50 percent.

So it is unlikely that overseas offices can match the profitability of their U.S. counterparts. And the U.S. market shows other signs of growth. Search firms, like management consultants, are now finding out there's lots of lucrative business to be had from small companies. "Five years ago," says Boyden's Putney Westerfield, "we didn't get search assignments from companies which were virtual start ups or those doing $2 to $5 million in sales. Now we have searches to recruit the whole management team for a $5 million company, and when that business grows from $10 to $50 million we get more business."

Westerfield, for example, initially recruited the vice-president of marketing for Galoob, a small San Francisco-based toy company. That assignment led to numerous others. "Now they need a whole management team, a vice-president of finance, a general counsel. And we just finished another search for a vice-president of engineering. That is happening all across the country. It's more important in the growth of the recruiting business than even the greater acceptance of search by big companies. From 1972 to 1982, the Fortune 1,000 companies didn't add a single new job to corporate America. We absorbed millions and millions of new jobs in our economy and it has all come from the small companies."

Will American executives remain as restless as they have been through the 1970s? While mindless company loyalty is a thing of the past, the music being played in the executive musical chair game has slowed down a few beats. The gamesman theory of corporation advancement, which promoted job mobility by job hopping, is losing ground. Executives and managers are returning, if only partially, to an old work ethic which demanded loyalty in exchange for advancement. Even some headhunters willingly concede this is true.

"Not so long ago, executives avidly responded to recruiters, leaving positions where they had accumulated considerable organizational equity," says Dwight E. Foster, who heads up Peat Marwick's search activities. "They were eager to pursue seemingly more rewarding assignments with new employers."

Things, of course, didn't always work out. "There were some failures, a lot of mismatches, and an increasing number of takeovers that left these mobile executives stranded and depleted," adds Foster. "Now, leaving a senior management sinecure to take a job in a new organization has become a risky business. While there are always a number of candidates who are in the process of actively seeking new jobs, those senior managers who are performing well in their current organizations are often more apt to gamble on their in-house prospects than risk jeopardizing what they've already achieved."

Critical, too, is that the idea of a "professional manager" who can run from one industry to the next as a Messiah or Savior has been partly discredited. Witness the failures of most of the mass marketers at companies like Atari and Osborne Computer Corp. "The notion that knowledge is interchangeable between different companies is coming into disfavor," says Dr. Robert Hayes of Harvard University's Graduate Business School. "The idea was that if you knew some basic tools you could run anything. You were the so-called professional manager. People are coming to understand that different businesses behave very differently and you have to have some degree of experience before you're qualified to run it. The bulk of the executive job-hopping movement has been composed of people who are selling specialized skills and the transferability of those skills to another environment. That is less accepted than it used to be."

This is a major setback for headhunters, because a good chunk of their business comes from moving executives from one industry to another. That's partly because in many industries the companies already know who the key players are, so there's less a need for the executive recruiter. Concerns are less aware of the Boy Wonders in industries in which they don't operate.

(CLICK.)

Continuous impact of technology on how we do research, reads the slide on the screen. "We may be able to shrink the candidate identification stage to one week or one day," envisions Neff. "So we could place greater emphasis on our sourcing skills, on screening and on evaluating candidates and counseling clients.

"How about videotaped candidate presentations?" he laughs. "The question here isn't if, but how much and how soon."

Addendum

The Top Ten U.S. Recruiting Firms

The accounting profession has its so-called Big Eight, an informal fraternity of the largest, most powerful numbers-crunching firms. In headhunting, though, it's more like the Big Four: Korn/Ferry International, Russell Reynolds Associates, Inc., Spencer Stuart & Associates and Heidrick & Struggles, Inc. All of these firms boast annual revenues of $30 million or more. And all of them are listed in the following mini-directory of the top ten executive search firms headquartered in the U.S.

Together the top ten employ over 700 headhunting consultants who stalk tens of thousands of executive prey in the corporate jungle every year. They carry out roughly 8,500 searches a year. Yet the top ten reflect just a small slice of the overall business. They bill less than $250 million annually, representing only 10 percent of the total search business. Revenues at the ten largest firms nearly doubled in the past five years. The biggest gains were racked up by Russell Reynolds and Handy Associates. Reynolds grew an average 45% a year since 1980; Handy by 35%. Among the top ten laggards were Heidrick & Struggles and Boyden Associates, which both eked out 4% annual growth rates.

While the majors continue to grow in power and size, most executive game hunts are the province of the smaller local and regional firms. For a more complete and authoritative guide, listing 2,000 U.S. search firms, refer to the *Directory of Executive Recruiters* ($24, pps. 354; Consultants News; Templeton Road; Fitzwilliam, New Hampshire 03447).

◧ Korn/Ferry International
1800 Century Park East
Los Angeles, California 90067

Total (1985) revenues: $58 million*
Five-year annual growth rate: 17 percent
Billings per consultant: $379,000

Total searches per year: 1,500+, $75,000 salary minimum.

Major searches: Raymond Dempsey, chief executive officer European American Bancorp; Peter Ueberroth, executive director Olympic Organizing Committee; Ryal R. Poppa, chief executive officer Storage Technology Corp.; Richard Cooley, chief executive officer Seafirst Corp.; Marvin Runyon, chief executive officer Nissan Motor Manufacturing Corp. USA; William H. Waltrip, chief executive officer Purolator Courier Corp. (resigned June 1985).

Profile: Founded in 1969 by former Peat, Marwick & Mitchell partners Lester Korn and Richard Ferry. Most aggressive of all the major search firms. A pioneer in the business, bringing the disciplines of an accounting firm to a small fragmented profession. Korn and Ferry own 55 percent of firm; remaining equity spread among all 106 partners. Total (1985) professional and support staff of about 400, with 153 partners and managing associates. With 36 offices in U.S., Canada, Europe, Latin America, Asia/Pacific and Australia. Overseas revenues account for roughly 25 percent of total.

Firm also pioneered the creation of specialty divisions boasting expertise in specific industries.

Specialty practices: Financial Services (Windle Priem, manager, New York); High Technology (Robert LoPresto, manager, Palo Alto); Energy (R. Larry Snider, manager, Houston); Fashion/Retail (Robert Nesbit, manager, New York); Real Estate (Lee Van Leeuwen, manager, Los Angeles); Hospitality/Leisure (Charles Ollinger, manager, Boston); Entertainment (Richard Ferry, acting manager, Los Angeles); Health Care (James Heuerman, manager, San Francisco); Government/Not-For-Profit/Education (Norman Roberts, manager, Los Angeles); Board Services (Virgil Baldi, manager, New York); Venture Capital (Bernard H. Schulte, manager, San Francisco).

Research Directors: Laura Rockwell, corporate director. Nancie Streger, New York; Henrietta Davis, Los Angeles; Eunice Azzani, San Francisco; Victoria Cheshire, Chicago.

U.S. offices:

Charles D. Ollinger, Manager
1 Post Office Square
Boston, Massachusetts 02109
(617) 423-4100

Dulany Foster, Jr., Manager
3 Landmark Square
Stamford, Connecticut 06901
(203) 359-3350

Thomas H. Hall III, Manager
233 Peachtree Street, NE
Atlanta, Georgia 30303
(404) 577-7542

Gary W. Silverman, Manager
120 South Riverside Plaza
Chicago, Illinois 60606
(312) 726-1841

R. Larry Snider, Manager
1100 Milam Building
Houston, Texas 77002
(713) 651-1834

John G. Harlow, Manager
600 Montgomery Street
San Francisco, California 94111
(415) 956-1834

Robert L. LoPresto, Manager
5 Palo Alto Square
Palo Alto, California 94306
(415) 856-2611

David F. Smith, Manager
237 Park Avenue
New York, New York 10017
(212) 687-1834

Ronald H. Walker, Manager
1825 K Street, NW
Washington, DC 20006
(202) 822-9444

Roland W. Stuebner, Manager
350 North St. Paul–1 Dallas Center
Dallas, Texas 75201
(214) 651-1801

Lewis F. Lenkaitis, Manager
1900 East Ninth Street
Cleveland, Ohio 44114
(216) 861-5656

George L. Reisinger, Manager
1801 California Street
Denver, Colorado 80202
(303) 292-1834

Thomas Burnham, Manager
1300 Dove Street
Newport Beach, California 92660
(714) 851-1834

Robert S. Rollo, Manager
1800 Century Park East
Los Angeles, California 90067
(213) 879-1834

Morgan H. Harris, Jr., Manager
911 Wilshire Boulevard
Los Angeles, California 90017
(213) 879-1834

James C. Hawkanson, Manager
999 Third Avenue
Seattle, Washington 98104
(206) 621-1834

Allan H. Raymond, Manager
2508 IDS Center
80 South Eighth Street
Minneapolis, Minnesota 55402
(612) 333-1834

Officers: Chairman Lester B. Korn; President Richard M. Ferry; Managing Partners Windle B. Priem, Morgan H. Harris, Jr., David F. Smith.

Top producer: Windle B. Priem, $1.4 million annually.

*Estimate for fiscal year ended April 30, 1986.

◻ Russell Reynolds Associates, Inc.   Total (1985) revenues: $47 million *
245 Park Avenue   Five-year annual growth rate: 45
New York, New York 10167   percent
   Billings per professional: $392,000

Total searches per year: 1,600, $75,000, salary minimum.

Major searches: Paul Ely, chief executive officer Convergent Technologies, Inc.; G. Kirk Raab, president Genentech, Inc.; Nolan D. Archibald, president Black & Decker Corp.; Barry Sullivan, chairman First Chicago Corp.; George Ball, chief executive officer Prudential-Bache Securities, Inc.; Frank Cahouet, chairman Crocker National Bank; Donald Ogilvie, executive vice-president American Bankers Association.

Profile: Founded in 1969 by Russell Reynolds, a former Morgan Guaranty Trust Co. officer who cut his teeth on the headhunting business with a three-year stint with William H. Clark Associates. Modeling itself after premier service firms, like McKinsey & Co. and Morgan Stanley, it is the most elite and the most arrogant of the firms, populated by Ivy League headhunters. Firm initially specialized in recruiting financial types, later branching out as a generalist. Reynolds and Vice-Chairman H. Leland Getz together hold 60 percent stake in firm with remainder spread among some 45 consultants. Total (1985) professional staff of 120. With 19 offices in U.S., Europe, Asia and Australia.

Specialty practices: Communications (Roger Bullard, manager, New York); Consumer Products & Services (Roger Bullard, manager, New York); Energy & Natural Resources (George Donnelly, manager, Houston); Financial Services (Richard Lannamann, manager, New York); High Technology (Ed Unterberg, manager, Chicago); Industrial Products & Services (Robert Crumbaker, manager, Cleveland); Not-for-Profit (William Olsen, manager, New York); Professional Services (Beth Olesky, manager, New York); Real Estate (Jim Phillips, manager, New York); Health Care (Richard Gifford, manager, Chicago); Information Systems (Norbert Gottenberg, manager, New York).

Research director: Brian O'Conner, New York.

U.S. offices:

Hobson Brown, Jr., Manager
245 Park Avenue
New York, New York 10167
(212) 953-4300

Jack Vernon, Manager
45 School Street
Boston, Massachusetts 02108
(617) 523-1111

Robert Seebeck, Manager
200 S. Wacker Drive/Suite 3600
Chicago, Illinois 60606
(312) 993-9696

John Stanton, Manager
2001 Ross Avenue/Suite 1900
Dallas, Texas 75201
(214) 220-2033

Edward A. Kister, Jr., Manager
333 S. Grand Avenue/Suite 4200
Los Angeles, California 90071
(213) 489-1520

Richard Gostyla, Manager
3000 Sand Hill Road/Suite 245
Menlo Park, California 94025
(415) 854-3330

Thomas McLane, Manager
3 Landmark Square/Suite 405
Stamford, Connecticut 06901
(203) 356-1940

Robert Crumbaker, Manager
1900 E. 9th Street
Cleveland, Ohio 44114
(216) 575-1750

John Franklin, Jr.
1850 K Street, NW
Washington, DC 20006
(202) 628-2150

David Morris, Manager
1000 Louisiana Street/Suite 4800
Houston, Texas 77002
(713) 658-1776

P. Anthony Price, Manager
101 California Street/Suite 3140
San Francisco, California 94111
(415) 392-3130

Officers: Chairman Russell S. Reynolds, Jr.; Vice-Chairman H. Leland Getz; President Ferdinand Nadherny; Executive Vice-President Andrew D. Hart, Jr.

*Estimate for fiscal year ended January 31, 1986.

◻ Spencer Stuart & Associates
55 East 52nd Street
New York, New York 10055

Total (1985) revenues: $43 million *
Five-year annual growth rate: 20 percent
Billings per consultant: $358,000

Total searches per year: 1,200 +, $75,000 salary minimum.

Major searches: Edward Acker, chairman Pan American World Airways; John S. Chamberlin, president Avon Products Inc.; Grant Gentry, chairman Food Fair (now resigned); William T. Knowles, chief operating officer (now chief executive officer), National Westminster Bank USA.

Profile: Founded in 1956 by former Booz, Allen & Hamilton consultant Spencer R. Stuart. First U.S. search firm to establish a successful international practice which today accounts for roughly half its billings. Stuart mistakingly neglected the U.S. market. In 1973 there were 55 headhunters in nine offices, and only two in the U.S. Greatest growth occurred after Stuart departed. Firm owned by roughly 90 of its consultants, none of whom have more than 5 percent stake. Among largest holders are Thomas Neff, president, and Arnold Tempel, chairman. Total (1985) professional staff of 120 consultants. With 29 offices in U.S., Canada, Europe, Australia, Asia and Latin America. Overseas revenues account for half of total.

Specialty practices: Boards of Directors (Thomas Neff and Jack Lohnes, managers, New York); Communications (Tony Thompson, manager, New York); Energy (Richard Kalen, manager, Dallas); Banking and Financial Services (Denis B. Lyons, manager, New York); Not-for-Profit/Health Care (Toni Smith, manager, Chicago); High Technology (Daniel Cruse, manager, Dallas); Real Estate (Dayton Ogden, manager, New York).

Research directors: Christine Clark, New York; Cindy Harris, Chicago.

U.S. offices:

Dayton Ogden, Managing Director
55 East 52nd Street
New York, New York 10055
(212) 407-0200

Robert Benson, Managing Director
693 E. Main Street/Suite 201
Stamford, Connecticut 06904
(203) 324-6333

George Henn, Managing Director
1100 Superior Avenue, NE
Cleveland, Ohio 44114
(216) 575-0500

Jerry Bump, Managing Director
245 Perimeter Center Parkway
Atlanta, Georgia 30346
(404) 396-2900

James Drury, Managing Director
401 North Michigan Avenue
Chicago, Illinois 60611
(312) 822-0080

Robert Slater, Managing Director
1200 First City Center
Dallas, Texas 75201
(214) 880-0400

Lou Rieger, Managing Director
4350 InterFirst Plaza
Houston, Texas 77002
(713) 225-1621

Joseph Griesedieck, Jr., Managing Director
333 Market Street/Suite 3140
San Francisco, California 94105
(415) 495-4141

Daniel Wier, Managing Director
400 South Hope Street
Los Angeles, California 90071
(213) 620-0814

Officers: Chairman Arnold Tempel; President Thomas Neff; Managing Director (U.S.) Robert Slater; Chief Financial Officer Richard Chapman.

Top producer: Thomas Neff, $1 million+ in 1985.

*Fiscal year ended September 30, 1985.

◻ Heidrick & Struggles, Inc.　　Total (1985) revenues: $30 million *
　245 Park Avenue　　　　　　Five-year annual growth rate: 4 percent
　New York, New York 10169　Billings per consultant: $385,000

Total searches per year: 1,000+, $50,000 salary minimum.

Major searches: John Sculley, chief executive officer Apple Computer, Inc.; Joseph Henson, chief executive officer Prime Computer, Inc.; Thomas Vanderslice, chief executive officer Apollo Computer, Inc.; Edward Hennessy, chief executive officer Allied Signal; Robert Frederick, president (now chief executive officer) RCA Corp.; Thomas Wyman, director (now chief executive officer) CBS Corp.; Philip Beekman, president Seagram Co.; Richard Voell, chief executive officer Rockefeller Center, Inc.

Profile: Founded in 1953 by ex-Booz, Allen & Hamilton consultant Gardner Heidrick and ex-Montgomery Ward & Co. vice-president John Struggles. Topped the business in billings in 1978 but internal management problems spurred a mass exodus of consultants between 1979 and 1981. Boasts headhunting superstar Gerry Roche, now chairman, who has put more chief executive officers and presidents in U.S. companies than any other single recruiter. Ownership of firm shared among some 30 consultants with Roche holding largest stake (20 percent). Total (1985) professional staff of 78, with 59 in the U.S. With 15 offices in U.S. and Europe (Heidrick & Struggles restructured its European operations in early 1984, reportedly selling 51 percent to locals).

Research managers: Karen Carruthers, New York; Claudia Casabat, San Francisco; Joelle Jennings, Los Angeles.

U.S. offices:

David Peasback, Manager
245 Park Avenue
New York, New York 10167
(212) 867-9876

R. William Funk, Manager
3690 RepublicBank Center
Houston, Texas 77002
(713) 237-9000

Eugene Rackley III, Manager
225 Peachtree Street, NE
Atlanta, Georgia 30303
(404) 577-2410

Thomas Friel, Manager
2200 Geng Road
Palo Alto, California 94303
(415) 856-3400

William Tipping, Manager
125 South Wacker Drive
Chicago, Illinois 60606
(312) 372-8811

Michael Boxberger, Manager
1999 Bryan Street
Dallas, Texas 75201
(214) 220-2130

Ray Foote, Jr., Manager
104 Field Point Road
Greenwich, Connecticut 06830
(203) 629-3200

Robert Hallagan, Manager
One Post Office Square
Boston, Massachusetts 02109
(617) 423-1140

John Richmond, Manager
1100 Superior Avenue
Cleveland, Ohio 44114
(216) 241-7410

Michael Schoettle, Manager
445 South Figueroa Street
Los Angeles, California 90071
(213) 624-8891

David Elliott, Manager
4 Embarcadero Center
San Francisco, California 94111
(415) 981-2854

Officers: Chairman Gerard Roche; Vice-Chairman Bill Bowen; Chief Executive and President David Peasback; Chief Financial Officer Rick Nelson.

Top producer: Gerard Roche, estimated $1.5 million annually.

*Estimate for fiscal year ended January 31, 1986.

■ Boyden Associates, Inc.   Total (1985) revenues: $17 million
260 Madison Avenue   Five-year annual growth rate: 4 percent
New York, New York   Billings per consultant: $233,000
  10016

Total searches per year: 900, $60,000 salary minimum.

Major searches: Boyden was first of the big-league executive game hunters, plucking Harold Geneen from Raytheon to ITT in 1959 and putting in place presidents and chief executive officers of many major U.S. companies. In recent years, though, the firm has performed few big assignments. Alan Gilman, president Murjani International; Harry J. Bolwell, president Midland-Ross Corp. (now chairman); Ray Adam, chief operating officer NL Industries (retired as chairman in 1983).

Profile: One of the oldest headhunting firms, founded in 1946 by Sidney Boyden, a former Booz, Allen & Hamilton consultant. It also was the biggest during most of the 1960s. Boyden retired in 1971 after selling the firm to Los Angeles-based Shareholders Capital Corp., his biggest error which led to massive turnover. Four years later, recruiters bought back the loss-making business. Now owned by 60 headhunting shareholders with President Putney Westerfield, former publisher of *Fortune* magazine, having largest single stake of 6 percent. Total (1985) professional staff of 73. With 40 offices in U.S., Europe, Australia, Asia and South Africa. (In 1984 overseas offices were required to purchase their local assets, a maneuver some interpreted as a move toward a franchised international system. Overseas consultants, however, own 40 percent of the entire firm and account for 50 percent of total billings.)

Research director: Laurie Billings, New York.

U.S. offices:

John M. Foster, Manager
260 Madison Avenue/Suite 2000
New York, New York 10016
(212) 685-3400

Paul C. Richardson, Manager
3003 Summer Street
Stamford, Connecticut 06905
(203) 324-4300

Peter R. Schmidt, Manager
55 Madison Avenue
Morristown, New Jersey 07960
(201) 267-0980

Ed Bitar, Manager
1625 Eye Street, NW/Suite 412
Washington, DC 20006
(202) 293-5561

Malcolm MacGregor, Manager
625 Stanwix Street/Suite 2405
Pittsburgh, Pennsylvania 15222
(412) 391-3020

J. David Morgan, Manager
3390 Peachtree Road, NE/Suite 1738
Atlanta, Georgia 30326
(404) 261-6532

David H. Hoffmann, Manager
10 South Riverside Plaza
Chicago, Illinois 60606
(312) 782-1581

Victor Viglino, Manager
2400 E. Commerical Boulevard
Fort Lauderdale, Florida 33308
(305) 491-5949

Bruce F. Brownson, Manager
2000 West Loop South
Houston, Texas 77027
(713) 626-4790

Robert A. Whitt, Manager
5420 LBJ Freeway/Suite 1868
Dallas, Texas 75240
(214) 387-7973

Jack Groban, Manager
800 South Figueroa Street
Los Angeles, California 90017
(213) 622-0411

Putney Westerfield, Manager
1 Maritime Plaza
San Francisco, California 94111
(415) 981-7900

Carl M. Olsen, Manager
3000 Sand Hill Road/Suite 280
Menlo Park, California 94025
(415) 854-9090

Robert MacLachlan, Manager
40 Grove Street
Wellesley, Massachusetts 02181
(617) 239-0190

Officers: President Putney Westerfield; Senior Vice-President of Finance & Administration Richard Foy; Managing Directors Michael Curlewis, G. Nicola daVinci, John Foster, Stanley Holt, Malcolm MacGregor, Paul C. Richardson, Peter R. Schmidt, Putney Westerfield.

Top producer: Bills $500,000 annually.

▣ Ward Howell International, Inc. Total (1985) revenues: $9.7 million
99 Park Avenue Five-year annual growth rate: 11 per-
New York, New York 10016 cent
                                  Billings per partner: $277,000

Total searches per year: 750, $75,000 salary minimum.

Major searches: chairman-designate Blue Cross/Blue Shield of New York; Michael Michaelowski, president Carter Weber; Hugh Williamson, chief executive officer Revere Copper and Glass; Dr. Frank Van Diver, president Texas A&M.

Profile: Founded in 1951 by former McKinsey & Co. consultant Henry Wardwell Howell. Howell retired in 1974. Died in automobile accident in 1980 at age 70. Only major firm owned equally by its partners. Stock held by 29 of them. Headhunters, on average older than other firms, are paid on 100 percent commission basis. Total (1985) U.S. professional staff of 35 consultants. With 20 offices in U.S., Europe and Australia. Overseas offices not owned by U.S. company, but are "affiliated" with Ward Howell. If included, total revenues would hit $17.5 million with worldwide professional staff of 83.

Research director: Reeva Friedman, New York.

U.S. offices:

Arthur L. Armitage, Manager
99 Park Avenue
New York, New York 10016
(212) 697-3730

Robert Butterfield, Manager
10100 Santa Monica Boulevard
Los Angeles, California 90067
(213) 553-6638

Stephen A. Garrison, Manager
1601 Elm Street/Suite 900
Dallas, Texas 75201
(214) 749-0099

Stephen A. Garrison, Manager
1000 Louisiana Street/Suite 2970
Houston, Texas 77002
(713) 655-7155

Donald G. Gaertner, Manager
20 North Wacker Drive/Suite 2920
Chicago, Illinois 60606
(312) 236-2211

James W. Cameron, Manager
3 Embarcadero Center/Suite 1060
San Francisco, California 94111
(415) 398-3900

Hans Ullstein, Manager
115 East Putnam Avenue
Greenwich, Connecticut 06830
(203) 629-2994

Officers: Office of the President, John H. Callen, Jr., Stephen M. Mc-Pherson and Stephen A. Garrison.

Top producer: Steven A. Garrison, $600,000 + annually.

■ Paul R. Ray & Co., Inc.
1208 Ridglea Bank Building
Fort Worth, Texas
76116

Total (1985) revenues: $8 million *
Five-year annual growth rate: 7 percent
Billings per consultant: $267,000

Total searches per year: 300 +, $50,000 salary minimum.

Major searches: Stanley Pace, chairman General Dynamics; Oliver Boileau, president General Dynamics; Allan Glueck, president, Armour Fresh Meat.

Profile: Founded in 1965 by Paul R. Ray, Sr., an ex-Boyden Associates consultant who had been an executive in the grain and feed industry for over a decade. Dominates Texas market with more professionals in Lone Star State than any other firm. Ray, Sr. sold firm to American Appraisal in 1971; consultants purchased it back in 1981. Ownership spread among 23 shareholders with largest single stake of 8 percent held by John Bohle, manager of the Los Angeles office. Total (1985) professional staff of 30. With seven offices in U.S. and Europe (London only).

Research director: David Vickers, Fort Worth.

U.S. offices:

Paul R. Ray, Sr., Manager
1208 Ridglea Bank Building
Fort Worth, Texas 76116
(817) 731-4111

Paul McKinnis, Manager
1201 Peachtree Street, NE/Suite 1718
Atlanta, Georgia 30361
(404) 892-2727

John Bradshaw, Manager
1010 Lamar/Suite 990
Houston, Texas 77002
(713) 757-1985

Peter Livingston, Manager
825 Third Avenue
New York, New York 10022
(212) 371-3000

David Radden, Manager
200 South Wacker Drive/38th Floor
Chicago, Illinois 60606
(312) 876-0730

Paul Kayser, Manager
777 East Tahquitz-McCallum Way
Palm Springs, California 92262
(619) 323-7705

Breck Ray, Manager
700 North Pearl Street
Dallas, Texas 75201
(214) 969-7620

John Bohle, Manager
1900 Avenue of the Stars/Suite 600
Los Angeles, California 90067
(213) 557-2828

Officers: Chairman and Chief Executive Paul R. Ray, Sr.; President and Chief Operating Officer Paul R. Ray, Jr.; Secretary and Treasurer Shelby Adams.

Top producer: Paul R. Ray, Sr., billing $1.2 million in 1984.

*Estimate for fiscal year ended February 28, 1986.

☐ Peat, Marwick, Mitchell & Co.
345 Park Avenue
New York, New York 10154

Total (1985) revenues: $7.4 million *
Five-year annual growth rate: 5 percent
Billings per consultant: $211,000

Total searches per year: 400, $50,000 salary minimum.

Major searches: Few, if any. Recruits primarily financial executives for medium-sized corporations. Only 5 percent of clients are Fortune 500 companies.

Profile: Although one of the last Big Eight accounting firms to move into executive search in 1962, it now boasts largest practice among the Big Eight. Dwight E. Foster, a 16-year Peat Marwick veteran, is national principal in charge of executive search. Growth extremely limited due to severe blockage problems. Under a regulatory agreement, headhunters cannot gain assignments to recruit top executives for SEC-registered clients. Nor can they pirate executives from any Peat Marwick auditing, accounting or management consultant client. Total (1985) professional staff of 35, with 11 U.S. offices. Overseas search work under the Peat Marwick banner is conducted separately from U.S. business.

U.S. offices:

Dwight Foster, Manager
345 Park Avenue
New York, New York 10154
(212) 758-9700

G. Charles Roy, Manager
3001 Summer Street
Stamford, Connecticut 06905
(203) 356-9800

Alexander K. Salmela, Manager
1 Boston Plaza
Boston, Massachusetts 02108
(617) 723-7700

John H. Telford, Jr., Manager
555 South Flower Street
Los Angeles, California 90071
(213) 972-4000

Donald F. Dvorak, Manager
303 East Wacker Drive
Chicago, Illinois 60601
(312) 938-1000

Lynne W. Dwigans, Manager
3 Embarcadero Center
San Francisco, California 94111
(415) 981-8230

David Kinsella, Manager
3000 Republic Bank Center
Houston, Texas 77002
(713) 224-4262

Mark E. Young, Manager
800 Brickell Avenue
Miami, Florida 33131
(305) 358-2300

William R. Robertson, Manager
225 Peachtree Street, NE
Atlanta, Georgia 30303
(404) 577-3240

J. Richard Davis, Manager
1601 Elm Street/Suite 1400
Dallas, Texas 75201
(214) 754-2000

Dale Schueffner, Manager
80 South 8th Street
Minneapolis, Minnesota 55402
(612) 341-2222

Terrence M. Gallagher, Manager
150 JFK Parkway
Short Hills, New Jersey 07078
(201) 467-9650

Officers: Principal Dwight E. Foster; Practice Committee Members Donald F. Dvorak, Lynn W. Dwigans, John H. Telford, Jr., Maurice "Moe" C. Paradis.

*Fiscal year ended June 30, 1985.

❑ Lamalie Associates, Inc.
13920 North Dale Mabry
   Highway
Tampa, Florida 33618

Total (1985) revenues: $7.0 million *
Five-year annual growth rate: 21 percent
Billings per consultant: $296,000

Total searches per year: 250, $60,000 salary minimum.

Major searches: Paul Tippett, chairman American Motors Corp. (now president Springs Industries, Inc.); C. W. Spangle, chairman Memorex Corp.; Roger Fridholm, vice-president Stroh Brewery Co. (now president); Ryal Poppa, chairman BMC Industries, Inc. (now chairman Storage Technology).

Profile: Founded in 1967 by Robert Lamalie, former human resources executive with The Glidden Co., Xerox Corp. and American Greetings Corp. Learned executive search during two-year stint at Booz, Allen & Hamilton. Lamalie is sole owner of firm. No international offices or linkups with foreign firms. Total (1985) professional staff of 25, with six U.S. offices.

Research director: Nancy M. Clausen, Tampa office.

U.S. offices:

Robert E. Lamalie, Chairman
John F. Johnson, President
101 Park Avenue
New York, New York 10178
(212) 953-7900

Michael Dunford, Managing Direct
120 South Riverside Plaza
Chicago, Illinois 60606
(312) 454-0525

Michael S. Reeder, Managing Director
3340 Peachtree Road, NE
Atlanta, Georgia 30026
(404) 237-6324

Robert Pearson, Managing Director
1601 Elm Street
Dallas, Texas 75201
(214) 754-0019

David Harbert, Managing Director
1900 East 9th Street
Cleveland, Ohio 44114
(216) 694-3000

Dennis M. Mummert, Vice-Presiden
13920 North Dale Mabry Highway
Tampa, Florida 33618
(813) 961-7494

Officers: Chairman and Chief Executive Robert E. Lamalie; President John F. Johnson; Vice-President/Finance Jack Wissman.

Top producer: John F. Johnson, setting Lamalie record of $615,000 billings in 1984.

*Fiscal year ended June 30, 1985.

◼ Handy Associates, Inc.　　Total (1985) revenues: $6 million
　245 Park Avenue　　　　 Five-year annual growth rate: 35 percent
　New York, New York　　　Billings per consultant: $429,000
　　10167
　(212) 867-8444

Total searches per year: 200 +, $75,000 salary minimum.

Profile: One of the first executive search firms, founded in 1944 by Jack Handy, an ex-McKinseyite. Handy retired in 1971; died at 88 in 1980. Firm owned by New Jersey-based Science Management Corp., a publicly-traded company. Only major search firm, other than Peat Marwick, with an executive compensation consulting arm which is headed by Pearl Meyer. Among a total (1985) professional staff of 14 is former Revlon vice-president Francis A. Shields, father of actress of Brooke Shields. With only one office in New York.

Research director: Ann S. Barry.

Officers: Chairman James A. Skidmore, Jr.; Chief Executive Officer and President J. Gerald Simmons.

Top producer: J. Gerard Simmons, bringing in $1.6 million in fees in 1984. (Simmons primarily does only business development.)

Index